CHAUCER STUDIES XXXII

THE LANGUAGE OF THE CHAUCER TRADITION

The manuscript copies of Chaucer's works preserve valuable information concerning Chaucer's linguistic practices and the ways in which scribes responded to these, but studies of Chaucerian language have generally neglected these primary resources in favour of edited texts. This book draws on recent developments in Middle English dialectology, textual criticism and the application of computers to manuscript studies to assess the evidence Chaucerian manuscripts provide for reconstructing Chaucer's own language and his linguistic environment. It considers how scribes, editors and Chaucerian poets transmitted and updated Chaucer's language, and the implications of this both for our understanding of Chaucerian book production and reception, and the processes of linguistic change in the fifteenth century.

Dr SIMON HOROBIN is Lecturer in English Language at the University of Glasgow.

CHAUCER STUDIES

ISSN 0261-9822

Previously published volumes in this series
are listed at the back of this book

THE LANGUAGE OF
THE CHAUCER TRADITION

SIMON HOROBIN

D. S. BREWER

© Simon Horobin 2003

All Rights Reserved. Except as permitted under current legislation
no part of this work may be photocopied, stored in a retrieval system,
published, performed in public, adapted, broadcast,
transmitted, recorded or reproduced in any form or by any means,
without the prior permission of the copyright owner

First published 2003
D. S. Brewer, Cambridge

ISBN 0 85991 780 0

D. S. Brewer is an imprint of Boydell & Brewer Ltd
PO Box 9, Woodbridge, Suffolk IP12 3DF, UK
and of Boydell & Brewer Inc.
PO Box 41026, Rochester, NY 14604–4126, USA
website: www.boydell.co.uk

A catalogue record for this book is available
from the British Library

Library of Congress Cataloging-in-Publication Data

Horobin, Simon.
 The language of the Chaucer tradition / Simon Horobin.
  p. cm. – (Chaucer studies, ISSN 0261–9822 ; 38)
 Includes bibliographical references (p.) and index.
  ISBN 0–85991–780–0 (alk. paper)
 1. Chaucer, Geoffrey, d. 1400 – Criticism, Textual. 2. English
 language – Middle English, 1100–1500 – Variation.   3. English
 language – Middle English, 1100–1500 – Texts.   4. Transmission of
 texts – History – To 1500.   5. Chaucer, Geoffrey, d. 1400 – Language.
 6. Manuscripts, Medieval – England.   7. Manuscripts, English (Middle)
 I. Title. II . Series.
 PR1939.H67 2003
 821′.1 – dc21   2002155053

This publication is printed on acid-free paper

Typeset by Joshua Associates Ltd, Oxford
Printed in Great Britain by
Antony Rowe Ltd, Chippenham, Wiltshire

Undergraduate Lending Library

GLASGOW
UNIVERSITY
LIBRARY

WITHDRAWN

Contents

For my parents

Preface

This is a book about Chaucer's language and specifically about the manuscripts of his works which transmit this language. In this book I attempt to harness recent developments in manuscript studies in order to reconsider the evidence such witnesses provide for reconstructing Chaucer's own language, and his linguistic environment. In the first chapter I survey new approaches to the study of Chaucerian manuscripts and Middle English dialectology to show how these developments provide new tools for analysing and interpreting these data. The aim of my second chapter is to consider the place of Chaucer's language within the development of the London dialect of Middle English during the fourteenth and fifteenth centuries. I also consider the way in which scribes responded to this language when factors such as linguistic change and standardisation made Chaucer's language appear old-fashioned. Chapter 3 focuses on the evidence of two manuscripts, the Hengwrt and Ellesmere manuscripts, in order to evaluate the evidence they offer for Chaucer's own linguistic practices. Linguistic differences between the texts of these two important manuscripts also highlight differences in the qualities of the texts of Chaucer's poem that they transmit and in the dating of the manuscripts. In addition to information regarding their attitudes towards Chaucerian language, the language of Chaucer's scribes also provides important evidence regarding the dialectal origin and the provenance of the manuscripts. In chapter 4 I draw on this evidence to provide a localisation of the fifty-four extant complete manuscript copies of the *Canterbury Tales*. This analysis presents a wealth of information concerning the provenance of individual manuscripts, including a large number of manuscripts produced outside London. Much scholarly attention has been focused on the metropolitan productions, marginalising our understanding of provincial book-production and Chaucer's reputation outside the capital. As well as discussing the dialectal input I also consider the influence of the language of the archetype and of the incipient standard written variety on the language of these manuscripts. Chapter 5 surveys the history of the Chaucerian print tradition from Caxton's first edition of the *Canterbury Tales* (1476) to the *Riverside Chaucer* (1987), and looks at the ways editors have treated Chaucer's language. This chapter considers how editors have tried to make Chaucer's language more accessible to readers through modernisation and translation, and the provision of linguistic apparatuses such as glossaries. Chapter 6 examines changes in English grammar in the fifteenth century, such as the loss of inflexions, and the corresponding impact such changes had on scribal understanding of Chaucer's metre and rhyming practices. Chapter 7 examines the influence of Chaucer's language upon later Chaucerian poets such as Thomas Hoccleve and John Lydgate, and considers the circulation of Chaucerian texts in Scottish anthologies, and the ways in which Chaucer's language was "translated" into Scots for a Scottish audience.

Acknowledgements

I owe a huge debt of gratitude to Professor Norman Blake who supervised my PhD thesis and who continues to influence and inspire my work. I am also grateful to the staff and students of The *Canterbury Tales* Project. I owe a particular debt to Michael Pidd and Estelle Stubbs whose technical and textual expertise has been of enormous benefit to my work. I am grateful to my colleagues in the English Language Department at Glasgow who have all encouraged and advised me during the writing of this book. In particular I wish to thank Professor Jeremy Smith who read the entire typescript and made detailed comments for its improvement. Jeremy's work on the language of the Gower tradition has provided a model for my own analysis and the debt I owe to the pioneering work of M.L. Samuels and J.J. Smith is apparent throughout the whole of this book. I have also profited from conversations and correspondence with the late Professor Charles Owen whose knowledge of the manuscripts of the *Canterbury Tales* was unparalleled. I am grateful to Professor David Burnley who was generous with his time and his comments in discussing many of the ideas presented here. I also wish to record my gratitude to Dr John Byrom who first introduced me to the study of medieval language and literature at Marlborough College and inspired me with his teaching. I am grateful to Caroline Palmer and to an anonymous reader for Boydell & Brewer who have helped to make this a much better book. I should add that I alone am responsible for any errors and shortcomings that remain. My final thanks go to my family who have all supported and encouraged me during the writing of this book. I am particularly grateful to my parents who have shown an interest in the work throughout and to Jennifer and Lucy who have helped to make it an enjoyable experience.

Earlier versions of parts of chapters 3 and 4 have appeared in *Anglia*, *English Studies* and *Notes and Queries* and I am grateful to the editors and publishers of these journals for permission to reproduce them here.

Abbreviations

BL	British Library
CUL	Cambridge University Library
EETS	Early English Text Society
ES	Extra Series
OS	Original Series
EN	East Norse
LALME	A. McIntosh, M.L. Samuels and M. Benskin (eds.), *A Linguistic Atlas of Late Mediaeval English*, 4 vols (Aberdeen, 1986)
Manly-Rickert	J.M. Manly, and E. Rickert (eds), *The Text of the Canterbury Tales: Studied on the Basis of All Known Manuscripts*, 8 vols (Chicago, 1940)
ME	Middle English
MED	H. Kurath et al. (eds), *Middle English Dictionary* (Ann Arbor, 1952–)
MS(S)	Manuscript(s)
n.s.	new series
OE	Old English
OED	*Oxford English Dictionary*
ON	Old Norse
P	Prologue
T	Tale
VB	Verb
WBP	Wife of Bath's Prologue
WN	West Norse

1

Introduction

E ver since the earliest critics and imitators of Chaucer's language and style, readers of Chaucer have praised his use of the English language. In the fifteenth and sixteenth centuries Chaucerian poets in both England and Scotland labelled Chaucer the master of rhetoric and eloquent diction. The following quotation from John Lydgate's *Life of Our Lady* is typical of the fifteenth-century response to Chaucer's linguistic legacy:

> And eke my maister Chauser is ygrave
> The noble Rethor, poete of Brytayne
> That worthy was the laurer to haue
> Of poetrye, and the palme atteyne
> That made firste, to distille and rayne
> The golde dewe dropes of speche and eloquence
> Into our tunge, thurgh his excellence[1]

These early readers credited Chaucer with revolutionising poetic diction in English, with many subsequent commentators echoing Thomas Hoccleve's effusive claim that Chaucer was the 'firste fyndere of oure faire langage'.[2] Such a view has endured well over the last four centuries with a number of nineteenth- and twentieth-century critics proclaiming the much-rehearsed claim that Chaucer created the English language. The history of the myth of Chaucer's "making" of the English language has recently been told by Christopher Cannon in his (1996) article 'The Myth of Origin and the Making of Chaucer's English'. However it is possible to overemphasise the influence of this viewpoint. A number of dissenting voices have been heard in opposition to this claim of Chaucer's linguistic originality. As early as 1778 Thomas Tyrwhitt prefaced his edition of Chaucer's poetry with an essay on Chaucer's language in which he contextualised Chaucer's usage within the historical development of the English language. He concluded that 'the English language must have imbibed a strong tincture of the French, long before the age of Chaucer, and consequently that he ought not to be charged as the importer of words and phrases, which he only used after the example of his predecessors and in common with his contemporaries'

---

[1] John Lydgate, *Life of Our Lady*, Book 2, lines 1628–34. Quotation from D. Brewer 1978: 46.
[2] Thomas Hoccleve, *The Regement of Princes*, line 4978. Quotation from D. Brewer 1978: 63.

(Tyrwhitt 1778: xxiii). Samuel Johnson's reasoned assessment of Chaucer's place within the linguistic history of English also counterbalances this claim.[3] Twentieth-century editors of Chaucer echoed Tyrwhitt's conclusions, as may be represented by F.N. Robinson's (1957) claim that 'Chaucer employed the London speech of his time, and a minute comparison of his usage with that of the contemporary London archives shows the two to correspond in all essentials. He not only did not invent or alter the grammatical inflections, but he also appears to have added few words to the English vocabulary' (xxx). More recently in his essay on language and versification in the *Riverside Chaucer* (1987), Norman Davis has stressed that 'Chaucer wrote in the English familiar to him from business as well as from court circles in London and Westminster' (xxvi). What is interesting about these different claims about Chaucer's linguistic novelty is their hugely contradictory conclusions. It is apparent from such contradictory statements that we have no certain means of assessing Chaucer's linguistic originality. One approach which has frequently been adopted has been to focus on the etymology of Chaucer's vocabulary as an indicator of his lexical innovation. However this is problematic as etymology provides little information concerning the status of particular words in the late fourteenth century. By the late fourteenth century many words of French origin had become thoroughly assimilated into the English language, and thus had become empty of any connotations of foreignness or high-status. Therefore any attempt to assess Chaucer's Romance vocabulary is complicated by difficulties concerning the status of the French words recorded in his verse. This problem has been stressed by Norman Davis: 'We need to know not only the bare fact of etymology but the associations and status of every word, and whether specific applications of it would seem to contemporary hearers in any way out of the ordinary' (Davis 1974: 73). Another related approach has been to discover which words were first used by Chaucer; an approach most recently associated with Joseph Mersand and his attribution of 1,180 neologisms 'to the word-wizard of the fourteenth century' (Mersand 1937: 2, 53). Recent criticism has suggested that Chaucer's lexical contribution to the English language was considerably less than earlier studies have suggested, although there remain a number of difficulties in determining the extent of Chaucer's originality in his use of vocabulary. For instance Christopher Cannon (1998) has shown that many words cited as first occurrences in Chaucer's works by the *Oxford English Dictionary* [*OED*] are revealed by the *Middle English Dictionary* [*MED*] to be recorded in earlier works. No doubt many other such words which are first recorded in Chaucer's poetry were already in use in the spoken language, and their lack of written attestation merely an accident of the historical record.

---

[3] See for instance Dr Johnson's 'History of the English Language' prefixed to his *Dictionary* (1755) in which he concluded that '[Chaucer's] diction was in general like that of his contemporaries'. Quoted in D. Brewer 1978: 209.

It is also apparent from the above discussion that much work on Chaucer's language has focused on Chaucer's vocabulary as indicative of his linguistic practice, and little account has been taken of other linguistic levels such as orthography, phonology and grammar. It is therefore the aim of this book to concentrate on these neglected aspects of Chaucer's language in order to consider the evidence they provide concerning the status of Chaucer's language within its contemporary context. The principal aim of this book is to situate these aspects of Chaucer's language within their textual, scribal and historical milieux. There have been a number of studies which assess the place of Chaucer's English within the development of the English language, although these studies have neglected the primary evidence for this language: the manuscripts of Chaucer's works. Recent advances in textual criticism and manuscript studies have provided a wealth of important information and resources for the understanding of Chaucer's language, although the full implications of these findings have not yet been fully explored. One of the principal arguments of this book is that studies of Chaucer's language must be firmly based upon an understanding of the manuscripts themselves, and on the relationships between these manuscripts. Furthermore I will argue that study of the language of the manuscripts has much to offer the textual study of these witnesses, and has further implications for our understanding of Chaucerian book production and reception.

Many discussions of Chaucer's language have continued to base their analyses upon the text of modern editions, such as the *Riverside Chaucer*, without questioning the extent to which these texts represent Chaucer's language. However such a position is problematic, given the status of this work as a product of the modern editorial process. As such the *Riverside Chaucer* presents a series of texts which are not the record of any single manuscript witness, but rather a mixture of scribal languages and texts. Each of these texts may contain traces of previous texts from which they were themselves copied, and many of these extant manuscripts contain mixtures of scribal dialects. An editor's choice of base manuscript will also affect the language of the edited text, as well as the extent to which this text represents that of Chaucer's original. For instance the Riverside text of the *Canterbury Tales* is based upon the Ellesmere manuscript, as was its predecessor edited by F.N. Robinson (1957). However the Riverside editors also recognised the importance of the Hengwrt [Hg] manuscript and introduced a substantial number of readings from this manuscript, thereby producing a 'hybrid' text (Benson 1987: 1120). Basing an analysis of Chaucer's language on an eclectic text of this kind is clearly problematic and also ignores recent work on the relationship between the Hengwrt and Ellesmere [El] manuscripts of the *Canterbury Tales*. In the remainder of this introduction I will sketch out some of the recent developments in studies of Chaucerian manuscripts in order to show how these affect our under-standing of Chaucer's language and its transmission throughout the fifteenth century.

The Status of the Hengwrt Manuscript

Much textual, linguistic and literary scholarship on the *Canterbury Tales* has been based upon the text of the Ellesmere manuscript which has historically been adopted as the base manuscript for editions of the *Tales*. However recent analysis of the manuscripts of the poem and of the relationship between the Hengwrt and Ellesmere manuscripts has argued that the Hg manuscript should form an important part of all such critical discussion. In this section I will survey critical and editorial responses to the Hg manuscript in order to assess their importance for a study of Chaucer's language.

The priority of the text of the Hg manuscript was first advanced by John Manly and Edith Rickert (1940) as a result of their collation of all extant manuscripts. The primary intention of this immense work is set out by the editors in the Prolegomena at the opening of the first volume. Here they explain that having studied the work of previous editors they observed that these editions 'indicated the need for a text of the Canterbury Tales based throughout upon the evidence afforded by all the extant MSS and such early editions as represented MSS no longer in existence' (I, 1). In order to undertake such a demanding task, Manly and Rickert divided their work into eight parts, only two of which contain the critical text itself. Volume I contains descriptions of all extant manuscripts, and Volume II supplies a classification of all these witnesses. The text and the critical notes fill Volumes III and IV, and the greatest part, Volumes V to VIII, comprises the Corpus of Variants: a record of all the variants of all the manuscripts. From it certain influential and important conclusions can be drawn. The text that is presented confirms the importance of the Hg text and the nature of El as an edited text. However Manly and Rickert's findings were not immediately addressed by scholars, partly on account of the timing of their publication and the difficulties in navigating the 8 volumes in which they were presented. Recently scholars have criticised the Manly and Rickert methodology as a result of a number of inconsistencies and paradoxes in their editorial procedures, some of which the editors were aware and others which appear beyond their control.[4] Despite the contradictions and inconsistencies that exist within the Manly-Rickert edition of the *Canterbury Tales*, the immense amount of variant readings considered and the high rate of accuracy lend authority to their work. Yet the Manly-Rickert text remains eclectic, incorporating most of the Hg text while retaining the ordering and extra inclusions of El. This paradoxical conclusion introduced a new period of editorial scholarship in which the text of Hg was regarded as the best although the ordering and contents of El were retained.

---

[4] For critiques of the Manly-Rickert methodology see the review by Root (1941) and articles by Blake (1983) and Kane (1984).

This situation may be exemplified by the work of the Variorum Chaucer project which aims to produce variorum editions of all of Chaucer's works, and facsimiles of the most important manuscripts. The texts of these editions of the *Canterbury Tales* use the Hg manuscript as a best-text, which is checked against collations of a small group of the principal manuscripts. These are Ad^3, Cp, Dd, El, Gg, Ha^4, He, La and Pw, and were chosen as they represent the major families used by Manly-Rickert in their corpus of variants. The editors of the individual volumes are free to include their own emendations, but are encouraged to do so only after careful consideration. Through their reliance on the Hengwrt text, and conviction of the superiority of its readings, the variorum editors attempt to discover the author's original, where Manly-Rickert aimed only to reconstruct the archetype of all manuscripts. Thus the variorum editors intend to compile a final text, described in the general editor's preface as, 'as close as we will come to Chaucer's own intentions for large parts of the *Canterbury Tales*' (Ruggiers 1979: xii). It is also significant that, despite their textual dependence on Hg, the editions retain the Ellesmere ordering and contents.

Norman Blake's (1980, 1985) work on the textual tradition of the manuscripts has drawn on the findings of Manly and Rickert but has advanced further in its advocacy of the importance of the Hg manuscript. Blake argues that the Hg scribe possessed the author's copytext in its entirety and that he organised the text according to a regular system of tale-link-tale wherever this was possible. The pieces that could not be fitted into such a system were placed first in the middle section, and were then followed by those that adhered to this sequence. The editor left gaps for the links that were missing, two of which were later filled by specially composed pieces which must therefore be regarded as spurious.[5] Proving these links to be scribal is central to Blake's argument, as it is only with such proof that Blake can explain the presence of gaps and later additions; which otherwise stand as testimonies to the concept of piecemeal acquisition proposed by Manly and Rickert. All this material was then copied by an experienced and accurate scribe, which resulted in an excellent text with very few additions. As Hg is our earliest extant manuscript, Blake concludes that it represents the first attempt to order Chaucer's papers, and that all subsequent orders are based upon this arrangement. Any revisions and additions shown by later manuscripts are therefore also scribal and consequently should not appear in an edition of the poem. These arguments informed the methodology that lies behind Blake's edition of 1980 which presents a lightly edited version of the Hg text, following its order of tales and its contents.

Blake's proposals have not found much support although the argument that the Hg manuscript preserves the earliest text of Chaucer's work has not been opposed. For instance in his work on the manuscripts of the *Canterbury Tales* Charles Owen severely criticised Blake's work but accepted that

---

[5] These are the Squire-Merchant and the Merchant-Franklin links.

the Hg manuscript was the earliest of the extant manuscripts. Palaeographical and codicological studies of Hg have also provided opposing conclusions to those proposed by Blake but continue to confirm the priority of Hg. In their 'Paleographical Introduction' to the Variorum Facsimile of Hg, Doyle and Parkes undertake a thorough study of the physical make-up of the manuscript, arguing that Hg displays many deficiencies and disconformities in its attempt to present a complete collection of the tales. Anomalies in the make-up of some of the quires, variations in the styles of writing and shades of ink, and the presence of blank pages are taken to suggest 'interruptions in the availability of exemplars of consecutive portions of the series of tales and links', and 'attempts to take advantage of what was available while it was so' (Ruggiers 1979: xxvi). These features are consonant with the view that the Hg manuscript was the first attempt to produce a complete copy of the *Tales* from the collection of links and tales left behind by Chaucer at his death. Ralph Hanna's (1989a) analysis of the planning and production of Hg also differs greatly from that suggested by Blake, but concurs in the view that Hg is the earliest of our extant manuscripts. Hanna argues that Hg was constructed as a series of discrete booklets and intended to present a collection of the canon of the work but with no concern for arrangement. However despite his very different conception of the make-up of Hg, Hanna concurs in his view of Hg as the earliest extant manuscript.[6]

In addition to the question of the priority of the Hg and El manuscripts, there have been important questions raised concerning the dating of these and other Chaucer manuscripts. Until recently scholars have accepted that no extant manuscript of any Chaucerian work may be dated to the fourteenth century, and that all our surviving witnesses are posthumous copies. This view is based upon factors such as the confused arrangement and make-up of the Hg manuscript and the use of the past tense in the marginal note that appears at the end of the unfinished *Cook's Tale* in Hg: 'Of this Cokes tale maked Chaucer na moore.' This view is found in the work of each of the critics discussed above, with the exception of Ralph Hanna. Hanna argues that Hg was copied as a series of discrete booklets because the production team had no clear guidelines as to the ordering of the various fragments. Therefore while Hanna argues that the Hg team did not have access to Chaucer's own papers, he suggests that the Hg manuscript was derived from *in vita* drafts of parts of the poem and that the manuscript itself may have been produced during the poet's lifetime: 'Hengwrt may, in fact, be totally an *in vita* manuscript, that is, one produced without any blessing from the author' (Hanna 1989a: 82). More recently the work of the art historian, Kathleen Scott, has forced Chaucer scholars to question the widespread assumption that Hg was copied after Chaucer's death. Scott has identified the

---

[6] See also his view as stated in the textual notes to the *Canterbury Tales* in the *Riverside Chaucer* that Hg is 'probably the oldest surviving manuscript' (Benson 1987: 1119).

work of the same illuminator responsible for the Ellesmere manuscript in another manuscript, Bodleian Library Hatton 4, an illuminated Hours of the Virgin, which may be dated on the basis of an ownership inscription to between 1397 and 1405 (Scott 1997). Comparison of the Ellesmere borders with those of the Hatton Hours and of the earlier Lapworth missal reveals that the El borders are 'stylistically even less "modern"' and that the date of the production of El should be shifted to the period 1400–1405. Moving the suggested date of the production of the Ellesmere manuscript earlier in the fifteenth century has implications for the dating of the older Hg manuscript. Scott suggests that on the basis of its border illumination Hg should be dated to 1395–1400, and adds in a footnote: 'The implication is of course that Hengwrt was made before the death of Chaucer' (Scott 1997: 119). As a result of this suggestion the question of whether Hg, and other early witnesses of the *Canterbury Tales*, might have been produced during Chaucer's lifetime, has been reconsidered by Norman Blake. Following Scott Blake has reassessed the textual and codicological evidence of Hg and other early manuscripts, concluding that there is no reason why these witnesses could not have been produced within Chaucer's lifetime: 'There would seem, then, in principle no reason for not accepting that some manuscripts of the *Canterbury Tales* and possibly some of *The Book of Troilus and Criseyde* were issued in Chaucer's lifetime and actually written under his guidance and supervision' (Blake 1997a: 116). In addition to these suggestions by art historians and textual scholars, the evidence of palaeographers may also lend tacit support to the suggestion that the Hg manuscript was produced before 1400. In their 'Paleographical Introduction' to the facsimile of the Hg manuscript Doyle and Parkes (1979) noted that the manuscript was copied in an old-fashioned Anglicana script which is more typical of the late fourteenth century than the early fifteenth century. More recently, work on the Digital Facsimile of the Hg manuscript by Estelle Stubbs (2000) has tentatively suggested that at least parts of the manuscript were produced under the poet's supervision. Stubbs concludes that the 'possibility of dating any part of either Hg or El to Chaucer's lifetime would have enormous repercussions for the study of the textual tradition of the *Canterbury Tales*'.

Discussion of whether copies of Chaucer's poems were produced during the fourteenth century has not been limited to copies of the *Canterbury Tales*. M.C. Seymour has recently argued for a date earlier than 1399 for the earliest of the manuscripts of *Troilus and Criseyde*, Corpus Christi College, Cambridge MS 61 (1995: 60). Seymour's proposal is based upon his interpretation of the famous frontispiece which he argues shows the figure of Richard II. The face of the monarch appears to have been considerably smudged and Seymour argues that this is a deliberate act of censorship following the deposition and murder of Richard in 1399. If Seymour's interpretation of the frontispiece is correct then the manuscript must have been produced before 1399 and therefore before Chaucer's own death in 1400.

The possibility that these manuscripts were produced during Chaucer's lifetime has implications for our understanding of Chaucer's language. For instance if we assume that Chaucer supervised or at least authorised the production of the Hg manuscript, then it is likely that the language of this manuscript is close to that of the poet. Even if we accept Hanna's suggestion that Hg was produced without Chaucer's involvement, it remains likely that a manuscript produced before 1400 would retain some relationship with the poet's own linguistic habits. The further possibility that parts of the El manuscript were also produced during Chaucer's lifetime raises the question of whether linguistic differences between the two manuscripts can be explained as a process of authorial revision. Furthermore it is likely that close examination of the language of these two manuscripts will shed further light on the relationship between their two texts and their relationship with Chaucer's own papers.

Studies of Chaucer's Language

Important discoveries by palaeographers have also had significant implications for the study of Chaucer's language. In a landmark analysis of John Gower's *Confessio Amantis* in Trinity College, Cambridge, MS R.3.2, A.I. Doyle and M.B. Parkes (1978) assessed the collaboration of five scribes in the production of this manuscript. In addition to their discussion of the methods of book production employed in London in the early fifteenth century Doyle and Parkes were also able to identify three of the hands in the Trinity Gower in a number of other important manuscripts. The second scribe in the Trinity Gower, termed Scribe B, also copied the Hengwrt and Ellesmere manuscripts of the *Canterbury Tales* and the Cecil Fragment of Chaucer's *Troilus and Criseyde*. In a subsequent article Doyle (1997) has also suggested that Scribe B may have copied a fragment of the *Prioress' Tale* which now survives as CUL MS Kk I.3/20. The fourth hand of the Trinity Gower, Doyle and Parkes' Scribe D, was responsible for copying a large number of other manuscripts and seems to have specialised in copying Gower's *Confessio Amantis*. The total number of manuscripts attributed to Scribe D is as follows: 8 copies of the *Confessio Amantis*, 2 copies of the *Canterbury Tales*, and single copies of Langland's *Piers Plowman* and Trevisa's translation of *De Proprietatibus Rerum*. The fifth contributor to the Trinity Gower, Scribe E, is identified as the poet and professional copyist Thomas Hoccleve. Hoccleve's hand has also been found in the autograph manuscript collections of his own poetry, in the *Formulary* in which he collected models of Privy Seal documents, and in two documents in the Public Record Office.[7]

The work of the palaeographers has subsequently been addressed by

---

[7] For details of these manuscripts and documents, and a discussion of the contents of the *Formulary* see Burrow 1994.

Middle English dialectologists who have exploited these findings in a number of important ways. For instance M.L. Samuels (1988b) has compared the language of Scribe B's contribution to the Trinity Gower with that of the Hg and El manuscripts in order to determine Chaucer's own spelling habits. By identifying linguistic features which are found in Hg and El and not in the Trinity Gower Samuels has attempted to isolate linguistic forms which derive from Chaucer's own foul-papers. Samuels' attempt to define Chaucer's own spelling forms has implications for editors of Chaucer's works and for the attribution of other works to Chaucer. Samuels himself compared the spellings he identified as those of Chaucer with those found in the manuscript of the *Equatorie of the Planetis*. This text is found in a manuscript, Peterhouse College, Cambridge MS 75.I, which has been argued by some scholars to be both composed and copied by Chaucer.[8] Samuels' attribution of this text to Chaucer on the basis of its language, has proved to be authoritative in discussions of the authorship of this text. In my discussion of Chaucer's language in chapter 3 I question Samuels' evidence and the attribution of the *Equatorie of the Planetis* to Chaucer. In addition to his work on Chaucer's spelling, Samuels has also analysed the spelling systems of the Hg and El manuscripts in order to support the conclusions of the palaeographers that these manuscripts are indeed the work of a single scribe (Samuels 1988c). Samuels identified a number of progressions in Scribe B's linguistic habits across these two manuscripts which led him to posit that 'there was a considerable period – perhaps almost a decade-between the copying of the two manuscripts' (p. 48). In chapter 3 I provide a detailed linguistic comparison between the Hg and El manuscripts in order to reconsider the length of time between the copying of their texts. I also draw upon these linguistic details for evidence of the different scribal and editorial policies adopted in the production of the two manuscripts.

Jeremy Smith (1988b) has analysed the language of all the manuscripts attributed by Doyle and Parkes to their Scribe D. Smith's analysis has revealed important facts concerning scribal behaviour during this period. By analysing the language of Scribe D's copies of different textual traditions Smith identified several different layers of linguistic forms belonging to different ME dialects. Smith showed that each of the manuscripts copied by Scribe D contained a West Midland layer which must therefore belong to the scribe himself, revealing Scribe D to be a London immigrant of West Midland origins. A surprising result of Smith's analysis was the identification of certain Kentish features in each of the manuscripts copied by Scribe D. Given that Scribe D was clearly a native West Midlander it seems unlikely that his repertoire could include a few stray Kentish spellings. However such Kentish forms do form part of the repertoire of John Gower,

---

[8] A facsimile of the manuscript and a summary of the authorship debate are found in Rand Schmidt 1993.

due to his family associations with Otford in North-West Kent (Fisher 1965). It appears therefore that, due to his long association with Gower's language and text, Scribe D inherited a number of distinctive Gowerian spelling forms and introduced these into his copies of works by Chaucer, Langland and Trevisa.

The studies by Samuels and Smith derive their orientation from the revolution in Middle English dialectology associated with the preparation and publication of the *Linguistic Atlas of Late Mediaeval English [LALME]* (1986). *LALME* provided a geographical localisation for the language of approximately 1000 Middle English manuscripts copied during the period 1350–1450. *LALME* also contains linguistic profiles of each of these ME texts and maps of salient spelling forms which allow other scholars to localise manuscripts not contained in the *LALME* survey. This resource has transformed our understanding of the geography of late Medieval literature and manuscript production. One of the starting points for the *LALME* survey was the localisation of all the manuscript witnesses of texts surviving in a large number of manuscript copies, such as the *Prick of Conscience*. However despite the large number of extant Chaucer manuscripts, many of these were not included in the Atlas, due to their comparatively late dates of copying and the corresponding influence of standardisation, which masked the diatopic variety characteristic of earlier Middle English texts. Analysis of the language of the extant manuscripts of other major textual traditions, notably those of Langland's *Piers Plowman* and Gower's *Confessio Amantis*, have revealed a number of important findings. For instance Samuels' localisation of many of the manuscripts of the three versions of *Piers Plowman* has shown that the different recensions enjoyed different circulations (Samuels 1988d and 1988f). The A and B texts appear to have been copied and read in the Greater London area while the C text survives in a number of manuscripts produced around Langland's West Midland home. These facts have important implications for our understanding of the transmission of the text, its readership and possibly Langland's biography. Jeremy Smith's discussions of the extant copies of Gower's *Confessio Amantis*, which were a by-product of his work on Scribe D, have also revealed important information concerning the reception of this poem in the fifteenth century (Smith 1985 and 1988c). Smith has shown that copyists of the poem were careful to preserve elements of Gower's idiosyncratic linguistic system, suggesting that Gower's language and text were regarded as authoritative. Smith's work on the language of the Gower tradition has also demonstrated the significance of the linguistic, particularly orthographic, evidence for identifying relationships between manuscripts. As such this evidence has a great potential value for textual and editorial studies which remains untapped. Smith writes: 'It can be argued that the study of orthography should become a key codicological tool, beside palaeography, textual criticism and the skills of the literary and art historian, for the researcher into fifteenth-century Middle English manuscripts' (Smith 1988c: 107–8).

Since the publications by Samuels and Smith, which were based on pen-and-paper analysis by selective questionnaire, and even since *LALME*, the whole approach to scholarly investigation of manuscripts has been massively enhanced by the use of computer technology. Of particular significance in the context of the present book is the work of The *Canterbury Tales* Project which aims to use sophisticated collation software to reconstruct the textual history of the poem.[9] As part of this enterprise the project has produced diplomatic transcriptions and linguistic databases of all the extant manuscript and pre-1500 printed witnesses to the *Wife of Bath's Prologue* (Robinson 1996). These transcriptions are accompanied by digitised images and bibliographical descriptions of each of the witnesses. No attempt, though, is made within these descriptions, or elsewhere on the CD-ROM, to provide an analysis of the language of these texts; but the functionality of the resource is such that it makes possible the programme of linguistic analysis flagged by Smith back in 1988c. One of the major purposes of this book is to address this programme.

Scribal Behaviour

In order to draw conclusions from linguistic data contained in Middle English manuscripts one must begin by considering the various ways in which a medieval scribe was likely to approach his task. While it is of course impossible to make exact predictions about such behaviour, sufficient work has been done to allow us to posit a theoretical model of scribal copying within which most ME scribes were likely to operate. One of the major breaks with traditional approaches to historical dialectology made by the ME Dialect Survey in the production of *LALME* was to treat the scribe as a linguistic informant. Previous studies tended to focus solely on the "pure" authorial language preserved in holograph manuscripts, ignoring scribal copies as dialectally mixed and corrupt. However in a seminal article of 1963 Angus McIntosh argued that when faced with copying a text in a dialect other than his own a scribe could approach his task in one of three ways:

A   He may leave the language of his copytext unchanged, producing a *literatim* transcription of the text.

B   He may "translate" the language of his copytext into his own dialect.

C   He may do something in between types A and B, thereby producing a mixture of his own forms and those of his exemplar.

It is evident that each of these different copying practices will produce different linguistic outputs. Type A will simply reproduce the language of

---

[9] For information concerning this project see Blake and Robinson 1993, 1997 and see the project's website at http://www.cta.dmu.ac.uk/projects/ctp/

the scribal exemplar, while Type B will result in the replacement of the language of the exemplar with a consistent scribal language. Type C will result in a mixed language containing both exemplar and scribal forms. Both types A and B will produce outputs which are suitable for dialectal analysis while Type C is unsuitable for such an analysis. While these distinctions are useful for making generalisations about scribal behaviour, it is apparent that the boundaries between these three types are fuzzy. For the purposes of identification of an individual scribe with a particular type it is probably safest to view types A and B as opposite poles of a cline, with type C copyists belonging somewhere along the cline, approximating closer to either Type A or B. While it is true that a text produced by a Type C copyist will produce a linguistic mixture, this mixture may reveal an internal consistency which enables it to be used for the purposes of ME dialectology. Where the language of the text is a random mixture of scribal and exemplar forms it is termed a *Mischsprache* and is unsuitable for dialectological analysis. However where the distribution of scribal and exemplar forms is orderly and may be distinguished as separate linguistic layers, such texts are known as *pseudo-Mischsprachen* and may be subjected to dialectological analysis. Such texts may be produced when a scribe begins copying an exemplar *literatim* and then switches to a process of dialectal translation at an identifiable point in the text. Similarly a scribe may in theory begin by translating his text into his own dialect and then switch to a process of *literatim* copying, although in practice such cases are less common. However it is common to find a period of "working-in" in a scribal text, where a scribe gradually settles down in his copying practice and adjusts himself to the language of the copytext from which he is working. More complex than these scenarios is the kind of scribal behaviour known as "constrained selection". This process defines a scribe who reproduces exemplar forms where they are familiar to him, but replaces unfamiliar forms with those from his own repertoire. The resulting linguistic mixture represents a compromise of forms, all of which are familiar to the scribe but which he would not produce as part of his spontaneous repertoire. Crucial to the concept of constraint is the distinction between active and passive repertoires. The former comprises those forms that the scribe would automatically produce when writing without any constraint from an exemplar, while a scribe's passive repertoire contains forms with which he is familiar and is willing to reproduce when confronted with them in a document which he is copying.

In addition to the kinds of copying practices and constraints outlined above there are other kinds of more restricted or specialised constraints which must be taken into consideration. For instance where a scribe copies a rhyming text his behaviour may be constrained by the use of a particular form in rhyme. In many cases this may lead to the preservation of an unusual form by a scribe who will otherwise produce a thorough translation of a text into his own dialect. However many scribes are quite content to translate words in rhyming position without any attempt to repair the resulting damage done to the rhyme scheme. Similar situations are also true of alliterative texts, where certain scribes are constrained to reproduce unfamiliar forms in alliterating position, while others translate these with no apparent concern for the alliterative metre.

The Emergence of Standardised Varieties of ME

So far we have focused on the influences of the scribe's own language and that of his exemplar. However in the late ME period other sociolinguistic influences began to appear surrounding the emergence of a written standard language. During the second half of the fourteenth century the functions of the vernacular changed and English began to be used as the language of government and administration, and for literary purposes. As a result of the general elaboration of English there was an increased need for a standardised written variety of Middle English which could be understood over a wide geographical area.

In a seminal discussion of the development of London English during the fourteenth and fifteenth centuries Michael Samuels (1963) distinguished 4 "types" of written standards which he labelled types I–IV. Type I, also known as the Central Midlands Standard, is found in a number of texts associated with John Wycliffe and the Lollard movement. This language is found in a large number of manuscripts of religious texts and Bible translations produced by the Lollards, copied and circulated widely throughout the country. This type of language is based upon the dialects of the Central Midlands and characteristic forms include 'sich' SUCH, 'mych', MUCH, 'ony' ANY, 'silf' SELF, 'stide' STEAD, 'ȝouun' GIVEN, 'siȝ' SAW. Samuels' Type II is found in a group of manuscripts copied in London in the mid to late fourteenth century. This group includes the Auchinleck manuscript which was produced in London around 1340 by a number of scribes, some of whom were Londoners and others native West Midlanders. Other Type II texts include three copies of the ME *Mirror*: BL MS Harley 5085; Corpus Christi College, Cambridge, MS 282; Glasgow University Library MS Hunter 250. Another important group of Type II manuscripts are those three manuscripts copied by a single hand dated by palaeographers to the 1380s: BL MS Harley 874; Bodleian Library MS Laud Misc. 622; Magdalene College, Cambridge, MS Pepys 2498. Characteristic Type II features include forms which are common to the Norfolk and Suffolk dialects and are thought to derive from immigration into the capital from those counties. Examples of such forms are 'þai', 'hij' THEY, 'þeiȝ' THOUGH, 'werld' WORLD, 'þat ilch(e), ilch(e)' THAT VERY. Type III is the language of London in the late fourteenth and early fifteenth centuries, recorded in, for example, the earliest Chaucer manuscripts: the Hengwrt and Ellesmere manuscripts of the *Canterbury Tales* and Corpus Christi College, Cambridge, MS 61 of *Troilus and Criseyde*. Other Type III documents are early civic documents such as the London guild returns and the Petition of the Mercers, and the holograph manuscripts of the poet Thomas Hoccleve. Characteristic features of this language are forms common to the Central Midlands dialects, including 'they' THEY, 'hir(e)' THEIR, 'though' THOUGH, 'yaf' GAVE, 'nat' NOT, 'swich' SUCH. Type III was subsequently replaced in the early fifteenth century by Type IV, also termed by Samuels 'Chancery Standard' which 'consists of that flood of government documents that starts in the years following 1430' (Samuels 1963, 1989: 71). Type IV also shows the influence of forms found in the Central Midlands dialects although these have been further supplemented by forms originally restricted to the North Midlands, e.g. 'theyre' THEIR, 'thorough' THROUGH, 'such(e)' SUCH, 'gaf' GAVE, 'not' NOT.

The importance of these standardised varieties for the study of scribal copying practice is however extremely complex. The term 'standard language' is a notoriously slippery term and one which is often not clearly defined when used to refer to medieval varieties. Samuels' use of the terms 'Central Midlands Standard' and 'Chancery Standard' has led to the misconception that these varieties were formally and functionally equivalent to our present-day written standard language. It will be useful therefore to consider the criteria by which a standard language may be identified in order to demonstrate the differences between our present-day standard written language and Samuels' types. Recent sociolinguistic study of the process of linguistic standardisation has drawn a distinction between social and linguistic aspects of standardisation (Milroy and Milroy 1985). The social aspect concerns what Milroy and Milroy have termed the "ideology of standardisation". This is concerned with the widespread belief in correct usage, and the notion that there are right and wrong ways of using language. The linguistic aspect of standardisation is concerned with the process of linguistic change whereby variation is reduced and a greater uniformity is achieved. Clearly both these factors are important in considering the rise of a standard language, and it is frequently difficult to determine whether the ideology of standardisation causes greater conformity in linguistic usage, or whether the increased uniformity in usage promotes notions of correct and incorrect linguistic behaviour. However it is important to distinguish between these in the following discussion which is concerned principally with the linguistic aspect of the process of standardisation. Sociolinguists have further demonstrated that a standard language must fulfill a number of criteria to be considered a standard; these are most clearly set out by Einar Haugen (cited in Hudson 1996: 33). According to Haugen a standard language must have undergone the following processes: selection, elaboration, codification, acceptance. Thus a variety must have been selected as the only acceptable variety and it must be codified and fixed either by an Academy or an educational system. It must also be elaborated so that it becomes the sole variety available to perform all linguistic functions and it must be accepted by all levels of society as the only acceptable usage.

It is evident that of Samuels' four types discussed above only the last of these, Type IV, eventually fulfilled the four criteria highlighted by Haugen. The process by which these criteria were achieved is extremely complex and as this is the subject of an authoritative forthcoming study by Benskin and Sandved it will not be pursued further in this book.[10] Here we will be concerned predominantly with Samuels' Type III, a variety of London language which never attained the status of a standard variety, but which nevertheless shows a degree of consistency across a number of texts copied in London during the late fourteenth and early fifteenth centuries. One of the questions that this book will address is what the function of this linguistic variety was and what the relationship is between the manuscripts copied in Type III London English.

One further type of language which must be discussed here is known as "colourless" language. This is a variety of language which is defined as neither regional nor standard language; a kind of compromise language in which strongly regional forms are replaced with those in wide use and therefore more communicatively efficient. Colourless language is made up of forms which are difficult to localise as they are drawn from a variety of regional dialects and conform to no one particular variety. *LALME* defines this usage as the process by which 'a writer replaces some or all of his distinctively local forms by equivalents which, although still native to the local or neighbouring dialects, are common currency over a wider area. The result is not a series of well-defined, regional standards . . . but a continuum in which the local element is muted, and one type shifts almost impercept-ibly into another' (*LALME* I, 47).

Having considered the various ways in which a scribe might respond to his copytext and the many linguistic and sociolinguistic constraints by which he might be influenced, it is now time to look in greater detail at the evidence for the variety with which we will be concerned in this book. This is the variety of London English termed by Samuels Type III, and the evidence, both linguistic and sociolinguistic, for this variety will be the subject of the following chapter.

---

[10] For preliminary discussions of this study see Sandved 1981 and Benskin 1992.

2

Chaucer's Language and the London Dialect

In the previous chapter we saw that Chaucer's language was a variety of Middle English current in London at the end of the fourteenth and beginning of the fifteenth centuries, termed Type III by M.L. Samuels in his study of the development of London English. It is therefore important that we do not attempt to discuss Chaucer's language in isolation, but rather consider it within the general development of London English during this important period in its evolution. Before examining Chaucer's language in detail, it will therefore be useful to consider the development of London English during this period more generally. In the previous chapter we saw that it was only at the very end of the Middle English period that the written language became standardised and this was a process which was ongoing throughout the fifteenth and sixteenth centuries. As a result of this lack of a written standard language, the late Middle English period is characterised by the huge degree of dialectal variation which is reflected in the written record. Chaucer himself drew attention to this in *Troilus and Criseyde*:

> And for ther is so gret diversite
> In Englissh and in writyng of oure tonge.[1]

The extent of this written variation may be exemplified by a consideration of the large number of different spellings of the common word SUCH recorded by the *Linguistic Atlas of Late Mediaeval English* [*LALME*]. While many of these spellings are relatively straightforward, for example 'swich', 'swech', 'soch', 'sych', others are less obviously recognisable to the modern reader, e.g. 'schch', 'slkyke', 'sik', 'sqwych', 'zueche'. During the second half of the fourteenth century the functions of the vernacular changed and English began to be used as the language of government and administration, and for literary purposes. As a result of the general elaboration of English there was an increased need for a standardised written variety of Middle English which could be understood over a wide geographical area. In the preceding chapter we saw that the emergence of a written standard language was focused on the London dialect during the fourteenth century. An alternative kind of standard written language has also been identified by

---

[1] Book V, lines 1793–4.

Samuels in various manuscripts of Lollard texts. As this language is based upon the dialects of the Central Midlands counties it will not be pursued further in this book which is concerned primarily with the language of London. The first of the London varieties identified by Samuels, known as Type II, is found in a group of manuscripts copied in London in the mid fourteenth century, such as the Auchinleck manuscript. The next London variety, termed Type III, is the language of London in the late fourteenth and early fifteenth centuries, recorded in, for example, the earliest Chaucer manuscripts and the Hoccleve holographs. Type III was subsequently replaced by Type IV, also termed by Samuels 'Chancery Standard' or, more recently by Benskin, 'King's English', which was used by the clerks employed in the various offices of the Medieval administration. The process by which Type III was replaced by Type IV and the relationship between this later variety and present-day standard written English is a highly complex and controversial subject which lies beyond the focus of this book. An authoritative survey of these processes will be provided by the forthcoming study by Benskin and Sandved to which the interested reader is referred.[2]

The language of the Hg manuscript therefore belongs to the variety of London English known as Type III. At this point it is important to emphasise that Samuels' types do not show the same degree of uniformity as does present-day standard written English. In considering the development of standard written English J.J. Smith (1996: 63–78) has stressed the difference between 'fixed' and 'focused' standard languages. Present-day standard written English is a 'fixed' standard as it consists of a fixed set of rules from which no deviation is permitted. Types I–IV were 'focused' standards as they incorporated a degree of internal variation. Smith has drawn a helpful parallel between Types I–IV and the present-day spoken standard, or reference accent, known as Received Pronunciation [RP]. While many speakers of English use RP few of these are likely to show all the features characteristic of this accent. RP is therefore an abstract set of prototypical features to which speakers tend, rather than a fixed set of linguistic shibboleths from which any deviation is stigmatised.

If we examine the evidence for Type III in greater detail we may identify the kind of variation found within this variety of ME. In his article Samuels listed a number of features as characteristic of Type III, including the following: 'though' THOUGH, 'nat' NOT, 'swich' SUCH, 'bot' BUT, 'hir(e)' THEIR, 'thurgh' THROUGH. While these forms appear regularly in Type III texts they are not the sole spellings adopted for these items. For instance the Hg manuscript has both 'nat' and 'noght' as spellings of NOT and these seem to be used in free variation. Similarly there are two dominant forms of the item THOUGH in Hg, 'thogh' and 'though', and both seem to have been equally acceptable. In fact there is a third form

---

[2] For a discussion of this projected work see Sandved 1981. A number of the issues involved in such a reappraisal are addressed in L. Wright 2000, although these contributions do not address the development of London English in the fourteenth century.

'theigh' not recorded by Samuels which appears in just 7 occurrences in Hg. For the purposes of localisation *LALME* merged the Hg and El manuscripts into a single linguistic profile. However to treat these two manuscripts as evidence for a single variety of ME ignores a degree of important variation between the two manuscripts. For instance while the two spellings 'thogh' and 'though' are both found in El, the Hg spelling 'theigh' is not used in El. The significance of linguistic differences of this kind between Hg and El will be pursued further in the following chapter. Comparison of the language of Hg and El with other Type III manuscripts reveals further evidence of the variation permitted within this variety. For example both Hg and El employ the spellings 'nat', 'noght' for the item NOT. The same forms are also found regularly in the holograph manuscripts of Thomas Hoccleve, although Hoccleve also used a third form 'naght' not recorded in the Hg and El manuscripts.[3] Such variation warns us against viewing these types of London English as discrete and unrelated developments. For instance the spelling 'theigh' recorded in the Hg manuscript is in fact characteristic of Type II, and is the regular form of Hand A of the Auchinleck manuscript. Two other manuscripts copied in Type III, Corpus Christi College, Cambridge, MS 61, a copy of Chaucer's *Troilus and Criseyde*, and Trinity College, Cambridge, MS B.15.17 also contain 7 and 14 occurrences of this spelling respectively alongside the more common Type III forms. Therefore we must view Samuels' typology as a linguistic continuum rather than as a series of discrete linguistic varieties.

We will now turn to consider the reasons behind the changes within the London dialect during the fourteenth century, focusing particularly on the shift from Type II to Type III. Samuels attributed the differences between these types of London English to waves of immigration into London from different parts of the country during the fourteenth century. Type II maintains a continuity with the earlier Essex-based usage found in the earliest surviving London documents, such as the Proclamation of Henry III (1258), while also showing the influence of forms common to East Anglian dialects. The presence of these forms in London English appears to correlate with patterns of immigration from these counties in the middle of fourteenth century. The move from Type II to Type III represents an influx of Midlands forms into the London dialect, a change which may also be linked to waves of immigration from the Central Midlands counties towards the end of the century. Type IV shows the influence of further Central Midlands forms and forms from the North Midlands which had filtered down into the Central Midlands dialects. These forms represent further immigration from these counties at the turn of the century. The explanation of the differences between these types of London English as the result of immigration was an attempt to explain the

---

[3] For texts contained in the Hoccleve holograph manuscripts see Furnivall 1970 and Burrow 1999.

apparently sudden and radical change in the nature of the London dialect in about 1380. Some of the Type II texts identified by Samuels may be dated on palaeographical grounds to c. 1380, while some of the earliest documents written in Type III are dated internally to 1383. Therefore Samuels argued that the only possible conclusion was that the 'London dialect changed suddenly and radically in the fourteenth century' (Samuels 1963, 1989: 70). Samuels' theory that these linguistic changes in the London dialect were the result of widespread immigration have recently been challenged by Laura Wright (1996).

Wright has argued that the evidence for a sudden population shift in the late fourteenth century is slight. Samuels based his argument of large-scale immigration into the capital from the Midlands counties upon the demographic work of Eilert Ekwall (1956), published in his book on the population of medieval London. Wright points out that Ekwall's claims were based upon problematic evidence, that of the provenance of London surnames during the period 1270–1350. Where such surnames were place-names Ekwall assumed that this place represented the origin of this individual Londoner. There are problems with such an approach, most obviously in the fact that the place-name might represent the origin of a previous generation of the family rather than the individual in question. As a result Ekwall's findings remained tentative and inconclusive, although Ekwall did conclude that: 'so far as can be judged from the Subsidy Rolls, the contribution to the London population from Southern counties about the beginning of the fourteenth century was larger than that from the Midland counties, and that the Midland character of the later London language could hardly be due to immigration on a larger scale from the Midlands than from the South' (xii–xiii). Sylvia Thrupp has also emphasised the diversity of origins of London immigrants throughout the fourteenth century: 'From the earliest years of the fourteenth century, London was drawing on the entire kingdom, any large sample of names conjuring up a map of the length and breadth of England' (1948: 208). Thrupp also highlighted the difficulties of using surnames as evidence of place of origin, showing that as these names were often passed down the male line of families they are not proof of recent migration. It was a common practice for an apprentice to adopt the surname of his master thereby further complicating the use of such evidence for demographic research. For example Chaucer's grandfather is thought to have adopted the name Chaucer as a mark of respect and gratitude towards his former employer and benefactor John le Chaucer (Pearsall 1992: 12). Thrupp's study of London immigrants during this period also revealed that immigrants were drawn from all levels of society, not just the wealthier and more prosperous classes. These factors complicate our understanding of the changes in the London dialect during this period. It is possible that immigration was a major factor in explaining the appearance of such dialectally diverse forms in the London dialect during this period.

However it seems that these population shifts can not be the only factor to explain these changes as the movement of immigrants, and the impact of their language, were unlikely to have been as sudden and dramatic as has been claimed. It is not possible to chart the origins of London immigrants during this period with any degree of precision, while it also appears that immigrants were drawn from throughout the country as a whole. It is also difficult to understand why the appearance of these immigrants in London should have had such a dramatic effect on the local dialect. Thrupp has shown that these immigrants were drawn from all levels of society and it is unclear why local Londoners should be concerned to adopt dialect features of these newcomers so soon after their arrival in the capital. Indeed sociolinguists have shown that immigrants traditionally show evidence of weak social ties both to their geographical and social networks. As a result of these weak ties these speakers tend to imitate the linguistic behaviour of those who belong to the social class to which they aspire.[4] In their efforts to mimic a prestigious accent weakly tied individuals have a tendency to overshoot or "hypercorrect", thereby producing forms alien to both their own and the target accent. Linguistic behaviour of this kind has frequently been identified as providing the trigger for linguistic change. While it is apparent that immigration into the capital may have produced the socio-linguistic context and the raw material for linguistic change, it is less clear why the native Londoners should choose to adopt the linguistic forms introduced by the immigrants. It is more common for the incomers to adapt their own linguistic behaviour rather than influence that of the local population. Londoners during this period demonstrated great civic pride and citizens were clearly marked by their legal status and their membership of a guild. Without such status residents of London were considered to be foreigners, even when born within the city itself. Londoners who had come from overseas were set apart further from natives and were termed 'aliens' (Thrupp 1948). It is apparent from the above discussion that there is a need for a re-examination of the documents themselves in order to build upon Samuels' conclusions. In the following discussion I will reexamine both the textual and linguistic evidence for the London dialect during this period in order to show how an understanding of the texts themselves and their textual environment can help to provide an assessment of the evolution of the London dialect, and the place of Chaucer's language within this dialect during this important period in its development.

I will begin by considering the textual evidence for Type III London English, found in texts dating from the late fourteenth and early fifteenth centuries. In the late fourteenth century its uses were primarily in official documents, such as the London Guild returns, the Appeal of Thomas Usk and the Petition of the Mercers.[5] Early fifteenth century texts copied in Type

---

[4] Social network theory and the importance of weak social ties for linguistic change are discussed in Milroy 1992.
[5] These texts are printed in Chambers and Daunt 1931.

III are the Hengwrt [Hg] and Ellesmere [El] manuscripts of the *Canterbury Tales*, Corpus Christi College, Cambridge, MS 61 of *Troilus and Criseyde*, Trinity College, Cambridge, MS B.15.17 of Langland's *Piers Plowman* and the holograph manuscripts of Thomas Hoccleve. There is a clear distinction between the functions of Type III in the fourteenth and fifteenth centuries. All extant texts from the fourteenth century are administrative or official documents and all extant Type III texts from the fifteenth century are literary texts. This apparent change in function may be partly explained by the appearance of another type of standardised written English, Type IV, in the early fifteenth century. Type IV was used in various government offices replacing the earlier Type III usage. This system subsequently became adopted outside these administrative offices and was used in a variety of written functions, including the copying of literary texts and private letters.[6] The process by which Type IV became adopted for a wider variety of functions was gradual and it seems likely that Types III and IV were able to coexist, at least for a short while, fulfilling distinct linguistic functions.[7]

I have highlighted that all extant texts of Type III in the fifteenth century are literary, although it is important to stress that there is no evidence that it was regarded as a literary standard language. It was not used by some prestigious London poets, such as John Gower, nor was it used in poetry composed and copied outside London, such as in the works of the *Gawain*-poet.[8] However what is striking about the Type III texts from the fifteenth century is their close association with the poetry of Chaucer. Type III copies of Chaucer's *Troilus and Criseyde* and *Canterbury Tales* are among the earliest and textually most important of Chaucer's major poetic works.[9] The Ellesmere and Corpus manuscripts are also among the most elaborate and deluxe of all Chaucer manuscripts, certainly of those produced in the early fifteenth century. Their early dates and textual accuracy suggest close associations with Chaucer's own papers and perhaps with Chaucer himself. Previous studies of the language of the Hg and El manuscripts and the work of their common scribe, labelled Scribe B, has suggested that the language of these manuscripts is that of the scribe rather than that of Chaucer.[10] Comparison of the language of Hg and El with Scribe B's contribution to a copy of John Gower's *Confessio Amantis*, Trinity College, Cambridge, MS R.3.2, suggested that Scribe B consistently "translated" the language of his exemplar

[6] For the adoption of standardised written features in the Paston Letters see Davis 1951–2, 1952, 1983.

[7] For a discussion of the process of elaboration of the functions of Chancery Standard see *LALME* I, 'General Introduction' and Smith 1996, chapter 4.

[8] Gower's language has been shown to comprise a mixture of the Kentish and Suffolk dialects. See Samuels and Smith 1988.

[9] The importance of the Hengwrt and Ellesmere manuscripts as witnesses to the text of the *Canterbury Tales* is discussed in Blake 1985 and Owen 1991. Corpus 61 is the basis of B.A. Windeatt's (1984) edition of *Troilus and Criseyde*.

[10] See Samuels 1988b. Doyle and Parkes 1978 identified the hand of Scribe B, the copyist of Hg and El.

into his own linguistic system. However study of the distribution of certain forms across the Hg and El manuscripts suggests that these conclusions are in need of modification and that at least some forms derive from the exemplar of these manuscripts (Horobin 1998b). Given that these manuscripts are early and authoritative witnesses to the text of the *Canterbury Tales*, it seems likely that these inherited exemplar forms derive from the archetype of the tradition and therefore possibly from Chaucer himself. Another important association with Chaucerian verse is the use of Type III in the holograph manuscripts of Thomas Hoccleve. Hoccleve was one of earliest imitators of the Chaucerian style and frequently praised Chaucer's use of the English language. It is therefore significant that Hoccleve adopted the Type III system for producing manuscripts of his own poetry. Hoccleve of course claimed to have known Chaucer personally and his knowledge of Chaucer's language may have been first hand. Another important link between Hoccleve and the Hg and El manuscripts is Hoccleve's collaboration with the scribe of Hg and El in the production of the Trinity R.3.2 manuscript of Gower's *Confessio Amantis*.[11] These factors suggest a close-knit community of people composing Chaucerian verse and producing deluxe and authoritative copies of this verse.

Trinity College, Cambridge MS B.15.17, a manuscript of the B-text of *Piers Plowman*, may not on the surface appear to belong within this textual community. Langland was a West Midlander writing alliterative verse. However *Piers Plowman* contains many topographical and political references to London and Langland may have been living in London when he composed the poem.[12] Michael Samuels' study of the language of the extant manuscripts has shown that the B-text was copied and circulated in London (Samuels 1988d and 1988f). Like the other Type III texts Trinity B.15.17 contains an early and authoritative copy of the B-text which was used by Kane and Donaldson as the base-text for their edition of the B-text, although the archetype of the B tradition is generally thought to represent a considerably corrupt version of Langland's text (Kane and Donaldson 1988: 70–97).[13] The manuscript was copied in an anglicana formata hand which closely resembles that of Scribe B, who was responsible for both Hg and El. Kane and Donaldson describe the two hands as 'pretty certainly of the same school and period' (1988: 13).[14] In addition to the similarity in hand the Trinity manuscript further resembles Hg and El in what Kane-Donaldson (1988: 214) refer to as 'the exceptional consistency of its spelling, and the conformity of its grammar with "standard" late fourteenth-century usage as this is instanced in the best known manuscripts of Chaucer and

---

[11] Hoccleve is Scribe E in Cambridge, Trinity College MS R.3.2. See Doyle and Parkes 1978.
[12] For some details of Langland's London associations see Barron 1992 and Pearsall 1997.
[13] The theory of the corrupt archetype has recently been criticised by C. Brewer 1996: chapter 21.
[14] An electronic facsimile of the manuscript has been published as volume 2 in the *Piers Plowman Electronic Archive*, see Turville-Petre and Duggan 2000.

Gower'. It seems therefore that the production of the Trinity manuscript
has much in common with the other manuscripts in this group, and
especially with the Hg and El manuscripts. All of these copies of Chaucer,
Hoccleve and Langland are deluxe copies of major vernacular poets,
working in London, copied in similar hands using a similar variety of
London English.

Having examined the textual evidence we will now turn to the linguistic
evidence for Type III to see how it differed from Types II and IV. The
following table details a number of the salient differences between Types II,
III and IV identified by Samuels.

	Type II	Type III	Type IV
NOT	nouȝt	nat	not
THEY	þai, hij	they	they
THOUGH	þei(ȝ)	though	though
GAVE	ȝef	yaf	gaf
SUCH	swich	swich	such
THEIR	hir(e)	hir(e)	theyre, þeir

However these general differences conceal an important degree of internal
variation within each type of language which creates a significant overlap
between these three linguistic varieties. In order to demonstrate the presence
of this variation and its significance for an assessment of the evolution of
the London dialect I will consider the spellings of a single word, SUCH,
across a number of late fourteenth- and early fifteenth-century London
texts. The older Type II spelling of SUCH is 'swich' and this is the only
form found in, for instance, Hand 1 of the Auchinleck manuscript. This is
also the main spelling of Type III texts, although in some texts the Type IV
form 'such' is introduced. Therefore during the period in question we have
two competing spelling forms: the older form 'swich' and the new form
'such'. The distribution of these two forms across a number of London
documents is given in the following table.

	London docs.	Gower	Hengwrt	Ellesmere
Swich	4	6	294	333
Such	19	800	0	0

	Corpus 61	Trinity B.15.17	Hoccleve
Swich	151	109	148
Such	0	0	0

The first column presents the spellings of SUCH found in the London
documents in Chambers and Daunt's *A Book of London English*.[15] The
documents in this collection date from 1384–1425 and it is interesting to note

---

[15] Chambers and Daunt 1931.

that 3 of the 4 appearances of 'swich' are found in documents dating from the beginning of this period. Two of these occurrences appear in the Proclamations of Nicholas Brembre (1383) and another in a Guild Return of 1389. The only other appearance of 'swich' is found in a document relating to the Grocers' Company of 1419. The newer 'such' spellings are much more common throughout these documents and account for almost all instances of 'such' after 1389. A similar situation is found in Gower's language, as recorded in the Fairfax and Stafford manuscripts of the *Confessio Amantis*.[16] Gower's spellings of SUCH are given in the second column. Here we see that Gower agrees broadly with the London documents in preferring the form 'such' against just 6 occurrences of 'swich'. However when we compare these usages with those of the literary Type III texts, all dating from the early fifteenth century, we find the opposite situation. Here we find an overwhelming preference for the 'swich' spellings, found in both the Hengwrt and Ellesmere manuscripts of the *Canterbury Tales*, Corpus 61 of *Troilus and Criseyde*, Trinity B.15.17 of *Piers Plowman* and the Hoccleve holographs. None of these manuscripts has a single occurrence of the 'such' spelling. Given that these manuscripts all date from at least one or two decades after the main occurrences of 'swich' in the London documents it seems clear that the distinction between 'swich' and 'such' is not one of chronology. It is not the case that older texts have the 'swich' spelling and later texts have the 'such' form. So how can we explain this distribution? It seems that the distinction between these forms may be explained by reference to the linguistic term "register". The term register is one used by sociolinguists to define a linguistic variety according to use, in contrast with a variety defined according to the user, termed a "dialect". The term register is employed to account for variation according to situational context, where a speaker may vary an utterance according to situation, rather than according to the message to be communicated. For instance one might compare the linguistic choices which are appropriate to the register of letter-writing and informal conversation. Of course the concept of a register is an abstract one and it would be impossible to quantify the number of registers available to an individual speaker or the linguistic items which make up a particular register. In discussing the nature of the linguistic register R.A. Hudson writes: 'We can only speak of registers as varieties in the rather weak sense of sets of linguistic items which all have the same social distribution, i.e. all occur under the same circumstances' (Hudson 1996: 47). Such a position forces us to locate our analysis initially upon the status of the individual linguistic item and subsequently to generalise to the abstracted level of the variety. This theoretical basis is an important notion and one we shall return to in our interpretation of the development of London English.

So to return to our analysis of the data themselves. The distribution of individual linguistic items appears to correlate with textual register; the 'such'

[16] Bodleian Library MS Fairfax 3 and Huntington Library MS El 26 A 17.

spelling is dominant in official documents while the 'swich' spelling is dominant in this closely related group of literary texts. So it would appear that far from representing a dramatic shift in the London dialect after 1430, the 'such' spelling was available to London writers throughout the second half of the fourteenth century. It was used by Thomas Usk in his Appeal (1383), in the Petition of the Folk of Mercerye (1386), and then in most official documents copied after 1389. The early appearance of this form in Thomas Usk's Appeal indicates something of the status of these Type IV forms during this period. Usk was a professional scribe and was first employed by John of Northampton as a secretary: 'to write thair billes', and must therefore have received professional training as a copyist.[17] The function of Usk's Appeal is also suggestive of the status of this language at this time. Paul Strohm has written of the way in which Usk adapted various genres of legal documents for his own political ends (Strohm 1992). Usk's intentions to employ the formal language and generic conventions of the appeal and to demonstrate his control over the power of the written word is further demonstrated by the fact that rather than dictating the text of his Appeal to the city coroner, Usk supplied a copy of the document written in his own hand: 'Thom*as* Vsk ...of london knowleched thes wordes & wrote hem with myn owne [honde]'.[18] The 'swich' spelling was common in Type II texts and continued to be used in some official documents of the 1380s, e.g. the Proclamations of Nicholas Brembre (1384), and then ceased to be used in official texts after 1389. However this form did continue to be used in literary texts of the early fifteenth century, such as the Hengwrt and Ellesmere manuscripts of the *Canterbury Tales*.

The emergence of Type IV during the early fifteenth century and its eventual success as standard written English is often seen as heralding the end of Type III. However Type III was not immediately and completely replaced by Type IV, and certain distinctive Type III features continued to appear in texts produced throughout the fifteenth and into the sixteenth centuries. In order to illustrate the survival of Type III we will briefly look at what happened to this type of London English when Type IV began to be adopted for use in a wider variety of linguistic functions, in the period after about 1430. As the Type IV spelling system began to be used in the London book trade for the copying of literary manuscripts we would expect to see all Type III spellings replaced with those of the new London standard. In order to consider the impact of Type IV on Type III I want to look at the spellings of SUCH across the fifteenth-century manuscript tradition of the *Canterbury Tales*, in order to discern to what extent scribes preserved the 'swich' spelling or introduced the 'such' spelling.[19] The following analysis is

---

[17] See Usk's 'Appeal' in Chambers and Daunt 1931: 23. For a discussion of Usk's career and his attempts to use his literacy for his own political ambitions see Strohm 1990.

[18] Chambers and Daunt 1931: 22.

[19] The spellings of this item provide a useful test-case as the complete replacement of 'swich' by 'such' is generally considered to have been an early development. Michael Benskin has written: 'Some of the Type III forms were replaced faster than others: *swich* 'such' looks to have been recessive by the 1420s.' See Benskin 1992: 80. See also Fisher et al. 1984, esp. p. 27.

based on the fifty-four extant manuscript and four pre-1500 printed witnesses of the *Wife of Bath's Prologue*.[20] These manuscripts were copied in various parts of the country, showing influences from a number of different dialects, covering the West and East Midlands, the Northern counties, the South-West and Kent. In addition there are a number of manuscripts which were copied in London.[21] These manuscripts were produced throughout the fifteenth century and we would therefore also expect to see the influence of the emerging Type IV across these manuscripts. The table below gives a comparison of the number of occurrences of the two spellings of SUCH across the manuscript tradition of the *Wife of Bath's Prologue*, divided into chronological periods of twenty-five years.

SWICH	1400–1425	54
	1425–1450	7
	1450–1475	13
	1475–1500	2
SUCH	1400–1425	37
	1425–1450	188
	1450–1475	185
	1475–1500	126

This table shows that while the impact of Type IV is apparent it did not immediately replace the Type III form, which continued to be used as late as 1482, in Caxton's second edition of the *Canterbury Tales*. While the number of appearances of the 'swich' form is reduced throughout the fifteenth century the occurrences increase in the period 1450–1475.

In order to attempt to understand this situation, I want to break this information down into two examples: one from the first twenty-five years and the other from the final twenty-five years of the fifteenth century. My first example concerns Doyle and Parkes' Scribe D who copied two manuscripts of the *Canterbury Tales*, probably within the first decade of the fifteenth century: BL MS Harley 7334 [Ha⁴] and Corpus Christi College, Oxford, MS 198 [Cp]. Scribe D's manuscripts are particularly useful because he copied a large number of manuscripts of different texts: in addition to the two *Canterbury Tales* manuscripts he copied 8 manuscripts of the *Confessio Amantis*, and single manuscripts of *Piers Plowman* and Trevisa's translation of *De Proprietatibus Rerum*. As a result of Jeremy Smith's work on these manuscripts we know that when Scribe D copied each of these texts his dominant spelling for SUCH was the Type IV form 'such'. However the situation is more complicated for the Chaucer manu-

---

[20] My analysis is based on the diplomatic transcripts and spelling databases available in P.M.W. Robinson 1996.

[21] The dialectal distribution of these manuscripts is the subject of chapter 4 and appendix 1.

scripts copied by Scribe D which also contain occurrences of the Type III spelling 'swich'. It is by no means as common as the Type IV form 'such' but its appearance in both these manuscripts is of interest. Cp has more occurrences than Ha4: Cp has 56 instances of 'swich' compared with 252 uses of 'such', while Ha[4] has 'swich' 13 times and 350 occurrences of 'such'. It could be argued that these are simply mistakes where Scribe D has neglected to change an occurrence of 'swich' in his copytext into his preferred spelling 'such'. However these spellings of 'swich' are not entirely isolated occurrences. A number of other Type III spellings are also found consistently throughout both the Cp and Ha[4] manuscripts, such as 'nat', 'hem', 'thurgh', 'ayein'. The survival of this group of forms into both manuscripts seems striking, especially given that London English was not Scribe D's native dialect. Jeremy Smith's work on Scribe D's manuscripts has shown that Scribe D was a West Midlander by birth and an immigrant into the capital (Smith 1988b). Each of Scribe D's manuscripts contains a layer of West Midlands spellings, and it seems likely that the inclusion of Type III forms was therefore a conscious decision to preserve these forms from the copytext. This theory is confirmed by the evidence that a number of these minor London forms appear in exactly the same positions in both Ha[4] and Cp. If these forms were simply careless copying errors we would expect to see a random distribution throughout the texts of the two manuscripts. However the preservation of these spellings in the same places in both manuscripts confirms that their appearance in the two manuscripts cannot be accidental.[22]

Let us turn now from Scribe D to the end of the fifteenth century and look at the two printed editions of the *Canterbury Tales* issued by William Caxton in 1476 and 1482. As with Scribe D, the evidence of Caxton's printed editions is useful as we may compare it with his editions of other authors and with printed editions of his own prose. The evidence of Caxton's two printed editions is also useful as Caxton tells us in his preface to his second edition that he corrected the first edition against a better manuscript in order to produce the text of the second edition.[23] Caxton's preferred spelling of SUCH is the Type IV spelling 'such' although there is a single occurrence in the *Wife of Bath's Prologue* of 'swhich' at line 147. Given Caxton's preference for the Type IV spelling of this word we would expect that when he came to correct his first edition for a second edition that he would replace the single occurrence of 'swhich' with 'such'. However this is not the case and the single use of 'swhich' is retained at line 147 of the *Wife of Bath's Prologue* in Caxton's second edition. It might be argued that this is simply laziness on Caxton's part. The single occurrence of 'swhich' in his first edition could be simply an error: one that Caxton was unconcerned to remove in his second edition. It might therefore be assumed that Caxton

---

[22] Consider for instance the remarkable correlation in the occurrences of ⟨ay-⟩ spellings of 'again(st)' in Ha[4] and Cp discussed in chapter 3.
[23] The text of this preface is printed in Blake 1973: 61–3.

was only interested in correcting the substantive details of the text, and was not interested in minor details such as spelling. However there is evidence that Caxton was interested in spelling. For not only did Caxton preserve a number of Type III spellings from his first edition into his second edition but he even introduced Type III spellings not found in the first edition. Comparison of these forms with those used by Caxton in his own prose writings reveals that Caxton's preferred usage for these items were the Type IV forms. So we cannot explain these changes as Caxton inadvertently introducing his own spellings into Chaucer's text. It seems that Caxton felt that certain spelling forms were distinctively Chaucerian and he therefore introduced them into his second edition, presumably having encountered them in the better manuscript which he used to correct his erratic first edition.[24]

The example of the two spellings of SUCH outlined above demonstrates that apparent changes in the London dialect during this period may in fact be indicative of ongoing linguistic variation rather than completed linguistic change. It seems that these two variants were available throughout the fourteenth and fifteenth centuries but that they acquired different connotations. The 'swich' spelling seems to have become associated with literary texts while the 'such' form appears to have been associated with official documents. Whether variation of this kind is representative of the spoken as well as the written language is difficult to assess in the example given above, and the question of the relationship between speech and writing is a notoriously difficult problem. However it is possible to demonstrate the continued tolerance of linguistic variation at the spoken level by a consideration of features of London phonology and morphology across these same texts. In order to demonstrate the preservation of phonological variation in the London dialect in this period I will now examine the various reflexes of OE *y* as found in London documents throughout this period. The diatopic distribution of the various Middle English reflexes of this vowel is as follows. In the East Midlands OE *y* was unrounded and written as ⟨i, y⟩ while in East Anglia and in the South-Eastern counties this vowel was reflected as ⟨e⟩. In the West Midlands and in the South-West the rounded vowel was preserved and represented as ⟨u, uy⟩ (Jordan 1974: 66–72). However it is a characteristic of London English to show considerable variation in the representation of this OE vowel and London texts frequently contain examples of each of these different spellings. This tolerance of linguistic variation is found in London documents produced over a time period of almost two centuries. The Proclamation of Henry III (1258) contains forms showing all three types of variant, ⟨i, e, u⟩, e.g. 'king', 'iwersed', 'kuneriche'.[25] A similar situation is found in Type II documents as may be exemplified by Hand III of the Auchinleck manuscript which contains examples of each of these forms within a single text. For instance

---

[24] The language of the early printed editions of the *Canterbury Tales* is treated in greater detail in chapter 5.

[25] For a printed text of the Proclamation see Dickins and Wilson 1951: 7–9.

the *Seven Sages* contains the following spellings of the verb KISS (OE 'cyssan'): 'kes', 'kest', 'kyste', 'kiste' and the following forms of the adjective MERRY (OE 'myrge'): 'mery', 'murie'. Both of these latter forms are found in rhyme, therby confirming that these belong to the authorial language and are not the result of scribal interference. Similar variation is evidenced in the spellings of the noun FIRE (OE 'fyr') which is spelled as both 'fir' and 'fer' in the following rhymes: 'fir: matir', 'fer: cher'. If we turn from the language of Type II to texts copied in Type III we find a similar situation. For instance the Hg manuscript of the *Canterbury Tales* shows considerable tolerance of variation in the reflection of OE *y* both within the line and in rhyme, as demonstrated by the following spellings of the adjective MERRY, all found in rhyming position: 'merye: berye', 'mury: Caunterbury', 'myrye: pirye'. It is clear that variation of this kind was tolerated at both the spoken and written levels and that there was little pressure towards standardisation and the reduction of variation.

The continuity and stability of the evolution of the London dialect throughout this period in its development may be further demonstrated by a consideration of certain aspects of its morphology. For instance the presence of morphological variation throughout the fourteenth century is demonstrated by the forms of the third person singular present tense inflexions recorded in these texts. The common form found in London English in this period is the Southern inflexion ⟨-(e)th⟩. For instance this form is the principal inflexion adopted by the scribe of the Hengwrt and Ellesmere manuscripts of the *Canterbury Tales*. This form survived into the fifteenth century where it was subsequently gradually replaced by the originally Northern form ⟨-(e)s⟩. However the ⟨-(e)s⟩ form is found in a number of instances in Type II London texts, where it is frequently employed in rhyme position. For example the copy of *King Alisaunder* contained in the Type II manuscript Bodleian Library MS Laud Misc. 622 shows the following forms: 'beres', 'shiftes', 'spedes', 'lookes'. The ⟨-es⟩ inflexion is also recorded in a number of Chaucerian texts, although it is restricted to early works such as the *Book of the Duchess* and the *House of Fame*, where it is often used for rhyming purposes. An example of the use of the inflexion in rhyme is found at lines 73–4 of the *Book of the Duchess*:

> That never was founded, as it telles,
> Bord ne man, ne nothing elles

Later in his career Chaucer seems to have preferred the ⟨-(e)th⟩ variant, reserving the ⟨-(e)s⟩ form as a dialect marker in the speech of the Northern undergraduates in the *Reeve's Tale*. Perhaps Chaucer, as a young poet, was forced to draw on this variant to cope with the 'skarsete of rym in Englissh', but as a more mature writer he considered it to be stylistically inappropriate.[26]

---

[26] For Chaucer's complaint that 'rym in Englissh hath such skarsete' see line 80 of the *Complaint of Venus*.

Or perhaps the status of this variant changed within the period between the composition of the *Book of the Duchess* and the *Reeve's Tale*. This situation illustrates the range of linguistic variation available within the London dialect throughout the fifteenth century, and the process by which the status of certain variants was subject to change. It is not the case that the older ⟨-(e)th⟩ variant was used until it was replaced by the arrival of the Northern variant. The two forms were available within the variational space found within the London dialect and a particular variant was selected for specific stylistic effect.

A similar situation may be illustrated by another important change in the development of London English during this period. This is the gradual adoption of the Norse-derived pronouns 'THEY, THEIR, THEM' as replacements for the native OE equivalents. Towards the end of the Old English period the native OE third person plural pronoun system became increasingly indistinct, particularly in reduced-stressed situations. In addition to this the replacement of grammatical gender with natural gender added to the ambiguity and the need for a formally distinct pronominal system.[27] The Old Norse pronouns first appeared as replacements for the OE forms in the *Ormulum*, a text copied in Lincolnshire c. 1200. They are gradually adopted more widely over the following two centuries, with the nominative form, 'they', becoming adopted in the London dialect in the fourteenth century. These pronouns were adopted in the London dialect at different times and the oblique forms are apparently not accepted until the emergence of Type IV in the early fifteenth century. The standard textbook description of the process by which these forms were accepted into London English may be summarised conveniently by the following table:

	Type II	Type III	Type IV
THEY	hij, þai	they	they
THEIR	hir(e)	hir(e)	thair, their
THEM	hem	hem	them, theym

However this standard account masks a degree of important variation within this paradigm. For example the scribe of the Type II manuscript Laud Misc. 622 has the following spellings of the nominative form of the pronoun: 'hij', 'hee', 'hi', 'þai', 'þay'. The evidence of Type III usages for these items appears more stable. The Hengwrt and Ellesmere manuscripts are extremely consistent in their use of the forms 'they, hir(e), hem' and the only example of variation is the use of the Old Norse form 'thair' where it is used for deliberate stylistic effect in the Northern speech of the

---

[27] For a detailed discussion of the factors conditioning the adoption of the Norse pronouns see the discussion in Smith 1996: 128–34.

Reeve's Tale. The same system is also consistently adopted by the scribe of Corpus 61. However the ⟨th-⟩ forms are not unknown in spellings of the possessive pronoun in Type III documents from this period. Thomas Usk used the forms 'thair', 'ther' alongside the form 'hem' in his Appeal of 1384. Usk was a native Londoner as he himself states in his 'Testament of Love': 'Also the citee of London, that is to me so dere and swete, in whiche I was forth growen'.[28] The form 'þam' appears in the will of another Londoner, John Pyncheon, dated to 1392 (Furnivall 1882: 3). It appears that the ⟨th-⟩ forms were available to Type III users although these forms were not adopted by writers such as Chaucer. It seems possible that the ⟨h-⟩ forms of the pronoun were associated with the tradition of literary composition while the ⟨th-⟩ forms were principally associated with official texts. This hypothesis is strengthened by a consideration of the treatment of these ⟨h-⟩ forms by later copyists of Chaucer's work. If the ⟨h-⟩ pronouns were considered to be archaic and old-fashioned we would expect to see fifteenth-century copyists replacing these with the more advanced ⟨th-⟩ equivalents. However a study of the treatment of these pronouns by copyists of Chaucer's *Wife of Bath's Prologue* throughout the fifteenth century indicates a strong tendency to preserve these forms:[29]

Line	No. of 'hem'	No. of 'them'
43	55	3
137	54	4
222	50	2
396	57	1
664	51	4

Line	No. of 'hir(e)' etc.	No. of 'their' etc.
101	55	2
206	53	5
392	52	6
672	55	3
722	57	1

It is apparent from the above table that scribes were careful to preserve forms of the pronouns with initial ⟨h-⟩ as found in Type III London English, despite the availability of the forms with initial ⟨th-⟩, 'them', 'their'. We have seen above that these forms derived from Old Norse were current in London English from at least as early as the 1384 when they are used by Thomas Usk in his 'Appeal'. This deliberate avoidance of these forms and careful preservation of the Type III equivalents throughout the fifteenth

---

[28] Book I, chapter 6. The text is edited in Skeat 1894: vol. VII.

[29] Differences in the total number of occurrences of these forms for each line may be explained by the fact that some manuscripts do not contain any form of 'their' in the line in question.

century, suggests that scribes considered the older pronouns to be appropriate to copies of Chaucer's verse and preserved them accordingly.

Changes in the pronoun system of the London dialect are also considered to have affected spellings of the item THOUGH in this period. It is argued that the forms derived from Old Norse 'þó' were adopted as a therapeutic measure to avoid the homonymic clash which arose following the loss of the final fricative in the forms 'þeigh', 'þeih', 'þeiȝ' and the adoption of the Old Norse third person plural pronoun, 'they'. In his discussion of this process Samuels provided schematic maps to indicate the forms found for these items in the Southern dialects of late Middle English. Samuels argued that in all Southern dialects the adoption of 'though' always followed the adoption of 'they' and never vice versa, and that when there was a time interval between the adoption of both forms this was always short.[30] The following table summarises the received view of the development of London forms of this item:

Type II	Type III	Type IV
þeiȝ	thogh, though	though

However the evidence of the texts themselves reveals that both the innovative Old Norse forms 'they' and 'though' were adopted early in London, and both are attested in Type II texts. Another piece of evidence which appears to conflict with the theory of replacement on the grounds of homonymy is the appearance of constructions such as 'þei þai' in Hand 1 of the Auchinleck manuscript for THOUGH THEY, where a diphthongal difference appears to be sufficiently distinctive.[31] A similar construction has also been identified by the editor of *Floris and Blaunche-flur* who observes that Hand 3 of the Auchinleck manuscript used the sequence 'þai þai' (e.g. line 554) (De Vries 1996: 48). Consequently the suggestion that the 'though' forms were adopted as a replacement for the 'theigh' spelling in order to prevent confusion seems less obvious. If this were the case we would expect that the introduction of the 'though' form would result in the immediate loss of the earlier 'theigh' spelling. However it seems that in the London dialect in this period there was a considerable period of overlap where both innovating and traditional forms remained available for the item 'though'. For instance while the dominant form in the Type II texts is indeed 'þeiȝ', both Hand 3 of the Auchinleck manuscript and Laud Misc. 622 also include the Type III spelling 'þouȝ'. Similarly the main forms recorded in the Type III Hengwrt manuscript are 'thogh', 'though' although there are a further 7 occurrences of the Type II spelling 'theigh'. The Corpus manuscript of the

---

[30] See Samuels 1972: 71–2.
[31] For examples of this construction see *Of Arthour and of Merlin*, lines 1011, 1781, edited by Macrae-Gibson 1973.

Troilus and Criseyde also favours the Type III spellings, but also contains 7 examples of the Type II form 'theigh'. The Trinity manuscript of *Piers Plowman* has 14 instances of 'theigh', including 4 instances of the construction 'theigh thei'. Late fourteenth-century official documents also show a tolerance of both forms. For instance in his Appeal Thomas Usk used the older spelling 'altheigh' while the 'Petition of the Folk of the Mercerye' has the spelling 'though'. Therefore the evidence of the spellings of THOUGH across texts copied in Types II and III shows that the replacement of the older form 'theigh' with the newer form 'though' was neither sudden nor comprehensive. Both forms were available throughout the period with a number of writers using both forms. This suggests that the adoption of the 'though' form was not a result of the pressures of homonymy, otherwise we would expect a complete replacement of 'theigh' forms with 'though' forms. It seems that the forms 'they' and 'theigh' coexisted within the London dialect for at least a century. It is possible that any potential confusion was avoided by the fact that these items belong to different word classes. It is instructive to note that a much greater potential for confusion existed in Type III forms for the pronouns 'her' and 'their', both spelled 'hir(e)'. Yet despite the similarity of these two forms the Old Norse form 'their' is not adopted as a replacement for 'hir(e)' until relatively late. It seems unlikely therefore that the adoption of the pronoun 'they' was the result of a homonymic clash with 'theigh' given the continued tolerance of such a clash concerning the pronouns 'her' and 'their'.

We do however see a major change in the ratio of usages for these items as the 'theigh' form becomes progressively less common and the 'though' form is increasingly adopted. By the early fifteenth century the number of occurrences of the 'theigh' form has decreased considerably, as shown by the small number of appearances of this form in the earliest Chaucer manuscripts. However the form does not entirely die out in the fifteenth century as it is preserved by a number of copyists of Chaucer's works. While it is evident that these fifteenth-century scribes did not have this form in their active linguistic repertoires, they were careful to preserve the form when they encountered it in their copytexts. In order to demonstrate the deliberate preservation of the 'theigh' form by fifteenth century scribes the following figure shows the treatment by later copyists of four occurrences of this form in the Hengwrt manuscript. The 12 manuscripts chosen for analysis are the 9 manuscripts which, with Hg itself, comprise the O Group of manuscripts: manuscripts argued to be related by their common descent from a single exemplar.[32] These manuscripts have been selected as they are likely to have had the 'theigh' form in their exemplars. Similarly the El manuscript and the two manuscripts copied by Scribe D have been included as early and authoritative witnesses.

---

[32] For the identification of the O Group and a list of the readings which are shared by this group of manuscripts see P.M.W. Robinson 1997.

MS	Dominant form	III.1327	V.325	V.612	III.53
Hg	**thogh, though**	**theigh**	**theigh**	**theigh**	**theigh**
Ad[1]	thouh	thouh	thouh	—	thouh
Ad[3]	thogh, though	theigh	theigh	thei	theigh
Bo[2]	þogh	þeigh	thei	—	þogh
Ch	though	theigh	though	though	theigh
Cp	þough	þough	þeigh	þeigh	þough
El	thogh, though	thogh	though	though	thogh
En[3]	thouh	thowh	thouh	—	thouh
Ha[4]	þough	þough	though	þeigh	—
Ha[5]	though	theigh	though	—	Out
Ht	þogh	thogh	though	þogh	þoughe
Ra[3]	thouȝ	they	thouȝ	they	thouȝ
Tc[1]	thouȝ	thouȝ	thouȝ	—	thouȝ

It seems clear that despite their own use of the Type IV forms, a number of these scribes deliberately preserved the Type II forms when they encountered these in their copytexts.[33] It seems therefore that the 'theigh' forms were stylistically salient, suggesting a situation similar to that proposed above concerning the 'swich' forms of SUCH. Rather than exhibiting a process by which the older 'theigh' spelling is completely replaced by the innovative form 'though', it appears that both types of form were used throughout the second half of the fourteenth and the fifteenth century. It seems that by the fifteenth century the 'theigh' spellings of THOUGH had adopted a specifically literary connotation, while the 'though' form gradually became the exclusive form of the documentary record.

The evidence of the fifteenth-century copies of the *Canterbury Tales* shows that a number of Chaucer's scribes preserved features of Type III London English despite the influence of a new written standard language, Type IV. This seems to represent a collective response to aspects of the language which were regarded as "Chaucerian", and therefore integral to a text of Chaucer's work. It seems that in the early fifteenth century Type III London English became associated primarily with literary texts due to its use by a small community of scribes producing important and deluxe manuscripts of the major English poets. The authority of these manuscripts was not simply a result of their expensive appearance. These manuscripts also reveal a textual accuracy which testifies to a close relationship with the author's foul-papers and possibly with the author himself. This situation is particularly apparent in the case of the Hg and El manuscripts of the *Canterbury Tales*, which represent early and accurate copies of Chaucer's work. The question of the relationship

---

[33] In the table the symbol '—' indicates that the relevant form is missing from the text in question.

between the language of the Hg and El manuscripts and Chaucer himself is therefore crucial to an understanding of the nature of Type III and its uses, and this will be the subject of the following chapter.

3

Evidence for Chaucer's Language

In the previous chapter I situated Chaucer's language within the development of the dialect of London in the fourteenth and fifteenth centuries. In
this chapter we will look more closely at the Type III variety of London
English, and particularly the Hg and El manuscripts, in order to consider
the evidence these texts offer for Chaucer's own linguistic usage. As no
Chaucerian holograph manuscript survives we have to rely on scribal copies
of Chaucer's works for evidence of the poet's own language. It has
traditionally been agreed by scholars that none of the extant copies of
Chaucer's works dates from the poet's lifetime, and that many of the earliest
manuscripts were written one or two decades after Chaucer's death in 1400.
However the question of whether extant manuscripts of his verse date from
Chaucer's own lifetime has recently been reopened by some scholars. The
possibility that early manuscripts of the *Canterbury Tales* were copied
before Chaucer's death is discussed by N.F. Blake (1997a), and the proposal
that the Hg manuscript may date from this period has been suggested more
recently by E. Stubbs (2000). The possibility that Hg and other early
witnesses date from Chaucer's lifetime has obvious implications for our
understanding of their status as records of Chaucer's language. It has
generally been accepted that the language of Hg and El is that of their
common scribe, Scribe B, and that this language is distinct from that of the
author. However if one or both these manuscripts were produced during
Chaucer's lifetime and possibly even under his supervision then their status
as evidence for Chaucer's language must be reconsidered. This chapter will
begin by examining the language of these early manuscripts in order to
reevaluate the evidence they offer for Chaucer's own linguistic habits. I will
then provide a detailed comparison of select linguistic features of the Hg
and El manuscripts in order to consider the nature of the differences in their
treatment of Chaucer's language, and the evidence these provide concerning
ongoing changes in the London dialect and the transmission of Chaucer's
text.

Previous work on the identification of Chaucer's own spelling habits has
been advanced by the identification of the language of the Fairfax and
Stafford[1] manuscripts of Gower's *Confessio Amantis* as the poet's own

---

[1] Bodleian Library MS Fairfax 3 and San Marino, Huntington Library MS EL 26 A 17.

usage. This identification has thus established a "control" for analysis of the language of subsequent copies of the *Confessio Amantis*.[2] Doyle and Parkes' demonstration of the presence of two scribal hands at work on both *Confessio Amantis* and *Canterbury Tales* manuscripts, Scribes B and D in their nomenclature, has allowed this "control" to be applied to the study of Chaucer's own orthographic practice.[3] Despite the apparent scientific certainty with which scholars have approached this problem, such studies continue to display fundamental disagreements, as is exemplified by the conclusions to articles on Chaucer's spelling by M.L. Samuels (1988b) and L.D. Benson (1992). Having identified certain forms which he claimed to be Chaucerian, Samuels demonstrated their similarity to the spelling system of the *Equatorie of the Planetis*, advising future editors of Chaucer to 'alter spellings in the directions indicated by the *Equatorie*' (p. 34). Benson's consideration of the same forms selected by Samuels, however, led him to the conclusion that 'the *Equatorie* is not in what was probably Chaucer's system of forms and spellings and that an editor would therefore be very ill advised to alter the spellings of an authentic text, as Samuels suggests, "in the directions indicated by the *Equatorie*"' (p. 23).

The reason for such disagreement lies in the approaches upon which such studies of Chaucer's spelling system are founded. These approaches include how the data used are collected and the methods with which these data are subsequently interpreted. The first section of this chapter will address the restrictions of the current methodology, and will attempt to demonstrate how, with the application of computers to manuscript studies, we may seek solutions to the problem with greater confidence.

A primary flaw in the assembling of data for the study of the spelling systems of Chaucer manuscripts is that such studies are often carried out without reference to the manuscripts themselves. The inaccessibility of many of these primary sources makes such reference difficult, but does not justify the reliance on untrustworthy material. Despite the publication of facsimiles of several important *Canterbury Tales* codices (Ruggiers 1979, Hanna 1989b, Stubbs 2000, Parkes and Beadle 1979), scholars have continued to rely on the Chaucer Society transcripts compiled by F.J. Furnivall in the late nineteenth century (1868–84). These transcripts often fill manuscript lacunae by introducing text from other witnesses and thus creating an appearance of completeness. As such they may be open to misinterpretation, as is demonstrated by Benson's article in which some data is taken from the text of CUL MS Gg.4.27 [Gg]. However, the

[2] Samuels and Smith (1988) claim that 'the Fairfax and Stafford MSS are, in all respects except their actual handwriting, as good as autograph copies' (21–2).

[3] Scribes B and D are shown to have co-operated in the production of Trinity College, Cambridge, MS R.3.2 of the *Confessio Amantis*, while B was individually responsible for Hg and El, and D for Cp and Ha[4]. Scribe D's hand has been recognised in a further 9 manuscripts, including 7 copies of the *Confessio Amantis*. Scribe B also copied the 'Cecil Fragment' of Chaucer's *Troilus and Criseyde* and possibly CUL MS Kk.I.3/20. See Doyle and Parkes 1978 and Doyle 1997.

facsimile of Gg reveals this manuscript to be defective, due to the wide-spread removal of its illuminations. In these portions of Gg, the spellings that Benson used to demonstrate the preservation of certain archetypal forms are those of BL MS Sloane 1685, used by Furnivall to supply the text missing from Gg for his Chaucer Society transcripts.[4] Similarly one must also beware the practice of modern editions, where spellings may be silently emended to conform to editorial preconceptions of metre and language, and readings may be supplied from elsewhere with a similar lack of acknow-ledgement. In this respect Benson fell foul of emendation in the *Riverside Chaucer*, recording a single use of 'suche' in the work of Scribe B at line X.894 in Ellesmere [El], a line found in this edition but not in El itself. The single appearance of a particular spelling is suggestive of the accidental preservation of an exemplar spelling, and possibly an authorial one, as Benson suggested for the case of 'suche'.[5] It is therefore extremely import-ant that such claims are founded on the evidence of the manuscripts themselves and not on outdated transcripts or edited texts.

The methods used in assembling the data may also prejudice the interpretation, as such studies rely on spellings taken from samples of text, the length and position of which restrict and determine the ultimate conclusions. The range of forms available to a scribe, from both active and passive repertoires, and the many external influences that determine the resultant choice of spelling demand that for the identification of an author's own forms the text must be analysed in its entirety. Certain tranches of text may yield quite different ratios of usage, or even unique forms, and the distribution of these ratios is crucial to an evaluation of the overall linguistic structure of the text. Distribution of forms across the entire text may further allow us to identify switches in exemplar, or the progress of copying, were a scribe to move from a graphemic to a logographic transcription policy. The analysis of variant spelling forms must similarly be free from assumptions imposed by our conception of ME dialect variation. For example, in his examination of Chaucerian orthography Benson explained his methodo-logy in this way:

> In most cases the distinction between the spelling chosen as Chaucerian and the alternative is a matter of form rather than spelling – between, for example, the form *ay-n(s)* and the form *ag-n(s)*, with a phonetic contrast in the first consonant, rather than between *ageyns* and *agayns*, in which the contrast between *-eyn-* or *-ayn-* is most likely a matter of spelling rather than sound. Though these differences in form are accidentals and therefore greatly at the mercy of scribal variation, they are somewhat more stable than spelling variants. They can thus be investigated by the ordinary means of comparing manuscript readings and by comparisons to contemporary usage; though in almost every case we must remain

---

[4] For example Benson recorded the following spellings in 3 lines in Fragment V where Gg is out: 'ayeyn' (53), 'ayeyne' (57) and 'agayne' (670). These are the forms given in the Chaucer Society transcript, although the text of these lines is that of Sloane 1685.

[5] Benson 1992: 27, n. 28.

uncertain about Chaucer's own preferred forms, we can make informed guesses about some of them. (Benson 1992: 1–2)

Although it is difficult to understand the distinction being made in this quotation, Benson seems to assume a correspondence between phonemic and graphemic usage that predetermines the data that he selected for his analysis. He assumes a simple binary distinction between the phonemes /g/ and /j/, and that these sounds were equivalent to the graphemes ⟨g⟩ and ⟨y⟩ which could not be used interchangeably for phonetic realisation in fourteenth and fifteenth-century dialectal usage. On the basis of these assumptions Benson silently regularised all spellings of 'AGAIN(ST)' which adopt the basic form ⟨aȝ-⟩, although he was not able to assimilate this third grapheme to his binary phonetic framework.[6] Any study of ME orthographic practice must operate on a graphemic level, analysing all variation regardless of possible phonetic value. Where a scribe used distinct orthographic forms we must not prejudge the significance of this usage, but examine the occurrences of all constituent spellings and judge possible phonetic or grammatical significance from the resulting data.

Analysis of scribal behaviour has traditionally been founded on McIntosh's (1963) description of the three basic types of copyist represented in our extant ME corpus. The first type of copyist (A) makes a *literatim* transcription of the exemplar, the second (B) attempts a thorough translation into his own scribal idiolect, and the third (C) combines these two processes with a variety of results. However the detection of types A and B is particularly tentative, as certainty can only truly be achieved through comparison of a scribal copy with its immediate exemplar: a very rare privilege given the erratic survival of ME manuscripts. The distinction between these two types and C is therefore one of degree rather than kind, and depends greatly on the amount of text analysed.

This becomes especially clear when we turn to the analysis of *mischsprachen*, where a single scribal output is found to contain a mixture of dialectal features. In their comprehensive account of *mischsprachen*, Benskin and Laing posited three possible scenarios to explain the appearance of 'exotic' forms in the work of a single scribe (Benskin and Laing 1981). The first type are relicts, lone exemplar spellings which do not form part of the scribe's own repertoire, transcribed by an otherwise consistent translator. The second type, uncommon forms found grouped in specific textual segments particularly at the beginning of a stint of copying, are deemed the result of a distinct move from transcription to translation. The third type are due to "constrained selection": the scribe's accommodation of his spontaneous usage to that of his exemplar. A scribe operating in this way will distribute forms from within the limits of both active and passive repertoires throughout the entire text. The distinctions made in this analysis

---

[6] It is unclear whether Benson regarded ⟨aȝ-⟩ as phonetically equivalent to ⟨ag-⟩ or ⟨ay-⟩. Two examples of 'aȝen(s)' in Fragment I in Gg are recorded as 'ayen' (1509) and 'ageyns' (1787).

rely on the identification of three important factors: the type of copyist, the language of the immediate exemplar, and the range and distribution of forms throughout the entire scribal copy. Having highlighted these three crucial factors I shall now discuss their application to the manuscripts of the *Canterbury Tales*.

Although traditional scholarly opinion currently accepts that no holograph manuscript of Chaucer's work survives[7] scholars have attempted to recover Chaucer's own spelling system from the extant fifteenth-century witnesses. This work has been centred on the El and Hg manuscripts: manuscripts close to the Chaucerian archetype and copied by a single scribe with a consistent grammatical practice. By comparing the orthographic features of his stint on the Trinity copy of the *Confessio Amantis* with the authentic Gowerian forms of the Fairfax and Stafford manuscripts, scholars have argued that Scribe B consistently translated the archetypal forms of *Confessio Amantis* and thus belongs to McIntosh's second category (Samuels 1988b). This same copying practice has then been assumed for his work on the Chaucer manuscripts, and forms common to Hg and El only are argued to be due to constrained selection. These forms are thus preserved from the exemplar and, given the textual authority of these manuscripts, ultimately from the archetype, and are therefore argued to be Chaucerian. Using this method Samuels compared the spellings of four words in the Fairfax and Trinity Gowers and the Hg and El Chaucers, identifying the following spellings, unique to both Hg and El, as authorial: 'agayn(s)/ageyn(s)', 'biforn/bifore', 'wirke' (vb.), 'say/saw'. The acceptance of these forms as authorial is thus based on a string of hypotheses that assume a straightforward textual history. While the claim that Fairfax and Stafford are linguistic autographs may be authoritative, we can be less sure that they represent the immediate exemplar of the Trinity Gower. To assume therefore that Scribe B consistently translated the Trinity exemplar is similarly open to debate, and simplifies the problem further. The subsequent assumption that Scribe B would behave identically when presented with the Chaucer exemplars requires a similar leap of faith. Any intermediary copy between the Gowerian archetype and the Trinity manuscript could transform the authorial language, and alterations in the frequency and distribution of authorial forms would be inevitable. Identification of a consistent translator must be firmly based on factual evidence from an immediate exemplar, and as this does not apply to Scribe B it is safest to assume that he was more likely to operate as a Type C copyist, mixing transcription with translation. Rather than relying on the evidence of the Trinity Gower to determine Scribe B's copying practice for his work on Chaucer, we must turn to the Hg and El manuscripts themselves, where

---

[7] Scholars remain undecided whether Peterhouse College, Cambridge, MS 75.I of the *Equatorie of the Planetis* is a Chaucerian holograph. However recent lexical, stylistic and codicological studies have argued strongly that the manuscript is neither Chaucerian nor an autograph. The debate over authorship is summarised in Rand Schmidt 1993.

the evidence reveals the problem to be less straightforward than Samuels suggested.

Samuels did not provide any of the data used in his analysis, nor did he specify which portions of the text he examined to construct his linguistic profiles, making it difficult to examine the evidence behind his conclusions. In the following table I give the figures for all the spellings of the forms Samuels cited as authorial on the basis of constrained selection, across the entire text of both witnesses.[8]

		Hengwrt	Ellesmere
AGAIN(ST)	'again(s,st)'	1	3
	'agayn(e,es)'	172	230
	'ageyn(s)'	16	20
	'ayein(s)'	9	0
	'ayeyn(s,es)'	0	11
BEFORE	'tofor-'	0	1
	'b-for-'	112	131
WORK (VB)	'werch-', 'wirch-'	12	17
	'werk-', 'wirk-'	39	42
SAW (VB)	'saugh(e)'	31	124
	'saw(e)'	43	5
	'say(e)'	48	12
	'seigh'	13	3
	'sy'	0	1

The distribution of forms across the two manuscripts certainly calls into question Samuels' conclusions, as one could support claims for the authority of quite different forms. For example, a hypothesis that Scribe B consistently translated his exemplar would mean that the forms 'ayeyn/ ayein' and 'tofor-' could be relics and therefore possibly archetypal. Similarly, if it was assumed that the scribe was generally a meticulous transcriber, these minor forms could be understood as the result of the unconscious use of his own spelling system. The number of different spellings for WORK and SAW testify to a range of variant forms, making such analysis complicated and highly subjective.

Samuels' argument is constructed upon selected data and the figures for the exact counts and the amount of text analysed are not given. Comparative frequency of usage is shown, although the distribution of this usage is ignored. Furthermore his methodology is based upon a set of assumptions concerning the textual history of these manuscripts which may not be

---

[8] These figures have been assembled using the electronic transcripts prepared by The *Canterbury Tales* Project, which allow the examination of individual spellings across entire manuscripts. Complete transcripts of Hg and El are available in Stubbs 2000, while the spellings found in Hg are also accessible in Blake et al. 1994.

accurate. In such a situation, where immediate exemplar and type of copyist remain unknown, confidence can only be acquired through an analysis of the distribution of the forms and the influences that may have prompted these orthographic choices. Benson does discuss the question of distribution, but as shown above the data upon which his analysis is constructed is flawed by inaccuracies and a further set of assumptions. In what follows I demonstrate a methodology which will allow us to approach the questions of exemplar spellings and copying type from a more objective standpoint. I use the word AGAIN(ST) as a model for this example, as Samuels' selection of the spelling 'agayn' as Chaucerian has been regarded as authoritative.[9]

In his work on Hg and El Scribe B employed five alternative spellings for AGAIN(ST): 'again', 'agayn', 'ageyn', 'ayein' and 'ayeyn'. In the following discussion I concentrate on the variation between the ⟨g⟩ and ⟨y⟩ graphemes. The ⟨ag-⟩ spelling is clearly the most common form throughout the entire text of both manuscripts, although the use of *ayein/ayeyn* is found alongside this spelling, concentrated in certain portions of text. There are 9 and 11 uses of the form ⟨ay-⟩ in Hg and El respectively, all clustered in restricted textual segments with remarkable correlation. Here are the line references:

	Hengwrt	Ellesmere
Fragment I		
KN	I.892	I.892
	I.1509	I.1509
		I.1787
MIP	[Hg out]	I.3155
RE	I.4067	
CO		I.4380
Fragment IV		
CL	IV.320	IV.320
MER	IV.2260	IV.2260
	IV.2313	
Fragment V		
SQ		V.96
		V.127
	V.670	V.670
Fragment VII		
TM	VII.1236	
NP	VII.3409	
Fragment X		
PA		X.448

---

[9] P. Robinson (1991) used the consistent appearance of the 'highly idiosyncratic' Chaucerian spelling 'agayn(s)' in the *Equatorie* as conclusive proof that 'Peterhouse 75.I is Geoffrey Chaucer's holograph'.

Such close correlation cannot reasonably be explained as the result of accidental transcription by a scribe transforming the spellings of his exemplar with the 'practised ease and consistency' Samuels assumed. The clustering of these forms in Hg alone warns against such a hypothesis, while the close agreement with the positioning of these spellings in El allows us to dismiss such a theory. The most likely explanation is that the use of these spellings reflects a change in usage in a common exemplar for these tales, or a change of the exemplar itself, preserved by direct scribal transcription. The differences that do remain in the exact uses of ⟨ag-⟩ and ⟨ay-⟩ forms in these tales may either be the result of an intermediate stage of copying of the common exemplar, or the mixed transcription and translation policy adopted by this scribe. Benson has also demonstrated a close correlation between the spellings 'ayein/ayeyn' in the Hg and El manuscripts, and he used the evidence of Gg to reinforce his claim that such forms are archetypal, and therefore authorial. However his conclusions are undermined by the initial assumptions he adopted and the incorrect data upon which he based his interpretation.[10] While Gg does not support the evidence drawn from Hg and El, significant conclusions can be drawn from the two manuscripts copied by Scribe D: Corpus 198 [Cp] and Harley 7334 [Ha^4]. Each manuscript has just two examples of spellings of AGAIN(ST) which adopt the form ⟨ay-⟩ throughout the entire text, and their positioning shows startling consistency. The form 'ayayn' appears at line VII.1769 in both manuscripts, while 'ayein' is found at line V.330 in Cp and in an extra line added after X.592 in Ha^4. The preservation of these four closely related spellings cannot be accidental, and must argue for the existence of these forms at these positions in their exemplars. The preservation of these spellings is especially marked given the strong West Midlands dialectal layer that their exemplars had passed through.[11] A further piece of supporting evidence comes from the distribution of these spellings in a later manuscript, although one whose text has close affiliations with Hg: BL MS Additional 35286 [Ad^3]. The Ad^3 scribe uses the ⟨ay-⟩ spelling just 15 times, and the distribution reaffirms the findings discussed above. All uses are grouped within the following tales, with 4 agreements with the exact line reference in Hg, El or both: KN, MIP, MI, RE, CL, MER, SQ, PR, SH, TM, PA. This evidence is also compelling for the survival of these forms despite the influence of the incipient Chancery Standard or Type IV, the influence of which is found in the Ad^3 language.[12] When we look beyond the evidence of the earliest manuscripts to a slightly later generation of copying, we see

[10] Many of the figures Benson assembles for Gg are inaccurate. The scribe of Gg never uses the spelling ⟨ay-⟩; all forms of AGAIN(ST) have the ⟨ag-⟩ spelling, with the exception of 27 examples of 'aȝens'.

[11] For a detailed analysis of the dialectal layers in the language of Scribe D, see Smith 1988b.

[12] The Signet, Privy Seal and Chancery documents record 22 forms of AGAIN with ⟨ag-⟩, 8 with ⟨ay-⟩ and 2 with ⟨aȝ-⟩. See Fisher et al. 1984.

the almost total removal of the ⟨ay-⟩ spellings. This is demonstrated in the complete lack of such forms in both CUL MS Dd.4.24 [Dd], the head of the *a* tradition, and BL MS Lansdowne 851 [La], a *c* manuscript whose exemplar was close to that of Cp.

Thus the spellings of AGAIN(ST) using the form ⟨ay-⟩ display a consistency among the earliest and most authoritative *Canterbury Tales* manuscripts. As we move further from the archetype the ⟨ay-⟩ spellings are completely removed across different textual traditions. That the presence of the ⟨ay-⟩ spellings in these five authoritative manuscripts could be due to coincidental scribal error or conflation seems highly unlikely, and we must surely assume that they are the result of one ultimate common exemplar. Thus by close analysis of the distribution of individual spelling forms in this manner we are able to deduce the degree of transcription and translation carried out by individual scribes in their work on specific manuscripts. Where the direct preservation of exemplar spellings is clear we are able to compile a profile of spellings that derive from the common archetype. Where such manuscripts are known to be of high textual authority, this archetype will be close to the authorial holograph and thus significant for an assessment of the author's own spelling habits. The evidence presented above suggests that the spelling 'ayein/ayeyn' repre-sents at least part of Chaucer's own usage, thus contradicting Samuels' conclusions and the argument that the *Equatorie* is in Chaucer's own spelling system. However we must always remember that an ultimate common archetype may be at least one stage removed from that of the author, and any reconstruction of Chaucer's own spelling practice remains speculative. This caveat is reinforced by Samuels's attempt to justify his choice of the forms 'agayn(s)/ageyn(s)' as Chaucerian against the collective testimony to forms beginning ⟨ay-⟩ and ⟨aʒ-⟩ common to most of his other Type III documents.[13]

There are a number of other minor forms in Hengwrt and Ellesmere which also appear in exactly the same positions in both manuscripts. As suggested above with the spellings of AGAIN(ST), this consistency points to the possibility that such forms represent exemplar forms preserved by *literatim* scribal transcription. Several of these forms serve to highlight further the degree of dialectal variation tolerated within the London dialect and within Chaucer's usage. For instance the form 'ar' ARE is a distinctly Northern form and is very much more common in the North of England during this period (see *LALME* I map 118). Chaucer's dominant forms for the verb BE are derived from the OE 'beon': 'ben', 'been' etc.,

---

[13] In order to justify his theory of constrained selection Samuels claimed that ' "agayn(s)" was an exceptionally progressive form for Chaucer to use', and provided a highly speculative hypothesis to account for its appearance in the poet's repertoire: 'We may surmise that Chaucer's adoption of it was due to his having encountered it more than most Londoners as a man of travel and affairs, but, since so pronounced a feature is more likely to have been adopted earlier in his life, it might equally well be due to his period of service as a page at Hatfield, Yorks., in the later 1350s', see Samuels 1988b: 30.

which are much more common in the Southern dialects of ME (see *LALME* I map 124). The Northern form 'ar' appears twice in Chaucer's depiction of the Northern dialect in the language of the students in the *Reeve's Tale*, thereby apparently reinforcing its Northern status. However there is a third appearance of this form which appears at line 350 of the *Shipman's Tale* in both Hg and El. The retention of this single instance of this form at the exact same position in both manuscripts suggests that it is a genuine exemplar form, and that it is likely to be Chaucerian. There are a handful of further related uses of the Northern form of the verb BE in Hg which appear as follows: 'are' (II.286), 'arn' (IV.342, VII.1642). It seems very likely that these are also survivals from the Hg exemplar as all 3 instances are also recorded in El. In addition to the preservation of these forms at the same positions, the El manuscript also contains an extra occurrence of 'are' at VIII.914 (a tale not found in Hg) and two appearances of 'arn' in the *Parson's Tale*. That these forms are likely to be derived from the Chaucerian exemplar is further reinforced by the appearance of 3 occurrences of 'arn' in Corpus 61 of the *Troilus and Criseyde*. Survivals of this kind warn us against the view of Scribe B as a ruthless dialect translator, and against an over-restrictive view of the variety of Chaucer's language. One further example concerns the use of the Northern forms of the verb GIVE with the initial ⟨g-⟩ alongside Chaucer's dominant form with initial ⟨y-⟩. There are two occurrences of the form 'gaf' in Hg at lines I.1441 and I.4411, and a single appearance of the form 'gyue' at III.501. The El manuscript contains just one example of the form 'gaf' which appears at the same point in the *Knight's Tale* as in Hg. In addition to their preservation of this form, both manuscripts contain a single occurrence of the form 'Forgyue' at line 425 of the *Shipman's Tale*. Once again this evidence strongly suggests that these Northern variant forms are genuinely Chaucerian forms.

Analysis of this kind is also significant for studies of the textual tradition of the *Canterbury Tales*, as the evidence of shared spelling forms in specific segments of text suggests common exemplars, and thus genetic affiliations between manuscripts. The close correlation in the appearance of certain rare spelling forms in both Hg and El suggests that, for these sections of the text at least, the two manuscripts were copied from the same exemplar. Evidence of this kind adds weight to the hypothesis that these manuscripts were produced from closely related exemplars, contradicting the view that differences in the text and language of the El manuscript are the result of a different copytext. Recently Jill Mann (2001) has argued that many of the differences found in El may be explained as the result of the scribe's use of a different exemplar, thus enabling her to dismiss the theory that the El manuscript is the product of scribal editing. However the evidence of the scribe's spelling practices across the two manuscripts appears to support the view that the two manuscripts were copied from the same copytext for parts of the text. There are indeed differences in the orthography of the two manuscripts although these have been explained by Samuels as changes in Scribe B's spelling practices over the period in which he copied Hg, El and the Trinity Gower and the Cecil Fragment of *Troilus and Criseyde*. Samuels showed that Scribe B's spelling habits altered in a systematic way across these manuscripts, with a number of linguistic features showing a gradual progression from Hg to El with the Trinity Gower and Cecil Fragment occupying intermediate positions. Samuels explained these developments as the result of changes in the scribe's own habits, reflecting contemporary changes in the London dialect rather than changes in exemplar. He further argued that these linguistic differences may also reflect differences in the scribe's attitude to the Hg and El manuscripts: an attitude which may have been influenced by the differences in the functions of the manuscripts themselves. Such factors are not addressed by Mann who views all such differences as the direct influence of different exemplars used by Scribe B in the copying of Hg and El. Yet Mann's discussion of a passage from CUL MS Gg.4.27 which the scribe inadvertently copied twice further highlights the fact that a scribe's treatment of spelling, grammar and even lexis could vary even when the exemplar itself remained unchanged. Given that the Gg scribe presumably produced both versions of the same passage on the same day, as Mann argues, it seems perfectly plausible that Scribe B could copy the same exemplar of the *Canterbury Tales* very differently, especially given the likely time delay between the production of the two versions. However where differences in spelling between the two manuscripts are found to cluster in particular textual segments these may indicate switches in exemplar. The evidence considered above suggests that the tales containing ⟨ay-⟩ spellings of AGAIN(ST) may derive from a separate copytext, although clearly a much larger profile of spellings must be subjected to this form of analysis before such a conclusion can be confirmed. In the remainder of this chapter we will investigate the linguistic differences between Hg and El in greater detail in order to consider whether these differences are likely to be scribal, editorial or the result of changes in exemplar.

Linguistic Differences between Hg and El

Despite the close agreements between certain linguistic features in both the Hengwrt and Ellesmere manuscripts discussed above, there are a number of distinctions between the language of these two witnesses. These differences may be explained in a variety of ways. They may be indicative of the range of variation found within the Type III variety of London English, thereby providing further evidence of the range of variation tolerated within a single scribe's repertoire. In chapter 2 I discussed the distinction between fixed and focused standardised varieties of written language, and gave some examples concerning the variation found within Type III London English. However a close comparison of the language of

Hg and El, copied by a single Type III scribe, will provide a much more detailed picture of the degree of variation permitted within a standardised variety of this kind. The identification of consistent differences between the language of the two manuscripts may also provide insights into changes in the scribe's idiolect in the interval between the copying of these texts. Such differences may provide evidence of changes occurring within the London dialect during this critical period in its development. In addition to this, comparison of the language of these two manuscripts will cast light on the relationship between these two important witnesses to the text of Chaucer's *Canterbury Tales*. Consistent linguistic differences between the two texts may be indicative of different editorial policies between the production of the two manuscripts. For instance where linguistic changes consistently affect metre or rhyme their motivation may be explained as deliberate editorial intervention. Where such differences appear to be less systematically introduced they are potentially indicative of a change of exemplar. Differences introduced in this way are harder to isolate but may be identified by comparison with readings in other manuscripts across the *Canterbury Tales* textual tradition, as well as with familiar models of scribal error and sophistication. In order to consider these many different factors the following section will comprise a close linguistic comparison of the texts of the Hengwrt and Ellesmere manuscripts.

In the previous chapter I discussed the availability of various different reflexes of OE *y* within the London dialect, and the way in which poets exploited this variation for the purposes of rhyme. If we look more closely at this aspect of variation across Chaucer's works and the Hg and El manuscripts, we may observe a number of factors determining the choice between these phonetic variants. For instance despite the variation available to Chaucer with regard to this feature there are certain words which appear in rhyme only in their East Midland form. For instance the word SIN (OE 'synn') appears in rhyme in Chaucer's works only in the spelling 'synne' (e.g. III.51 and IV.1681). A similar situation is found in Chaucer's use of the word HILL which appears in rhyme in the form 'hil', as in BD 1319–20: 'hil: fil'. It may be that the preference of this form over its South-Eastern equivalent with ⟨e⟩ is due to the avoidance of a homonymic clash with the word HELL. The avoidance of certain phonetic variants is also found in non-rhyming environments. For instance the common word FIRST, which never appears in rhyme in the *Canterbury Tales*, is found in its East Midland form 'first(e)' in each of its of 140 occurrences in both the Hg and El manuscripts.

Some words rhyme most frequently on the East Midland form but admit sporadic use of the South-Eastern variant in certain rhymes. An example of this is found in the forms of the word THIN which is commonly used in rhyme in the form 'thynne' (e.g. VIII.740–1 'wynne: thynne'), but also appears in a single instance in rhyme in the form 'thenne' (I.4065–6 'renne:

thenne'). A similar example is found in the spellings of the word DINT which appears within the line and in rhyme in its East Midland spelling 'dynt' (e.g. III.276, HF 534), but also appears in one instance in rhyme in its South-Eastern form 'dent: yblent' (I.3807–8). The word MILL also appears only in its East Midland reflection 'mille' throughout Chaucer's works, except in three occurrences of 'melle' in rhyme. One of these occurrences is in the *Former Age* and two others in the *Reeve's Tale* both in the rhyme 'melle: telle' (I.3923–4, 4241–2). In addition to these instances of 'melle' there is a single further occurrence of this form in the Hg manuscript in the *Parson's Tale*. That this form does not appear in the equivalent line in El suggests that the South-Eastern spelling was increasingly recessive during the early fifteenth century. Another such form is the South-Eastern reflection of KIN which appears just once in rhyme in Chaucer's works (BD 437–8) alongside many instances of the East Midland spelling 'kyn' both within the line and in rhyme (e.g. I.3941–2). The South-Eastern spelling 'stere' is limited to appearances in rhyme in *Troilus and Criseyde* (III.910, IV.1451) and does not appear elsewhere in Chaucer's works. It seems likely therefore that Chaucer favoured the East Midland reflex 'stire' and that the use of 'stere' in the *Troilus* was necessitated by the demands of a more complex rhyme scheme.

In some words the South-Eastern form is the more common or even unique form in rhyming position. For example the verb STINT appears in a number of instances in rhyme with the spelling 'stente'. There are 3 occurrences of this form in rhyme in the *Knight's Tale* and others in the *Clerk's* and *Monk's Tales* (e.g. I.903–4, 1367–8, 2441–2). It is however significant that this form appears only in rhyme and the East Midland equivalent 'stynte' appears a further 28 times in the *Canterbury Tales* in non-rhyming positions. It appears that Chaucer's use of the form 'stente' was conditioned by its usefulness in certain rhymes and that his preference was otherwise for the East Midland form 'stynte'. It is perhaps worth noting that the *Clerk's* and *Monk's Tales* employ rhyme schemes which are more demanding in terms of finding rhyme words, while the *Knight's Tale* is known to have been composed early in Chaucer's career. This distribution in the *Canterbury Tales* appears to be reinforced by the use of the form 'stente' in Chaucer's other works. This form appears in rhyme in a total of 10 instances in *Troilus and Criseyde*, often in rhyme with the common words 'wente', 'sente' (e.g. IV.340). Other appearances of the form in Chaucer's works are found in two rhymes in the *Book of the Duchess*, where 'stente' appears in rhyme with the verb 'wente' (BD 153–4, 357–8). This distribution outside the *Canterbury Tales* appears to reinforce the use of 'stente' observed above. It appears to be a form found largely in certain rhyming contexts, such as 'stente: wente: sente', and is generally restricted to earlier works and those composed in more demanding verse forms, such as the rhyme royal of the *Troilus*.

The verb SHUT is an example of a word which appears only in its South-

Eastern reflection throughout the Chaucer corpus in both rhyming and non-rhyming contexts. For instance there are a total of 11 instances of this verb in the *Troilus*, 8 of which are in rhyme and all are in the South-Eastern form 'shette'. The clear preference for the form 'shette' is highlighted by its appearance at III.1086 where it is found rhyming with the form 'knette'. The spelling 'knette' is also a South-Eastern form used alongside the more common East Midland 'knitte' by Chaucer and its appearance here seems to be determined by Chaucer's preference for the form 'shette'. It is perhaps likely that Chaucer's preference for the South-Eastern realisation of OE 'scyttan' is due to the avoidance of the homonymic clash with the taboo noun SHIT. The overwhelming adoption of the South-Eastern form 'shette' is also reinforced by the forms of this verb found in the *Canterbury Tales*. There are 8 examples of 'shette(n)' in the *Canterbury Tales*, 4 of which are in rhyme (e.g. I.3499–500). By comparison there are no instances of the East Midland form 'shitte' in either the Hg or the El manuscripts. One interesting exception to the complete avoidance of the East Midland form 'shitte' by Chaucer is the following rhyme found in Fragment A of the *Romaunt of the Rose*:

> For ther is noon so litil thyng
> So hid, ne closid with shittyng,   (1597–8)

The rhyme is clearly not dependent on the use of the East Midland form although the appearance of a distinctively non-Chaucerian form in rhyme in Fragment A of this work is striking. Scribes were often particularly careful to preserve authorial spellings in rhyming positions whether these were essential for the rhyme or not so it seems unlikely that this form is scribal.[14] Furthermore there are other instances of the South-Eastern form 'shette' within the line elsewhere in Fragment A suggesting that this is the scribe's preferred form (e.g. line 1082). It is possible that the unusual form 'shittyng' may be explained by the early date of composition of Chaucer's translation of the *Romaunt*, as has been observed in the appearance of other unfamiliar and subsequently recessive forms in Chaucer's earlier works (see above, p. 29.

In some words there appears to be a progression across Chaucer's career, as may be demonstrated by his use of the variant spellings 'knette' and 'knytte'. The South-Eastern form 'knet' appears in rhyme in the earliest works such as the *Romaunt* (RR 1397–8) and in those composed in rhyme royal, such as the *Parliament of Fowls* (PF 627–8) and the *Troilus* (III.1088, 1734). However in addition to its appearance in rhyme in the *Troilus* there is also a single further occurrence within the line at III.1748. There are a number of occurrences of the East Midland form 'knytte' in the *Canterbury Tales* (e.g. V.986) but only a single instance of the South-Eastern form

---

[14] Although of course this is not always the case. See the discussion in chapter 1 for a more detailed discussion of scribal treatment of forms in rhyme.

'knette' in the Hg manuscript, at X.28. The equivalent line in El has the East Midland 'knytte' demonstrating the ongoing process by which the South-Eastern form became less favoured and increasingly replaced by the preferred East Midland form.

A similar progression across Chaucer's works may be observed in the forms of the verb KISS (OE 'cyssan'). The East Midland spelling 'kisse' is the most common form across Chaucer's works and appears frequently both in rhyming and non-rhyming contexts. The forms 'kesse', 'keste' etc. appear in rhyme in both the *Troilus* (e.g. III.1129) and the *Canterbury Tales*, although there is a difference in the treatment of these forms in the Hg and El manuscripts. For instance the rhyme 'stedfastnesse: kesse' is found at IV.1056–7 in both Hg and El while the rhyme 'blesse: kesse' at IV.552–3 is found only in Hg; El has 'blisse: kisse'. A similar situation may be observed at lines 141–2 of the *Shipman's Tale* where Hg has the rhyme 'keste: leste', while El rhymes on the East Midland vowel 'kiste: liste'. It appears that tolerance of the South-Eastern form was reduced betwen the copying of the Hg and El manuscripts, and that in rhymes where it was possible, the scribe of El preferred to substitute a South-Eastern form with an East Midland equivalent.

The above discussion has shown that a number of changes may be observed in Chaucer's attitudes to dialectal variation available in London English and that the status of such variants was clearly changing throughout his career. However further changes have also been observed between the treatment of such variants between the Hg and El manuscripts, despite the fact that both were copied by the same scribe. I now want to examine this feature more closely by comparing the treatment of OE *y* reflexes in these two manuscripts in greater detail.

In the above discussion I concentrated on the exploitation of differences in spellings of this group of words in rhyme, but variation of this kind is not limited to rhyme words in the Hengwrt manuscript. For instance a consideration of the total number of spellings of the word MERRY in Hg shows a considerable amount of variation: 'mery(e)' 5, 'myry(e)' 20, 'mury(e)' 39. Of these occurrences only a small number may be explained by the demands of the rhyme scheme: 'mery(e)' 4, 'myry(e)' 6, 'mury(e)' 5. However it appears that the scribe had a different attitude to such forms when he copied the Ellesmere manuscript. In copying Ellesmere the scribe was careful to retain these variants where the rhyme demands it, but where the Hg manuscript has variation within the line El shows a clear preference for a single form. Where the Hg manuscript often shows a preference for spellings with OE *y* reflected in ⟨u, e⟩, in El the preference is clearly for spellings with ⟨i, y⟩. This preference may be exemplified by a consideration of the following differences between the spellings of words showing various reflections of OE *y* in the Hengwrt manuscript. These examples are taken from the *General Prologue* and the *Miller's Tale*:

		Hg	El
GP	I.757	murye	myrie
GP	I.759	murth	myrth
GP	I.764	murye	myrie
GP	I.782	murye	myrie
GP	I.857	murye	myrie
MI	I.3218	murye	myrie
MI	I.3325	murye	myrie
MI	I.3344	murye	myrie
MI	I.3491	thenk	thynk
MI	I.3575	murye	myrie
MI	I.3578	murye	myrie
GP	I.3654	busynesse	bisynesse

In addition to these evident preferences for spellings showing the reflection of OE *y* in ⟨y, i⟩ within the line, the scribe of the El manuscript also makes some adjustments in rhyme words where such words rhyme with each other. For instance lines I.3307–8 of the *Miller's Tale* have the following rhyme in Hg: 'cherche: werche'. However in El the spelling of both words has been adjusted to give the following rhyme: 'chirche: wirche'. In some instances the Hg manuscript has a spelling which appears to spoil the rhyme and these occurrences are frequently emended in El. An example of this occurs at lines 225–6 of the *General Prologue*:

Hg   For vn to a poure ordre for to yeue
       Is signe that a man is wel yshryue

El   For vn to a poure ordre for to yiue
       Is signe þat a man is wel yshryue

However there are also instances of the reverse situation: where the El scribe has a spelling which spoils the rhyme represented in the Hg spelling. For example lines 505–6 of the *General Prologue* read as follows in the two manuscripts:

Hg   Wel oghte a preest ensample for to yiue
       By his clennesse how þat his sheep sholde lyue

El   Wel oghte a preest ensample for to yeue
       By his clennesse how þat his sheep sholde lyue

The consistency of the differences in the representation of the reflex of OE *y* in the two manuscripts suggests that the intervening years between the production of Hg and El saw a change in the status of these linguistic variants. We saw in the previous chapter how this period witnessed the gradual reduction of such variation as a standardised spelling system began to emerge. It may be that this move towards a single preferred form for these items in this scribe's repertoire is indicative of this ongoing change. In fact there is evidence that a change in status was occurring and that the scribe was responding to such changes in his choice of these forms. In his eagerness to replace items in his repertoire which show OE *y* reflected in ⟨e, u⟩ with spellings with ⟨i, y⟩, the scribe produced a number of unusual forms. For instance in line I.3732 of the *Miller's Tale* in El the scribe writes the word 'pitte' for Hg's 'putte'. This may have seemed a perfectly appropriate form to the scribe but it is a very unusual spelling and one which does not appear elsewhere in Chaucer, apart from in the *Reeve's Tale* where it forms part of the students' Northern dialogue: 'Why ne had thow pit the capil in the lathe' (I.4088). In producing this rare form the scribe appears to be responding to an external linguistic pressure to replace examples of ⟨u, e⟩ with spellings with ⟨i, y⟩. However it is apparent that the impetus for this change is external as the scribe has also transferred this change to an environment where it is "correct" but not commonly found in London English. Therefore the scribe appears to have "hypercorrected" in applying a phonetic change to an environment where it is not appropriate. The sociolinguistic concept of hypercorrection was discussed in the preceding chapter and its importance as evidence for linguistic change was highlighted. Hypercorrection is commonly the result of a speaker imitating a more prestigious mode of speech, thereby demonstrating the availability and recognition of prestigious spoken systems within a particular social context. A good example of this phenomenon is the random spreading of initial [h] to unhistorical and non-standard environments by *h*-droppers in an effort to imitate Received Pronunciation (Hudson 1996: 173).[15] While it is a common phenomenon in modern sociolinguistic studies it also has a number of parallels in medieval scribal practice.[16] The identification of this kind of linguistic behaviour in the work of Scribe B provides important evidence concerning ongoing linguistic change within the London dialect, and the scribe's perception and response to the status of such changes.

In addition to the changes with respect to orthography and phonology discussed above, there are also a number of consistent differences in the morphology of these two manuscripts. Morphological differences frequently affect the number of syllables in a particular word and can therefore have an important impact upon the metre of the text. For instance in Chaucer's language there was considerable variation in the use of the ⟨y-⟩ prefix, a reduced form derived from OE ⟨ge-⟩, in past participles. This variation could therefore be exploited by poets such as Chaucer for metrical purposes. However comparison of the treatment of past participles in the Hg and El manuscripts suggests that in copying El the scribe had a different policy regarding the use of this prefix. Many occurrences of the past participle without the prefix in Hg, are found with the ⟨y-⟩ prefix in the equivalent occurrence in El. Consider the following

---

[15] For a discussion of the importance of hypercorrection in linguistic change see Labov 1972.
[16] See for instance J.J. Smith's discussion of the linguistic habits displayed in Farman's contribution to the Rushworth Gospel gloss: Smith 1996: 26–9.

examples taken from the *General Prologue*, the *Miller's*, *Shipman's* and *Summoner's Tales*:

		Hg	El
GP	I.77	come	ycome
GP	I.193	purfiled	ypurfiled
GP	I.324	falle	yfalle
GP	I.690	yshaue	shaue
MI	I.3235	barred	ybarred
MI	I.3429	born	yborn
SH	VII.309	shaue	yshaue
SU	III.2118	thonked	ythanked

A similar kind of variation was available in the inflexional endings added to present plural forms of the present indicative and to infinitives which could both end ⟨-e(n)⟩. This variation could also be exploited by poets for metrical purposes, as the addition or omission of a final ⟨-n⟩ will often prevent or allow elision with a following vowel, thereby affecting the syllable count. However despite the importance of this feature in determining the metre of the verse there is considerable variation between the Hg and El treatment of such forms. A comparison of the following examples of such differences in the *General Prologue* and the *Summoner's Tale* demonstrates the frequency of such discrepancies. These examples also show that there is a consistent tendency for the El scribe to add the final ⟨-n⟩ where it is omitted in Hg:

		Hg	El
GP	I.170	gyngle	gynglen
GP	I.186	swynke	swynken
GP	I.413	speken	speke
GP	I.578	weere	weren
GP	I.581	make	maken
GP	I.635	drynke	drynken
GP	I.642	knowe	knowen
GP	I.651	excuse	excusen
GP	I.806	spende	spenden
SU	III.1878	hadde	hadden
SU	III.2097	speke	speken
SU	III.2125	yeue	yeuen
SU	III.2236	deme	deemen
SU	III.2288	seyden	seyde

In addition to this variation in the addition or omission of a final nasal consonant in inflexional endings, there is also considerable difference in the representation of unstressed vowels in these endings. There is a greater tolerance of variation in the Hg treatment of unstressed vowels which may be written ⟨e, i, y⟩, while El shows a clear preference for ⟨e⟩. This difference may be demonstrated by a consideration of the following forms of the verb 'clepen':

	Hg	El
(y)cleped	5	46
(y)clepid	30	2
(y)clepyd	14	1

It seems that in copying Hg the scribe was much more tolerant of such variation whereas when the same scribe copied El his preference was clearly in favour of the use of ⟨e⟩ to represent the unstressed vowel. The single use of the form 'yclepyd' occurs at line 410 of the *General Prologue*: 'His Barge yclepyd was the Maudelayne', which might suggest that its appearance is the result of a scribal slip early in his work on the manuscript. It was common for scribes to use a greater range of forms in the opening folios of a manuscript during an initial period of "working in" (see Benskin and Laing 1981).

Another interesting aspect of variation found in Scribe B's verbal inflexions concerns the ending of the third person singular of the present tense. This ending is written ⟨-eth⟩ throughout both manuscripts, although the final fricative is represented by the runic ⟨þ⟩ in some instances. All of these uses of the ⟨-eþ⟩ inflexion are found in the two prose tales, the *Parson's Tale* and the *Tale of Melibee*. There are 12 occurrences of this inflexion in both Hg and El, although only one of these instances concerns the same verb in the same position ('ouercomeþ'). It is interesting to compare the restriction of this feature to prose with the same scribe's use of this inflexion in his stint on the Trinity Gower. In this text the runic ⟨þ⟩ is used frequently within the verse both in third person singular endings and in other words where it is extremely rare or never found in Hg or El. For instance the verb ending in ⟨-eþ⟩ is common, as are spellings such as 'þei', 'þere', 'þanne', 'þow'. The form 'þei' THEY is not found at all in Hg and is recorded just once in El in the *Parson's Tale* , while 'þow' is found once in Hg alone in the *Tale of Melibee*. It seems likely that the use of this letter in prose tales only in the Chaucer manuscripts is a result of the practical necessity of fitting longer lines onto the page. In fact a similar explanation may lie behind the increased use of this feature in the Trinity Gower as this is the only manuscript of these three which has two columns to a single folio, placing greater restrictions upon the scribe's writing space.

A slightly different kind of morphological variation between the two manuscripts concerns the use of the present and preterite tenses. There are a large number of instances where the two manuscripts differ in their use of the present and preterite tenses. While this variation rarely impacts upon concerns such as metre, it is frequently of stylistic significance. Consider for example the following readings taken from the *Squire's Tale* in the Hg and El manuscripts, and the *Riverside* edition of the poem.

16	*Riverside* [R], El	Hym lakked noght that longeth to a kyng
	Hg	Hym lakked noght þat longed to a kyng
430	R, El	She swowneth now and now for lakke of blood
	Hg	She swowned now and now for lakke of blood
443	R, El	Whan þat it swowned next for lakke of blood
	Hg	Whan þat it swowneth next for lakke of blood
602	R, El	Therfore bihoueth hir a ful long spoon
	Hg	Therfore bihoued hir a ful long spoon

These readings give examples of the variation between present and preterite forms in the Hg and El manuscripts, and the *Riverside* edition's dependence on the text of El. There does not appear to be any grammatical principle underlying the selection of one verb form over another by the *Riverside* editors, as is shown by the selection of different forms at line 430 and 443. Chaucer's tendency to switch between the present and the past tenses within a piece of narration has been the focus of a number of scholarly discussions, particularly concerning Chaucer's use of the historic present. For instance L.D. Benson demonstrated the stylistic significance of the historic present with an examination of the use of the preterite and present tenses in lines concerning Absolon in the *Miller's Tale*. Benson argued that the historic present is employed in the passages describing Absolon's wooing of Alison in order to emphasise the continuous nature of his courtship. However the consistent use of the historic present in this passage is only found in El, while Hg is less regular in its use. For example here are lines I.3371–4 in the Hg manuscript:

> Fro day to day this ioly Absolon
> So woweth hir þat hym is wo bigon.
> He waketh al the nyght and al the day.
> He kembed his lokkes brode and made hym gay

One of the central problems in interpreting Chaucer's use of the historic present is the frequent tendency to switch tenses abruptly within a short passage, or even within a single line. This has frequently been accounted for as the result of 'lack of sequence of tense', thereby arguing that single uses of the present within a passage cast otherwise entirely in the preterite are simply errors and not genuine examples of the historic present. Benson argued that sudden switches from the present to the preterite tense are a stylistic device indicating a move from continuous to finite action: 'The present verbs describe an action that continues until it is ended by a preterite verb which brings the action of the sentence to a climax' (Benson 1961: 67). However the extent to which this tendency is observed also varies according to the text one consults. In the following example the switch from the use of the historic present to the preterite in line 1046 to signal a shift from continuous to finite action is found only in the Ellesmere manuscript and not in Hg:

> The sesoun priketh euery gentil herte
> And maketh hym out of his slep to sterte
> And seith arys and do thyn obseruaunce
> This maked Emelye haue remembraunce   (I.1043–6)

Another use of the historic present identified by Benson concerns rhetorical passages where the narrator addresses the audience. However the use of the present tense in these instances is similarly prone to variation, as in the following example:

> Almyghty god that saueth al mankynde
> Have on Custaunce and on hir child som mynde
> That fallen is in hethen hand eft soone
> In point to spille as I shal telle yow soone   (II.907–10)

Here the use of the historic present 'saueth' seems appropriate not only for a direct address to the audience, but also to emphasise the timelessness of the event. Salvation is a continual and eternal process which is not bound by temporal constraints. However the present tense form is found only in the Hg manuscript and not in El, and here the *Riverside* edition adopts the Hg reading. A comparison of the use of present and preterite forms in the Hg and El manuscripts reveals a number of similar instances where the two texts differ.[17] Study of these differences reveals that Hg shows a greater tendency to switch between tenses within a piece of narration, while El is more consistent in the adoption of the present or the preterite. These differences reveal tendencies similar to those discussed above, in which the scribe is more tolerant of linguistic variation in Hg and more prone to consistency and standardisation in El. Despite the stylistic significance which has been drawn from such consistency in El, it seems unlikely that this feature is Chaucerian. It seems more likely that the consistent use of the present tense in a passage of narrative in El is the result of the scribe's desire to regularise the tenses rather than a reflection of deliberate stylistic policy by Chaucer. The different attitude towards variation between the present and preterite tenses in Hg does not necessarily reflect Chaucer's own practice either, although given its tendency to represent the linguistic details of its copytext more accurately it seems that a study of Chaucer's use of the historic present should be based upon the Hg rather than the El text. While Benson's study remains a valuable general discussion of the uses of the historic present, it cannot be relied upon in all its details as a study of Chaucer's own practice but rather as that of the El manuscript.

One further aspect of linguistic variation between the two manuscripts which affects the stylistic quality of the texts they transmit concerns the

---

[17] See for instance the examples in the following tales: *Knight's Tale*: I.978, 1046, 1260, 1278, 1362, 3063; *Miller's Tale*: I.3374, 3380, 3602, 3627, 3635; *Man of Law's Tale*: II.440, 463, 862, 907, 1058, 1158; *Clerk's Tale*: IV.687, 1085.

representation of the Northern dialect in the *Reeve's Tale*. It is generally recognised that there is an increased number of Northern features in the Ellesmere manuscript, suggesting that the scribe or editor of El attempted to make the characterisation more consistently Northern. In order to consider the scribe's motivations more closely I want to focus on several related forms which occur only in the Hg and El representations of the Northern dialect, with the following distribution: 'heem' HOME [Hg I.4032]; 'geen' GONE [El I.4078]; 'neen' NONE [El I.4185, 4187]. These forms have been the cause of some considerable confusion for philologists as they show an apparently unhistorical reflection of OE *ā* in ⟨ee⟩. J.R.R. Tolkien (1934) was unable to account for such forms and he dismissed them as 'ghostly', speculating that they may be the result of scribal confusion between the ⟨o⟩ and ⟨e⟩ graphs. Subsequent studies have generally grouped these forms among other Northernisms with no attempt to account for their appearance.[18] Jeremy Smith has recently argued (1994) that these spellings may be explained as attempts to adapt a Southern orthography to represent changes in the realisation of long vowels in Northern dialects following the Great Vowel Shift.

It is my view that none of these suggestions sufficiently accounts for these forms and for the evidence of their manuscript distribution. Tolkien's decision to base his text and his discussion on the El manuscript led him to focus his discussion on the El forms 'geen' and 'neen', and to dismiss the Hg form 'heem' from consideration. However we have seen that recent textual scholarship has argued for the primacy of the Hg text, and has suggested that the El text is the result of a degree of editorial activity (P.M.W. Robinson 1999). It is therefore important to base any explanation of these forms on the Hg form 'heem' rather than on the two El forms. If we attempt to explain this form alone it seems likely that the Hg spelling 'heem' does not represent an unhistorical reflection of OE 'ham' but rather a straightforward development of Old Norse 'heim'. Indeed the spelling 'heem' suggests a development from a specifically East Norse form 'hem', showing characteristic EN *ē* for West Norse *ei*, *æi*, e.g. EN 'en' for WN 'einn', EN 'hetir' for WN 'heita'.[19] The suggestion of an ON rather than an OE origin is of course appropriate for the representation of the Northern dialect, and the students' dialogue contains a large amount of ON vocabulary, e.g. 'hayl' [I.4022] (ON 'heill'), 'ille' [I.4045] (ON 'illr'), 'ymel' [I.4171] (ON 'í milli'). This last example is of particular importance for the present argument as it is derived from EN 'í melle' rather than WN 'í milli', thus showing a similar etymology as suggested above for the Hg spelling 'heem'.[20] However this explanation cannot account for the appear-

---

[18] For example the notes in the *Riverside Chaucer* simply mark 'geen' and 'neen' as (Nth). See Benson 1987: 81–2.

[19] For a convenient list of the most important differences between East and West Norse see Gordon and Taylor 1992: 320–6.

[20] I am grateful to Dr Richard Dance for drawing this to my attention. See further Dance 2000.

ance of the forms 'neen' and 'geen' in El, as such forms are not recorded in Old Norse. However these forms may be understood according to the editorial process which the El text has undergone. A number of differences between the Hg and El texts of the *Reeve's Tale* reveal attempts by the El scribe or editor to increase the representation of Northern dialect, and to regularise the inconsistencies found in Hg (Smith 1997, Horobin 2001a). For instance Hg's sole use of 'slyk' (ON 'slíkr') at line I.4170 alongside the usual Northern ME form 'swilk', is found in three further occurrences in El [lines I.4130 (2), 4173]. A similar tendency towards increasing and regularising the Hg usage might therefore explain the appearance of the forms 'geen' and 'neen'. It seems that in copying El the scribe or editor viewed the form 'heem' as showing a specifically Northern reflex of OE 'ham' and transferred this same development to the related forms 'nan' and 'gan'. Therefore these forms in the El manuscript may be explained by recourse to the sociolinguistic phenomenon of hypercorrection, already identified in the El scribe's linguistic behaviour above. Hypercorrection describes the process of overcompensation by which speakers who are weakly tied to their own linguistic network attempt to imitate the speech patterns of a different social group. It seems that in copying El the scribe or editor was attempting to emend the spelling of his copytext according to a system that he did not fully understand. This is well exemplified by a comparison of the treatment of adjectival final ⟨-e⟩ in line I.4175 in the Hg and El manuscripts. In Hg this line reads: 'This lang nyght ther tydes me na reste', while El has the weak form of the adjective: 'This lange nyght ther tydes me na reste'. While the El reading is grammatically correct according to Chaucer's own practice, it fails to notice that the uninflected form is appropriate to the Northern dialect of the students, following the much earlier loss of the distinction between weak and strong adjectives in the North of England. This example shows the scribe applying a grammatical principle to an environment where it was not appropriate, in a similar way as I have suggested for the spellings 'geen' and 'neen'. These readings suggest that while the El scribe or editor emended the language of his copytext intelligently, he was not always fully aware of the linguistic subtleties of Chaucer's text.

In this chapter we have examined the relationship of the language of the Hg and El manuscripts in order to determine which features of their language are likely to derive from Chaucer himself. We have seen that the conclusions of scholars such as Benson and Samuels that their language is that of Scribe B needs to be considerably modified in the light of study of the distribution of certain forms across both manuscripts. We have also noted a number of differences in their treatment of language and suggested that these are representative of ongoing changes in the London dialect during this period and also of differences in editorial policy between these two very different witnesses to Chaucer's text. In the next chapter we will examine the transmission of this language across the manuscript tradition of the *Canterbury Tales* as a whole in order to observe its treatment by scribes writing in different dialects and at different periods throughout the fifteenth century.

4

The Language of the Manuscripts of the *Canterbury Tales*

There is a long history of textual and editorial discussion of the manuscripts of the *Canterbury Tales*, and recent years have seen numerous studies of palaeographical and codicological issues concerning these manuscripts. Research has also been carried out into the provenance of these manuscripts, based upon inscriptions made on the manuscripts themselves, and records of copies in wills. As a result of this work we know a large amount about the production and ownership of the manuscripts of Chaucer's poem. However despite this comprehensive treatment of the many aspects of manuscript study, there has been little consideration of the language of a large proportion of the *Canterbury Tales* manuscripts. Such a study may provide crucial information concerning the production and readership of these manuscripts, in addition to its obvious linguistic value. Much scholarly attention has been focused on the metropolitan productions, such as Hg and El, at the expense of a consideration of provincial productions, and Chaucer's reputation outside the capital. A study of the language and dialect of the manuscripts of the *Canterbury Tales* will allow a much clearer picture of where these manuscripts were produced, and thus will lay the foundation for a fuller assessment of Chaucer's readership, and provincial book production. A linguistic survey of this kind will also aid the further identification of scribal hands in more than one such manuscript, thereby allowing us to construct a more detailed picture of the scribes active in fifteenth-century book production.

There have been previous efforts to classify the linguistic data contained in these manuscripts, although their methodologies are now largely outdated. In their description of all *Canterbury Tales* manuscripts, published as Volume I of the *Text of the Canterbury Tales*, Manly and Rickert (1940) supplied brief descriptions of language and spelling and included a broad localisation based upon the scribal dialect. However the linguistic criteria upon which these localisations are based are limited to a small selection of features whose diagnostic potential is somewhat restricted. For instance their criteria for identifying a scribal dialect as Southern are limited to two features: use of the ⟨-eth⟩ inflexion in present plural forms of verbs and the voicing of /f/ to /v/. It is perhaps not surprising that they localised few of the *Canterbury Tales* manuscripts to the Southern counties. Manly and Rickert were particularly unsure as to the diagnostic features of the Kentish dialect of this period. They wrote: 'It is difficult to apply tests for Kentish . . . The older conspicuous signs of Kentish had practically disappeared' (I, 547). It is a result of these difficulties that the dialect and spelling of the Delamere manuscript, copied in a consistent Kentish dialect, is described by Manly and Rickert as: 'East Midland. The usual dialectal features are overshadowed by the unique eccentricities in spelling which set the MS apart from all others' (I, 111). Manly and Rickert were aware of the limitations of their efforts in this area and emphasise the tentative nature of their conclusions:

> It would be absurd, even with the use of all available material, to hope for very positive results in attempting to locate a MS by dialect alone. The growth and spread of Standard English and the fluctuations within this Standard in the making, the present state of dialect studies, and certain features inherent in the nature of the CT material – all, in one way or another, operate to make difficult or to prevent entirely the reaching of definite conclusions. (I, 547)

However despite these caveats Manly and Rickert used their dialectal analyses as supporting evidence for much of their extensive work on the provenance of the manuscripts. Dialect evidence is also brought to bear upon the identification of textual affiliation in their efforts to find relationships between manuscripts. These are of course important uses of dialect studies, yet it is of course important that the dialect evidence is correctly interpreted if it is to be trusted. The discussions of provenance provided by Manly-Rickert remain influential in subsequent studies of the manuscript tradition, despite the fact that these are often not supported by the dialect evidence. For instance Manly and Rickert's identification of the scribe of Dd as Richard Wytton, Master of Mickle Hall, Oxford is not supported by his use of the Cambridgeshire dialect. However this identification is reproduced by Owen in his study of the manuscript tradition (Owen 1991: 121). There is clearly a need for a comprehensive study of the linguistic and dialectal characteristics of the manuscripts of the *Canterbury Tales*, taking account of recent developments in Middle English dialectology.

Since the work of Manly and Rickert there has been a renaissance of interest in Middle English dialectology, largely sparked off by the work of the Middle English Dialect Survey which culminated in the publication of the *Linguistic Atlas of Late Mediaeval English* [*LALME*] (1986). *LALME* provided localisations for a number of *Canterbury Tales* manuscripts, and also included the data to allow other manuscripts to be localised according to their representation of a range of linguistic criteria. The applications of the methodology devised by *LALME*, and the data it provided, to the manuscript traditions of late Middle English works were demonstrated in a number of subsequent publications. Examples of these applications are found in Lewis and McIntosh's (1982) analysis of the manuscripts of the *Prick of Conscience*, whose vast textual tradition presents a geographical range which covers most of the British Isles. M.L. Samuels' localisation of the manuscripts of the three texts of Langland's *Piers Plowman* is frequently cited in the literature and has been influential in an assessment of Langland's readership and popularity. An important result of Samuels' research was the discovery that while both A and B texts of *Piers Plowman* were copied mostly in and around London, the C-text seems to have enjoyed a circulation based largely upon the West Midlands. This view has also been used as support for Skeat's view that Langland returned to his Malvern home late in life (Samuels 1988d: 77). J.J. Smith's (1985) extensive description of the language of the manuscripts of Gower's *Confessio Amantis* provided much information on scribal responses to Gower's work, particularly evidenced by the tendency for scribes to preserve aspects of the author's own language. In addition Smith was able to provide an exhaustive study of a scribe who seems to have specialised in copying Gower's work, Scribe D, revealing important evidence for Scribe D's treatment of the language and text of the many other works he copied. However despite these many applications of dialectological studies to manuscript traditions, no attempts have been made to apply the same tools to the language of the Chaucer tradition. The most recent bibliographical catalogues of the manuscripts of the *Canterbury Tales* are those by Mosser (1996) and Seymour (1997). Mosser's descriptions include no information concerning language or dialect, while Seymour's catalogue does include an attempt at localising each manuscript. Seymour's localisations generally follow *LALME*, although he does incorporate his own adjustments. However he provides no data or explanation to clarify or support these localisations, and certain details of his modifications seem to be simply errors. For example Seymour localised the hand of the Petworth manuscript to Essex although the linguistic evidence points clearly to a provenance in the West Midlands (see appendix 1).

In addition to the availability of *LALME*, another important recent development relevant to such research is the application of computers to manuscript studies, as demonstrated by the work of The *Canterbury Tales* Project. As a result of the work of this project we now have access to diplomatic transcripts of a number of manuscripts of the *Canterbury Tales*, in electronic form. The *Wife of Bath's Prologue on CD-ROM* (1996) provides transcripts of all fifty-four manuscript witnesses of the *Wife of Bath's Prologue* [WBP] and four pre-1500 printed editions. The electronic format of these texts allow for rapid and extensive interrogation of the language of each of the manuscripts, supported by the spelling databases, which comprise a list of all spelling variation found in the manuscripts. The purpose of this chapter will be to use the data provided in the *Wife of Bath's Prologue on CD-ROM* in order to provide a full linguistic survey of each of the fifty-four manuscript witnesses of the *Wife of Bath's Prologue*. The four printed editions will be discussed in the following chapter. This analysis will adopt the techniques developed by the editors of *LALME* and will draw on the maps and linguistic profiles to attempt to localise the manuscripts of Chaucer's poem.[1] This chapter will present a discussion of this information while brief linguistic descriptions, including a number of diagnostic spellings, are presented as appendix 1.

In addition to a survey of the input of regional dialects in the language of these manuscripts, this chapter will also investigate two other important linguistic influences. The first of these is the influence of the Type III London English variety which is the language of the two earliest manuscripts of the textual tradition, Hg and El, and which we have seen in chapter 3 is likely to be close to that used by Chaucer himself. The second important influence to be considered is that of the incipient standardised variety known as Type IV. This variety was in the process of becoming adopted for a wider variety of linguistic functions and we shall therefore consider its impact upon the language of the *Canterbury Tales* textual tradition during this important period in its development. Previous studies of this kind, notably Smith (1985, 1988c), have observed the tendency for scribes to be constrained in their treatment of certain linguistic features in the copying of prestigious texts. In such situations scribes were likely to reproduce certain distinctive features of the author's own idiolect rather than translate them into their own dialects. By contrast, less prestigious textual traditions show the opposite tendency where scribes were happy to replace any unusual or distinctive authorial forms in favour of their own forms or those of the incipient standard language. In chapter 2 we observed the influence of certain Type III spellings across the tradition; in this chapter we will look more closely at this phenomenon to see the extent and the motivation for such a process. The influence of the standardised variety known as Type IV is much more difficult to quantify and any comprehensive or conclusive study must await the completion and publication of the authoritative study underway by Benskin and Sandved. However by restricting our attention to a single textual tradition where the number of potential linguistic variables has been minimised it will be possible to make some comments about the appearance of Type IV forms in these manuscripts. Where such forms can be shown to be alien to the dialect of the individual copyist and the language of the archetype, it seems likely that they derive from the external influence of a supra-regional variety such as Type IV. However we must also remember the importance of other non-regional varieties during this period, known as colourless language and representing a compromise blend of non-local and non-standard forms (see chapter 1 for a fuller discussion).

---

[1] These techniques are described in full in the 'General Introduction' to *LALME* (I, 3-55) and in Benskin 1991.

Dialect and Textual Tradition

In this section we will examine the dialect features found in the various manuscripts of the WBP and consider the ways in which dialect can be seen to correlate with textual tradition. The aims of this section will therefore be both linguistic and textual: providing further evidence of ME dialectology of the fifteenth century and the provenance and distribution of manuscripts and copytexts of the *Canterbury Tales* during this period. It is however important to stress that the localisation of the dialect of a particular manuscript does not necessarily identify its place of production. The fifteenth century was a period of social and geographical mobility and scribes are likely to have moved around the country quite considerably. Therefore a scribe writing in a distinctively West Midland dialect may have copied manuscripts in the East Midlands. This is particularly true when considering the London book trade during this period. The fourteenth and early fifteenth centuries saw large numbers of people migrating from the provinces into the capital, particularly those seeking employment in specialised crafts and trades such as scribal copying. Therefore we must be aware of the potential for a scribe using a provincial dialect to be working in London. The identification of the dialect of a particular manuscript therefore provides us with information about the scribe rather than the place of production of the manuscript itself. However it is of course possible that the language of the scribe does indeed reflect the place of copying of the manuscript, especially where there is corresponding evidence of early ownership. A further complicating factor concerns the type of copying practice employed by the scribe. In chapter 1 we looked at the three types of copying practice that were adopted by scribes and the ways in which these determine the linguistic output. Where a scribe consistently reproduced the language of his copytext we may identify only the dialect of the copytext and not that of the scribe. As such we may identify the place of production of the exemplar but not necessarily that of the manuscript itself.

The manuscripts of the *Canterbury Tales* may be arranged in groups according to both textual affiliation and similarities in the ordering of the tales. In their authoritative study of the text of the *Canterbury Tales*, based upon all extant manuscripts, Manly and Rickert (1940) identified four textual groups, labelled A–D. Recent stemmatic analysis of the manuscripts of the *Wife of Bath's Prologue* by P.M.W. Robinson (1997) has served both to confirm and further refine the genetic groupings first identified by Manly and Rickert. In addition to Manly and Rickert's groups A–D, Robinson argued for the existence of 3 further groups, E and F, and an O group of manuscripts related by their common descent from the archetype of the entire tradition. This O group is thus of extreme importance for the recovery of the archetypal text as the O manuscripts are not affected by intervening scribal error. In its close relationship to the archetype the O group is also of interest to the study of scribal responses to Chaucerian language, as each of these manuscripts represents a direct response to a copytext which is likely to have been copied in Type III London English. This aspect will be considered in further detail in the following section of this chapter. Here we are concerned with the appearance of dialectal features in these various manuscript groupings and whether these can be seen to correlate with textual affiliations or with data concerning their early provenance.

Consideration of the dialectal evidence in the light of our knowledge concerning the textual affiliations of the manuscripts reveals certain significant patterns. From an examination of the geographical and textual information it is apparent that the text of the two closely related A and B groups of the *Canterbury Tales* circulated predominantly in the East Midlands, as 6 manuscripts belonging to this group may be localised to this area:

Cn	Suffolk
Dd	Cambs
En[1]	Essex
He	Essex
Ne	Norfolk
Ii	Norfolk

The identification of this group of manuscripts with these counties is further strengthened with reference to the provenance studies carried out by Manly and Rickert. We need to be cautious in relying too much on these aspects of Manly and Rickert's work as many of their findings are rather tentative, however the coherence of provenance and dialect is certainly suggestive. Manly and Rickert's inquiries into provenance of the manuscripts have recently been pursued further by Estelle Stubbs (2001) who has argued for centres of copying and circulation of exemplars in religious houses and family seats in East Anglia. Stubbs has identified a number of names written in the margins of *Canterbury Tales* manuscripts with Augustinian Friars associated with Clare Priory in Suffolk and with connections with prominent local families, such as the De Vere family of Castle Hedingham in Essex. The clustering of this group of textually-related manuscripts in East Anglia certainly appears to indicate the existence of a pool of exemplars in the area from which local scribes made copies, presumably for local patrons and readers.[2]

In addition to the number of manuscripts associated with the East Midlands which belong to the AB tradition, there are also several manuscripts belonging to the O Group which can be localised to the same area.

---

[2] Samuel Moore first traced the network of associations concerning literary activity in the East Anglian counties during this period in an important pair of articles, see Moore 1912 and 1913.

The O Group is comprised of manuscripts which are related only by common descent from the archetype of the entire tradition. The manuscripts belonging to this group are accurate copies of an authoritative text close to the head of the tradition, and are therefore important witnesses to the text of the *Canterbury Tales*. The manuscripts belonging to this O Group localised to the Eastern counties are as follows:

Ad^1	Suffolk
Ad^3	Suffolk
En^3	Suffolk
Gl	Norwich
Ha^5	Suffolk

The evident clustering of these manuscripts of high textual authority in the Suffolk area is striking and is certainly suggestive of local connections with a single collection of exemplars. The date of these manuscripts is also interesting as each of these manuscripts was copied after 1450 and several, Ad^1, En^3 and Gl, as late as the 1470s.[3] These dates suggest that their copytext(s) must have remained intact and available in the local area for some considerable time. Given that the copytext(s) used by these manuscripts is closely related to Hg and the archetype of the entire tradition it must have survived for some time before its use by these scribes in the latter decades of the fifteenth century. Access to texts of such high authority also suggests networks connecting the areas of Suffolk and its environs with the capital, the centre of the manuscript book trade in this period. There were of course family connections between the Chaucer family and the Suffolk region, as Alice Chaucer, the poet's granddaughter, was married to the Duke of Suffolk William de la Pole (Pearsall 1992: 282). In fact it has been suggested by Manly and Rickert that Ha^5, a member of the O Group copied in a Suffolk dialect, has connections with Alice Chaucer (Manly and Rickert 1940: I, 235–7, 613). Stubbs extends these connections, arguing for an established network of links between London and Clare Priory in Suffolk via which friars and copytexts could pass frequently and easily. The dialect evidence of Ad^3 also appears to correlate with the fragmentary evidence which we have for its early provenance. Manly-Rickert's identification of the name 'Hocden' scribbled in the margin of folio 44v of Ad^3 with the Suffolk village of Hawkdon suggests that Ad^3 was copied or owned by someone in this area (I, 47). This inscription provides another link with the El manuscript which is also associated with this area early in its history. Despite being copied by Scribe B in a variety of the London dialect of ME, El does have several connections with certain locations in East Anglia. The presence of the

---

[3] It should be noted that Gl was copied from two separate exemplars and thus has two separate affiliations. Up to approximately WBP 192 it was copied from Mm (a manuscript belonging to the D group) and subsequently it was copied from an exemplar belonging to the O group.

inscription 'John Hedgeman of Hawkedoun' in El suggests connections with the same Suffolk village as Ad³, a manuscript with which it is further connected by text and marginalia.[4] Another East Anglian link is suggested by Doyle's identification of the motto of the Paston Family of Norfolk 'de mieulx en mieulx' which appears on several leaves of the El manuscript (Doyle 1983; see also Hanna and Edwards 1996: 14). The study of the early provenance of the El manuscript by Hanna and Edwards (1996) focuses on the poem by Rothely in praise of the De Vere family of Castle Hedingham copied onto one of the Ellesmere flyleaves. Hanna and Edwards describe a network of manuscript owners and patrons with connections with the El manuscript early in its history focused on the neighbourhood of Bury St Edmunds in Suffolk. This network encompasses important book-owning families such as the Pastons, the De Veres and the Drurys all with connections with El and with other important literary manuscripts in this period.

In addition to shared textual affiliations a number of these manuscripts also employ a similar order of tales, termed by Manly and Rickert the *a* order. This is the arrangement of tales employed by the Ellesmere manuscript and now familiar from many modern editions, such as the *Riverside Chaucer*. The *a* arrangement of tales is found in the following manuscripts which are associated dialectally with the East Midlands: Ad¹, Ad³, Cn, Dd, En¹, En³, Gg, Ha⁵. These connections are also suggestive. It is of course quite possible for manuscripts to be textually related but to use quite different arrangements of the tales. Similarly manuscripts with similar tale orders may be completely unrelated in the texts that they preserve. However the correlation in certain manuscripts of textual affiliation, tale order and dialect suggests that these manuscripts were produced in the same area from a stock of exemplars which were carefully ordered and which remained in such a state over a period of decades. The relationship between dialect and provenance of one further manuscript copied an in Eastern dialect is also of interest. Ne may be localised on the basis of its language to Norfolk, a localisation which coincides closely with Manly and Rickert's identification of the manuscript as the property in the sixteenth century of William Fermor of East Barsham, Norfolk (I, 384–6).

Examination of the manuscripts localised to the west of the country shows that many of these manuscripts employed the CD text of the *Tales*. Western copies of the *Canterbury Tales* containing copies of the CD tradition are: La, Ph³, Pw, Sl¹. It is significant that early members of the C and D traditions, La and Pw, were both copied in the west, suggesting that these closely related exemplars remained close to the place of copying of the CD ancestor. The contrast with the East Midlands is striking: there is only one manuscript copied in the west which contains the AB text,

---

[4] For a discussion of the connections between Ad³ and El see Horobin 1997a and 1997b.

Ma, which was produced in Warwickshire. It is also interesting to note that Ma is one of the latest of the A Group of manuscripts, copied c. 1485, suggesting that the AB text remained available solely in the East throughout much of the fifteenth century. There is also only one Western manuscript belonging to the O Group, Bo^2, produced in South Worcestershire. In addition to the use of closely related exemplars, these Western manuscripts also show similarities in their ordering of the tales. A characteristic feature of the arrangement of the tales in these manuscripts is the use of the *Man of Law's Endlink* as a link to the *Squire's Tale* which then follows this linking passage. The other major difference is found in the placement of Fragment VIII, the *Second Nun's* and *Canon's Yeoman's Tales*, which are placed between the *Franklin's Tale* and the *Physician's Tale* in this arrangement. As well as showing these differences in ordering this group of manuscripts commonly shows differences in its approach to the material as a whole. Many of these manuscripts aim to present the material in a more complete form and thus include spurious linking passages which are not present in other traditions. Although not exclusive to these traditions, these manuscripts commonly include the *Tale of Gamelyn* after the *Cook's Tale*, in order to compensate for the evident incompleteness of this tale. A different attitude towards the text as a whole is also demonstrated by the use of chapter numbers for some of the tales. This seems to represent another attempt to overcome the many gaps found in the prologue-tale arrangement. While no manuscript implements this system in a methodical and consistent way, traces of such a system are found in a number of manuscripts localised to the West Midlands (Fi, Ph^3, Pw, Sl^1).[5] Chapter numbers are found earliest in Cp, a manuscript probably copied in London, but by a scribe who was an immigrant from the West Midlands. It seems possible that the Cp scribe, Scribe D, maintained his links with the West Midlands and that features such as text, ordering and chapter numbering were passed to the West Midlands via these connections. Certainly the Cp copytext (or even Cp itself) was available in the West Midlands soon after its production as it was used by the scribe of La for the production of this manuscript. Scribe D's literary connections with the West Midlands have been demonstrated by Hanna in his discussion of Sir Thomas Berkeley's patronage and dissemination of the works of John Trevisa. Hanna (1989c) argues that Scribe D's copy of Trevisa's translation of *De Proprietatibus Rerum* (BL MS Additional 27944) was taken from a copy of Trevisa's holograph supplied by Berkeley himself. Evidently Scribe D, whether directly or indirectly, was able to obtain good quality exemplars of texts from important sources both in the West Midlands and in the capital, and may have acted as a channel through which such exemplars could be exchanged. It seems

---

[5] Other non-Western manuscripts which have chapter numbers are Cp (discussed below), Mm and Ry^1.

likely that the use of chapter numbers in these manuscripts was related to the adoption of this system in Cp rather than the result of independent decisions, as the very haphazard inclusion of chapter numbers frequently coincides across these manuscripts.[6]

Correlation of individual Western manuscripts with evidence concerning their early provenance also raises some interesting links. For instance Bo^2 shows a number of West Midland dialect features, specifically of South Worcestershire, a localisation which provides potential links with Manly and Rickert's identification of the name Beauchamp in a fifteenth-century hand on folio 139.[7] Manly and Rickert link the manuscript with Margaret Beauchamp, daughter of Richard Earl of Warwick, who married John Talbot, Earl of Shrewsbury. Both were prominent land-owning families in the West Midlands during this period, thus providing a tentative connection with the production of the manuscript in this area. The Ch manuscript has few prominent dialect features, although certain forms are suggestive of a Western, or specifically South-Western origin. This could accommodate the area of Hampshire which is suggested by the presence of the motto of Winchester College in a fifteenth-century hand on folio 1. Another manuscript copied in a Western dialect which can be located in the West early in its history is Mc. This manuscript is copied in the dialect of West Oxfordshire and was owned by Sir Thomas Baskervyle in Pershore, Worcestershire, in the sixteenth century (I, 359). Ry^2 is also marked by West Midlands dialect features which correlate with evidence of its early ownership. According to Manly and Rickert this manuscript was first owned by Philip Chetwynd of Ingestre, Staffordshire, whose name and family motto appear on folio 272v (I, 489–90). Si also shows links between the language of its copyist and early ownership. This manuscript was copied in a Warwickshire dialect which coheres with the information found in a sixteenth-century bill written on folio 78. According to Manly and Rickert the writer of this bill refers to himself as 'william Cooke of Leiceter [?] in the County of warwike', although they note that no such town is found in the county of Warwickshire (I, 502–3).

It is apparent from the above analysis that many copies of Chaucer's work were produced outside the capital and presumably therefore for a provincial readership. In some cases early provincial readers can be identified, further supporting the interpretation of the dialect evidence. However it is of course possible that in some instances the dialect features identified are indicative of the origins of the copyists rather than the manuscripts themselves. Scribes appear to have been extremely mobile during this period and it is certain that a number of scribes of provincial origins were working

---

[6] For example the first tale to be numbered in Cp, Fi, Mm, Pw is the *Reeve's Tale* as number 3. There seems no reason for this situation other than that this particular number, and none for the preceding tales, was recorded in their copytexts and faithfully transcribed.

[7] The interpretation of the name is however in doubt. Manly and Rickert (1940) are uncertain as to whether the name should be read as 'Belthiam' or 'Belchiam' (I.69).

in London, as evidenced by the infamous Scribe D. However it seems likely that the above localisations provide a preliminary identification of regional copies of Chaucer, which may be subsequently confirmed or rejected by subsequent codicological, palaeographical and provenance studies. It also seems apparent that scribes during this period were content to include a wide range of dialectal spellings in copies of Chaucer thus suggesting that such books were intended for readers familiar with such forms. However alongside such provincialisms we frequently find evidence of forms which correspond with those identified as Type III London English. It seems likely that these forms derive ultimately from the archetype of the tradition, deliberately preserved by *literatim* transcription. In order to investigate this phenomenon further the following section will examine the influence of Type III forms across the manuscript tradition of the *Canterbury Tales* in more detail.

The Influence of Type III

In addition to their use of regional spelling features which allow a localisation of their scribes, these manuscripts frequently reveal a number of Type III spellings which appear to derive ultimately from the archetype of the tradition. In this section we will look at the evidence for the survival of such forms across the manuscript tradition and attempt to determine the significance of this phenomenon. The following table records the presence or absence of a number of characteristic Type III spellings across each of the manuscripts of WBP divided into chronological periods of twenty-five years.

	MUCHE(L)	NAT	THURGH	S(C)HOLD-	YEUE-
1400–1425					
Cp	−	+	+	+	+
Dd	−	+	+	−	−
El	+	+	+	+	+
Gg	−	+	−	−	−
Ha[4]	−	−	+	+	−
Hg	+	+	+	+	+
La	+	−	−	+	−
1425–1450					
Ad[3]	−	+	−	+	+
Bo[2]	−	+	−	+	−
En[1]	−	+	+	+	−
En[2]	−	+	−	+	−
He	+	+	−	−	+
Ii	−	−	−	−	−
Lc	−	+	+	−	−
Ld[1]	−	+	−	+	+

	MUCHE(L)	NAT	THURGH	S(C)HOLD-	YEUE-
Ph³	+	−	−	+	−
Ps	−	−	+	−	−
Pw	−	+	−	−	−
Ry²	+	−	−	+	−
Sl¹	+	−	−	−	+
1450–1475					
Bo¹	+	+	+	−	+
Bw	−	+	−	−	−
Ch	−	+	−	+	+
Cn	+	+	−	−	−
Dl	−	−	−	+	+
Ds¹	−	+	−	−	+
Fi	−	−	−	−	−
Ha²	−	−	−	−	+
Ha⁵	−	+	+	+	+
Hk	+	+	−	+	−
Ht	−	−	−	−	+
Ln	+	−	−	−	+
Mc	+	−	−	+	−
Mg	−	+	+	+	+
Mm	−	+	−	−	−
Ne	+	+	−	+	+
Nl	−	+	−	−	+
Ph²	+	+	+	−	+
Py	−	+	+	−	−
Ra¹	−	+	−	+	+
Ra²	−	−	−	+	−
Ra³	−	+	−	−	+
Ry¹	−	−	−	−	+
Se	−	+	−	+	−
Tc¹	−	+	−	−	+
To¹	−	+	−	−	+
1475–1500					
Ad¹	−	+	−	+	−
En³	−	+	−	+	−
Gl	−	+	+	−	+
Ld²	+	−	+	−	−
Ma	−	+	−	+	+
Si	−	+	−	+	+
Sl²	−	+	−	+	+
Tc²	−	+	−	+	+

It is apparent from the above table that the treatment of these 5 forms across the entire manuscript tradition varies for each individual item. The first column documents the history of the spelling 'muchel' across the manuscripts, showing that few scribes use this form. This situation is reinforced by the evidence of *LALME* which shows clearly that this form is most commonly found in West Midlands dialects, with a small scattering of occurrences in London, Essex and Kent (*LALME* I map 104). As we saw in the previous section, many of the *Canterbury Tales* manuscripts were copied in the East and it seems that this characteristically Western form was not tolerated within their repertoires. A number of the manuscripts which do contain this spelling have other Western features which suggest that these forms derive from their scribes rather than the Type III language of the archetype of the tradition. These manuscripts are La, Ld[2], Mc, Ry[1], Sl[1]. By comparison the spelling 'nat' is found in a large number of manuscripts, appearing consistently throughout the fifteenth century. This form is quite widespread in dialects of Middle English and is found in texts copied in a variety of areas including both the West and East Midlands (see *LALME* I map 276). Therefore it may be that its presence in these manuscripts is due to coincidence with the scribe's active repertoire rather than the deliberate preservation of an archetypal Type III form. However its consistent use in manuscripts of the period 1475–1500 is striking as in this period dialect forms of this kind were generally recessive and it may be that these scribes are more consciously reproducing traditional Chaucerian features rather than simply using their own forms. In the third column the presence of the spelling 'thurgh' is recorded, based on a comparison of the spelling of this item in line 697 of the WBP. In addition to the Hg spelling 'thurgh' there are a number of manuscripts which record spellings of this item which reflect a similar monosyllabic form as that of Hg, as opposed to disyllabic forms such as the Type IV spelling 'thorough'. For instance the closely related spelling 'thorgh' is found in Ad[3], Bw, Gg, Ht and another similar spelling 'thourgh' is recorded in Ch, Ha[5], Mm, Pw. Other related forms are 'thorghw' (Dl), 'thorwhe' (La), 'þourh' (Mc), 'thurh' (Nl). The fourth column records the presence of spellings of SHOULD spelled 's(c)hold-', a form which appears reasonably frequently throughout the fifteenth century and is particularly frequent in the earliest and latest periods, with a slight decline in the middle. In the fifth column the distribution of the spellings 'yeue(n)' are noted. Not included in this column are forms with initial ⟨ȝ⟩ which are also recorded in Bw, Dd, En[2], Gg, Ha[4], La, Lc, Ln, Mg, Nl, Ph[3], Pw, Ry[2], Si, Sl[1]. Some manuscripts have both spellings e.g. Ln, Mg, Nl, Si, Sl[1].

It appears from this analysis that scribes did preserve spellings which are characteristic of Type III London English, the language which stands at the head of the textual tradition. However the influence of this variety was evidently complex. It appears that scribes were more likely to preserve such forms where they were reinforced by the practice of their own or other contiguous dialects. Where a form was not supported by local use scribes were unlikely to preserve it. Therefore while the language of the tradition did act as a constraining factor upon an individual scribe's linguistic choices, its influence was limited to instances where it was supported by wider use. This situation is similar to the concepts of active and passive scribal repertoires discussed by Benskin and Laing and described above in chapter 1. When a scribe encountered a Type III form which was familiar to him as part of his passive repertoire he was content to retain it. However where such a form was not part of the scribe's passive repertoire he was likely to replace it with an equivalent form from his own active repertoire.

Simply noting whether a particular spelling is present or absent in the text consulted may appear a rather crude way of determining scribal attitudes to the archetype but nevertheless certain striking patterns do emerge. The earliest manuscripts show the greatest consistency in the use of Type III spellings as we would expect. However beyond the first period of twenty-five years, date of copying does not appear to be a determining factor as to whether a manuscript contains a particular spelling or not. In fact it appears that the presence of certain spellings correlates more closely with textual affiliation. For instance, despite their relatively late dates of copying, manuscripts belonging to the O group contain a number of the Type III forms surveyed in the above table. In the period 1425–50 these are found in Ad^3 and Bo^2 as well as in the AB manuscripts En^1 and He. In the period 1450–75 a number of manuscripts show several Type III forms, including two from the O group, Ch and Ha^5 and another member of the AB group: Ne. In the final twenty-five years of the century these forms appear to have retained their currency and are found in O manuscripts, Ad^1, En^3, Gl and a member of the AB group: Ma. It is perhaps not surprising that these groups of manuscripts show the clearest tendency to preserve such forms, given that the O manuscripts are likely to have been copied from exemplars in Type III language, while members of other traditions are likely to derive from copytexts written in non-Chaucerian language. It appears that where a scribe did encounter Type III language in his copytext he was careful to preserve this despite the fact that such language would have appeared increasingly old-fashioned throughout the fifteenth century. In fact it appears that the tendency to preserve such language increased throughout the century rather than vice versa. It may be that the more archaic Chaucer's language appeared to scribes, the more they were concerned to preserve it as an integral part of the text they were transmitting. The preservation of such forms in the AB tradition may also be due to similar factors although as we observed earlier, manuscripts from this tradition are commonly copied in dialects of the East Midlands. As such the language of the scribes of these manuscripts coincided with that of Type III (which contains a number of Midlands forms) and therefore the scribes of these manuscripts were probably more familiar with such forms and therefore more likely to preserve them. By contrast manuscripts of the CD tradition were more commonly produced by scribes writing in Western dialects and therefore Type III forms were less likely to coincide with their habitual forms. It is therefore likely that these Type III features disappeared earlier in the CD tradition than in the predominantly eastern AB tradition. Given

these factors it is thus particularly striking that certain Western manuscripts, such as Ch, Bo^2, Ma, Ra^1 and Si, contain a large number of Type III
forms.

The Influence of Type IV

In addition to allowing an insight into the impact of scribal dialects and
Chaucerian language, this enquiry also enables us to observe the gradual
process by which the standardisation of written English progressed during
the fifteenth century. In order to allow comparison with the forms
considered above concerning the influence of Type III, the following table
records the presence or absence of equivalent Type IV forms across the
manuscript tradition.

	MOCH	NOT	TH(O)ROUGH	S(C)HULD-	GIUE-
1400–1425					
Cp	−	+	−	+	−
Dd	−	+	−	+	−
El	−	−	−	−	+
Gg	−	+	−	+	+
Ha^4	+	+	−	+	−
Hg	−	−	−	−	+
La	−	+	−	−	+
1425–1450					
Ad^3	+	+	−	+	+
Bo^2	−	+	−	+	+
En^1	−	−	−	−	−
En^2	−	+	−	−	−
He	−	+	−	+	−
Ii	−	+	+	+	+
Lc	+	+	−	+	−
Ld^1	−	+	−	+	+
Ph^3	−	+	−	−	−
Ps	−	+	−	+	+
Pw	+	+	−	+	−
Ry^2	+	+	−	+	−
Sl^1	+	+	+	+	−
1450–1475					
Bo^1	−	+	−	+	+
Bw	+	+	−	+	−
Ch	+	+	−	+	+
Cn	−	+	+	+	−
Dl	−	+	−	−	+
Ds^1	+	−	−	+	+
Fi	−	+	−	+	+
Ha^2	−	+	+	+	−

	MOCH	NOT	TH(O)ROUGH	S(C)HULD-	GIUE-
Ha[5]	+	–	–	+	+
Hk	–	+	–	+	–
Ht	+	+	–	+	+
Ln	–	+	–	+	–
Mc	–	+	–	+	+
Mg	+	+	–	+	–
Mm	–	+	–	+	–
Ne	+	+	–	–	+
Nl	–	–	–	+	+
Ph[2]	+	+	–	+	+
Py	–	–	–	+	+
Ra[1]	+	+	–	+	+
Ra[2]	+	+	+	–	–
Ra[3]	+	+	–	+	–
Ry[1]	–	–	+	+	+
Se	–	+	+	+	–
Tc[1]	+	+	–	+	+
To[1]	+	–	–	+	+
1475–1500					
Ad[1]	–	+	–	+	–
En[3]	+	+	–	+	–
Gl	+	–	–	+	+
Ld[2]	+	+	–	+	–
Ma	+	+	–	–	–
Si	+	+	–	–	+
Sl[2]	+	+	–	+	+
Tc[2]	+	+	+	+	+

It is apparent from the above table that chronology is a more significant factor than above for determining the presence or absence of a particular Type IV feature. For instance the first column shows that the spelling 'moche(l)' is relatively rare in the first half of the century, then more common from 1450–75 and subsequently found in almost all of the manuscripts copied between 1475–1500. The spelling 'not' becomes common very early in the century and remains consistently so throughout the period. A similar distribution is found for the spellings of SHOULD with medial ⟨u⟩ as listed in the fourth column. The spelling 'th(o)rough' shows a completely contrasting history and is found only infrequently, with just a handful of occurrences throughout the entire period. It may be that scribes were careful to preserve a monosyllabic form over a disyllabic one such as 'thorough' given the metrical implications which would be involved in such a change. The final column shows that spellings of the verb to give with initial ⟨g⟩, implying an initial velar as opposed to a palatal consonant, are rather rare across the manuscripts. In some instances, such as Ps, the use of this form correlates with other features characteristic of a Northern dialect of ME. It seems likely that in such instances the ⟨g-⟩ spellings of the verb GIVE are dialectal rather than Type IV features (see *LALME* I Map 424). There is however one instance of a spelling of the verb with initial ⟨g⟩ in Hg in WBP in the following line (501): 'Lat hym fare wel god gyue his soule reste'. It is interesting to note that a number of other manuscripts have the ⟨g⟩ spelling of the verb in this same instance, despite clear preferences for forms with initial ⟨y⟩ demonstrated elsewhere. The following manuscripts have forms with initial ⟨g⟩ in this line: Ad³, Ch, Ds¹, Fi, Ha⁵, Ht, Ld¹, Mc, Nl, Ps, Ra¹, Tc¹, To¹. There seems to be a correlation between the appearance of this form and textual tradition, as four of these manuscripts belong to the O Group identified by Robinson: Ad³, Ch, Ha⁵, Ht. This instance reminds us of the importance of textual tradition in assessing the language of these manuscripts. The appearance of spellings of GIVE with initial ⟨g⟩ in these manuscripts appears on the surface to represent the influence of Type IV usage. However once we have seen that the Hg manuscript has 'gyue' in this single instance then it is clear that the appearance of these forms in subsequent manuscripts is due to the influence of the language of the archetype of the textual tradition. Whether the form with initial ⟨g⟩ is Chaucerian or scribal, some scribes encountered it in their copytexts in this position and were careful to retain it despite their use elsewhere of forms with initial ⟨y⟩.

This discussion has shown that even in a prestigious textual tradition such as that of Chaucer's *Canterbury Tales* dialectal and archaic spellings were tolerated throughout the entirety of the century, frequently alongside the forms of the Type IV spelling system. This demonstrates that it is important not to view the standardisation of English spelling as a single decisive event, but rather a lengthy process during which Type IV forms existed alongside those associated with other varieties. Rather than viewing it as a prestige written variety which was adopted by scribes in an attempt to align their linguistic usage with an accepted and respected variety, Type IV should be seen as simply another influence acting upon an individual scribe, operating alongside influences such as those of a local dialect or of the copytext. The transition from a manuscript to a print culture towards the end of the fifteenth century is often viewed as representing a decisive shift towards linguistic standardisation. In order to consider this further the next chapter will look at how Chaucerian language is treated in early printed witnesses of his texts.

5

Chaucer in Print

In the previous chapter we examined the language of the manuscript tradition of Chaucer's *Canterbury Tales* in order to see how fifteenth-century scribes responded to his use of language. In this chapter I want to look beyond the fifteenth century and beyond the culture of manuscript book production, to see how Chaucerian language has been treated in printed editions of his works. As in the last chapter I will focus my examination on printed copies of the *Canterbury Tales*, although I will also consider editions of the complete works of Chaucer as they begin to appear with Thynne's edition of 1532. As a prelude to the following discussion I will begin by briefly summarising the history of Chaucer's text in print.

Chaucer's works have enjoyed a long career in print and large numbers of editions have appeared since William Caxton's first editions of Chaucer at the end of the fifteenth century. The first printed edition of Chaucer's works was Caxton's edition of the *Canterbury Tales* in 1476, and his second edition appeared in 1482. The rationale behind Caxton's second edition is recorded in the famous preface to the work, where he justified the necessity for a new edition by claiming that it represented a much closer witness to Chaucer's own text. Whether Caxton was really concerned with the accuracy of his text, or simply keen to justify the need for a new edition of a popular work, the methodology adopted for this second edition, supplementing the earlier text with readings from a manuscript with certain adjustments to the order, set the precedent for standard editorial practice of the next three centuries. Caxton's second edition formed the basis for Pynson's two editions of 1492 and 1526, while a copy of the same text was partly emended with another manuscript by Wynkyn de Worde for his edition of 1498. De Worde's edition formed the subsequent basis of the version in William Thynne's *The Workes of Geffray Chaucer*, printed in 1532, although under the authorisation of Henry VIII Thynne had special access to many *Canterbury Tales* manuscripts. The next two centuries saw many editions of Chaucer's works, particularly those of Stow (1561) and Speght (1598), which mostly represent reprints of Thynne's text of 1532. John Urry's posthumous edition of 1721 followed the order of Thynne, although he was aware of many manuscripts and earlier printed editions. While including the entire accepted Chaucerian canon, Urry's edition also contained a life of Chaucer and a glossary. The preface includes a list of the manuscripts consulted by the editor, complete with accurate descriptions, thus displaying not only an attempt to apply scholarly techniques but also to display materials as an aid to future scholarship. Thomas Tyrwhitt's edition of 1775–78 presents an eclectic text, based upon that of Speght, heavily edited with the readings from some 26 manuscripts. In creating his text, Tyrwhitt collated approximately 24 manuscripts, including Ha[5], Dd, Ad[1] and particularly Ha[4], a highly respected manuscript which became especially important to nineteenth-century editors. This is reflected in Thomas Wright's best-text edition of 1847–51 which used Ha[4] as a base. The later nineteenth century is characterised by the appearance of several collected editions which used Wright's text as a base, such as those of Robert Bell and Richard Morris.

The modern critical debate of the textual tradition of the *Canterbury Tales* begins with Frederick Furnivall and his work for the Chaucer Society. This society was founded by Furnivall himself in 1868, and over the following sixteen years it published transcriptions of six of the principal manuscripts of the *Canterbury Tales*. Through his close association with Bradshaw, Skeat and Morris, and an affection for Chaucer which allowed the society to flourish at the cost of his other various enterprises, Furnivall was able to achieve his goal: 'To do honour to Chaucer, and to let lovers and students of him see how far the best unprinted manuscripts of his works differed from the printed texts' (Benzie 1983: 162). The society's *The Six-text Edition of Chaucer's Canterbury Tales* consists of diplomatic editions of the manuscripts El, Hg, La, Pw, Cp, and Gg, and was later followed by supplementary publications of Ha[4] and Dd. Furnivall's study of the manuscripts, while not always strictly confined to matters of textuality, has received much praise and resulted in the felicitous first printing of Hg and El. However, while he was no doubt impressed with the linguistic value of El, it is clear that his judgement was swayed by the physical appearance of the manuscript. Furnivall was not an editor by his own admission, but he did produce a huge amount of accurate material which formed the basis for future editions, such as Skeat's *Clarendon Chaucer*. Skeat's edition of Chaucer's complete works appeared in six volumes published between 1894 and 1895, and set new standards in the editing of Chaucer's text. The twentieth century saw a number of further editions of Chaucer. F.N. Robinson's edition of 1933 remained the dominant text for a considerable time and was reprinted with few minor alterations in his second edition of 1957. Robinson's editions have also formed the basis of the standard reference text of current scholarship, the *Riverside Chaucer*, which appeared in 1987 under the general editorship of L.D. Benson.

Printing and Spelling

Here I will survey the language of the Chaucerian printed tradition in order to examine the way in which editors have treated linguistic details in their presentation of Chaucer's text. Such a survey will enable us to consider attitudes towards Chaucer's language throughout the history of the tradition and also to observe how the processes of linguistic change have affected those attitudes. Furthermore it is also possible to consider the significance of early printed editions of Chaucer's works in disseminating the standardised written variety of English. The establishment of the first printing press in Westminster in the 1470s by William Caxton had important implications for the development of written English during this period. During the fifteenth century a standardised written variety of English had emerged, focused on the official language used by government clerks based in Westminster. The diffusion and adoption of this written variety, known as Type IV, for written functions outside the government offices was a gradual process which was ongoing throughout the fifteenth century. Therefore the appearance of the printing press coincided with an important period in the process of standardisation and was clearly instrumental in spreading the standard written variety and encouraging its adoption. However the importance of the advent of printing for the standardisation of written English has been the subject of much controversy. The possibility that a single text could be produced in a large number of identical copies and circulated over a wide geographical area presented opportunities for linguistic stabilisation never possible in an age of manuscript copying. This possibility has been widely recognised and incorporated into histories of the language which frequently cite printing as a decisive factor in the establishment of standard written English. Baugh and Cable describe the impact of printing in the following way:

> A powerful force thus existed for promoting a standard, uniform language, and the means were now available for spreading that language throughout the territory in which it was understood. (Baugh and Cable 1993: 196)

In his recent *History of the English Language* N.F. Blake is more cautious in his assessment of the role of the printing press in disseminating the standard written language: 'The introduction of the press did not at first assist the adoption of the standard, but over time compositors became more familiar with it and helped to ensure its triumph' (Blake 1996: 205). In fact some scholars have argued that the initial impact of the printing press was to promote greater variation rather than uniformity. For example M. Görlach writes: 'it is an irony in the history of the development of the standard that the orthography of early printing represented a backward step when compared with the established conventions of chancery English' (Görlach 1990: 24; see also the discussion in Görlach 1991).

Despite the crucial, yet contradictory, role that printing has been allowed to play in our view of the history of standard written English, certain important questions have never been adequately addressed. There have been few studies of the language of the early printed books and those that have been undertaken have reached contradictory conclusions. In an earlier study N.F. Blake has argued that Caxton's erratic and careless attitude towards orthography demonstrates that he had 'no particular policy towards the spellings he used in his books' (Blake 1969: 174). However J.H. Fisher has claimed a greater role for Caxton in the standardisation of spelling, and his study of Caxton's usage concludes that Caxton was a 'transmitter' of standard written English, and 'should be thanked for supporting the foundation of a written standard' (Fisher 1996: 129).

Caxton's Spelling Practices

In his examination of Caxton's spelling practices in his editions of Malory's *Morte Darthur* and Gower's *Confessio Amantis* J.J. Smith (1986) has demonstrated that Caxton varied his treatment of orthography according to the text being printed. Smith has shown that Caxton's edition of Gower's *Confessio Amantis* preserves a large number of traditional 'Gowerian' spelling forms, which may be contrasted with Caxton's wholesale translation of the spelling system of the Winchester manuscript of Malory's *Morte Darthur*. Smith suggests that such a situation may be explained as a result of a higher respect accorded by Caxton to the work of Gower than Malory. In her study of the early printed editions of Nicholas Love's *Mirror of the Blessed Life of Jesus Christ* L. Hellinga (1997) has identified a similar tendency in Caxton's preservation of a number of provincial Northern spelling features associated with Nicholas Love's own usage. Hellinga suggests that Caxton's retention of authorial forms, such as 'mykel', 'clepe' and 'sythe', may be motivated either by the demands of a regional readership, or by 'a conscious wish to preserve the character of the author's language, his "voice"' (Hellinga 1997: 155).

So despite the availability of a standardised written system, Caxton appears not to have adopted this spelling system for these printed editions. It is also possible to compare Caxton's treatment of the spelling of works by other authors, with texts composed or translated by Caxton himself. In order to exemplify the kind of variation in spelling practice found in Caxton's own prose, the following is an extract from Caxton's prologue to his edition of the *History of Troy*, printed in 1476.

> Whan I remembre that every man is bounden by the comandement and counceyll
> of the wyse man to eschewe slouth and ydlenes, whyche is moder and nourysshar
> of vyces, and ought to put myself unto vertuous ocupacion and besynesse than I,
> havynge no grete charge of ocupacion, folowynge the sayd counceyll toke a
> Frenche booke and redde therin many strange and mervayllous historyes wherein
> I had grete pleasyr and delyte as well for the novelte of the same as for the fayr
> langage of Frenshe; whyche was in prose so well and compendiously sette and
> wreton whiche me thought I understood the sentence and substance of every
> mater. And for so moche as this booke was newe and late maad and drawen into
> Frenshe and never had seen hit in oure Englissh tonge, I thought in myself hit

shold be a good besynes to translate hyt into oure Englissh to th'ende that hyt myght be had as well in the royame of Englond as in other landes, and also for to passe therwyth the tyme; and thus concluded in myself to begynne this sayd w[e]rke. And forthwith toke penne and ynke and began boldly to renne forth as blynde Bayard in thys presente werke whyche is named the *Recuyell of the Trojan Historyes.*

And afterward whan I rememberyd myself of my symplenes and unperfightnes that I had in bothe langages, that is to wete in Frenshe and Englisshe, for in France was I never, and was born and lerned myn Englisshe in Kente in the Weeld, where I doubte not is spoken as brode and rude Englissh as is in ony place of Englond. (Blake 1973: 97–8)

It is clear from even a superficial glance at this passage that Caxton's spelling practice was inconsistent and admitted a good deal of non-standard variation. For instance the variation bewteen the use of ⟨a, o⟩ before nasal consonants, e.g. 'Englond', 'landes', 'many'. The representation of /ʃ/ also shows variation as demonstrated in the spellings showing ⟨ch, sh, ssh⟩, e.g. 'Frenche', 'Frenshe', 'Englissh', 'nourysshar'. Other non-standard features include the reflection of OE *y* in ⟨e⟩, 'besynes', 'besynesse', the retention of initial ⟨h⟩ in the pronoun IT, and the spellings 'ony' ANY and 'shold' SHOULD. Caxton's idiosyncratic spelling system remained influential for some time and many of the same 'colourless' features identified as part of Caxton's own repertoire are also found in the editions later published by his successor, Wynkyn de Worde.

However there has been no consideration of Caxton's treatment of orthography in his editions of Chaucer's works, despite the number of editions of Chaucer's poetry which issued from Caxton's press throughout his career. The aim of this part of the chapter is to make an initial contribution to this subject by considering Caxton's treatment of orthography in his two editions of Chaucer's *Canterbury Tales*. In order to consider subsequent developments my study will also incorporate the other fifteenth-century editions of the *Canterbury Tales* printed by de Worde and Pynson. So the aim of this part of the chapter is to consider the spelling systems adopted by the early printers of Chaucer's *Canterbury Tales*, in order to investigate the influence of standardisation on printed copies of this important and popular work. In addition to this I will consider any evidence for the preservation of a distinctively Chaucerian orthography, and discuss the implications for an assessment of the status of Chaucer's works at the close of the fifteenth century.

The Language of the Fifteenth-Century Printed Editions of the Canterbury Tales

In this section we will investigate the language of the four printed editions of the *Canterbury Tales* issued before 1500, those by Caxton (1476 [Cx^1], 1482 [Cx^2]), Wynkyn de Worde (1498) [Wy] and Richard Pynson (1492)

[Pn]. As in the previous chapter, data will be drawn from the transcripts and spelling databases made available on *The Wife of Bath's Prologue on CD-ROM* (Robinson 1996). In order to consider the evidence for the spelling systems employed by these printers we must first examine the textual relationships between each of these four copies of the poem. In producing an edition of a Middle English work printers, like scribes, were faced with three possible options. The first possibility was to reproduce the language of the copytext exactly, thus producing a *literatim* transcription of the exemplar. The second option available was to convert the language of the copytext into the printer's own system, thus carrying out a thorough translation of the exemplar. The third possibility was to combine the two processes of *literatim* transcription and translation thus producing a *mischsprache*.[1] In order to determine to what degree these printers reproduced the language of their copytexts or converted it into their own language we must first attempt to identify the likely language of their individual exemplars. Printed editions were commonly set up from an earlier edition and thus the interrelationship between these four editions will be important in determining the linguistic habits of their printers.

Caxton's first edition was classified by Manly and Rickert as a member of the b tradition of the poem, closely affiliated to New College, Oxford, MS D 314 [Ne], and a later manuscript, Trinity College, Cambridge, MS R3.15 [Tc²] which may have been copied directly from Caxton's edition (Manly and Rickert 1940: I, 79–81; Blake 1991b). Caxton subsequently issued a second edition of the poem which represented a reprint of the first edition corrected against another manuscript lent to the printer by a mysterious 'gentylman'. The manuscript used in the second edition has not been identified although recent stemmatic analysis of the extant manuscripts of the *Wife of Bath's Prologue* has suggested that its text was close to that of the archetype (Robinson 1997). The two subsequent editions, those of de Worde and Pynson, were both derived from Caxton's second edition (Robinson 1997: 108–9). Therefore these four manuscripts provide access to an important body of information concerning the spelling practices of the early printers. The six years between the publication of Caxton's two editions of the poem allow us to observe any changes in the printer's spelling policy through a comparison of the orthography of the two texts. Comparison of the spellings of the editions of de Worde and Pynson with those of Caxton will enable us to determine the habits of the later printers, and the influence of Caxton's practice.

As the manuscript used by Caxton in producing his first edition is no longer extant it is not possible to compare the spelling system of this edition with its immediate copytext. Therefore I shall use the Hengwrt manuscript as a

---

[1] For extended discussion of the three types of Middle English copyist see the 'General Introduction' to *LALME*, and chapter 1 above. Detailed consideration of *mischsprachen* may be found in Benskin and Laing 1981.

control for comparison as this is widely considered to be the earliest and most authoritative witness to Chaucer's work. Thus, in the absence of a Chaucerian holograph or a direct exemplar for Cx^1, the Hg manuscript provides a useful control for the purposes of comparison. In addition to this it will be helpful to compare the spellings of these printed books with that of Caxton's preferred usage. In order to consider this the following figure includes a comparison with equivalent forms found in Caxton's editions of his own prose translations, where interference from an intervening exemplar is likely to be minimal.

	Hg	Cx^1	Cx^2	Caxton
MANY	many	many, meny	many, meny	many
NOT	nat	not, nat	not, nat	not
ANY	any	ony	ony, eny	ony
SUCH	swich	suche, swhich	suche, swhyche	suche
THOUGH	thogh, though	though	though	though
THEIR	hir	here, her	her, here	their
HER	hir	hir, her	her	her
THEM	hem	hem, ((them))	hem, ((them))	them, hem
THESE	thise	thyse, these	thise, thyse	these ((thyse))
MUCH	muche	muche	muche, moche	moche

A comparison of the spelling systems found in Caxton's editions of the *Canterbury Tales* with that of the Hg manuscript demonstrates that Caxton translated the language of his copytext into a system similar to that found in his editions of his own prose. Although the immediate exemplar used in the production of Cx^1 has not survived, we may assume that it was written in a language similar to the the Type III of the Hg manuscript, because of a number of relict Type III forms that are found in Caxton's text. For instance 5 uses of the Chaucerian spelling 'nat' are found in Cx^1 and subsequently reduced to 3 in Cx^2, and a single instance of 'swhich' at line 147 of Cx^1 survives as 'swhyche' in Cx^2. That the language of Caxton's editions is due to the input of the printer rather than to an earlier layer of copying is further confirmed by the close correspondence with the language of Caxton's own prose as listed in the figure above. This may be further confirmed by comparison with the language of a number of Caxton's editions of other writers examined by Gómez-Soliño (1984). Thus the spelling system adopted by Caxton in his two copies of the *Canterbury Tales* is largely the same idiosyncratic mixture of forms found in a number of his other editions.

In order to consider the impact of standardisation on Caxton's usage we may compare these forms with those found in Samuels' Type IV. Type IV London English is used to describe the language of the mass of vernacular documents which issued from government offices such as the Chancery and the Privy Seal in the second quarter of the fifteenth century.[2] Caxton's spelling practice shows a degree of similarity with that of Type IV and the printer adopted a number of forms considered prototypical of Type IV usage, such as 'not', 'such' and 'though'. In addition to these Type IV features are a number of 'colourless' forms: non-standard spellings not tied to a particular dialect, such as the form 'ony'.[3] Caxton's practice remains reasonably unchanged in the six years that separate the two editions, although certain developments may be observed. For instance the shift from 'hir' to 'her' in the item HER which is underway in Cx^1 is completed by Cx^2, and there are no uses of the earlier spelling 'hir' in Cx^2.

There are however a small number of features in these texts which indicate a significant departure from Caxton's customary practice, thus indicating a different attitude to his editions of Chaucer's work. In his analysis of Caxton's treatment of spelling in his edition of the *Confessio Amantis* Jeremy Smith (1986) has shown that Caxton reproduced a number of archetypal Gowerisms, thus exhibiting the type of scribal behaviour termed "constrained selection". There is evidence of a similar motivation in the preservation of a number of Type III spellings in Caxton's editions of the *Canterbury Tales*. For instance, despite the widespread preference for 'them' displayed by Caxton in his other printed editions, Caxton preserved a significant number of examples of the Chaucerian 'hem' throughout both editions of the *Canterbury Tales*. Similarly the Chaucerian form 'thise' is maintained in spite of Caxton's general preference for the Type IV form 'these'. Where Caxton mixed the two forms in his first edition at III.560, he regularised the inconsistency in his second edition in the direction of Type III usage:

Cx^1 III.560   Thyse wormys ne these mowthis ne thyse mytis
Cx^2 III.560   Thise wormys ne thise mowthis ne thise mytis

Caxton also uses the Chaucerian spelling 'muche' on two occasions, against a single usage of his customary form 'moche'.

In order to consider the impact of Caxton's spelling practices on later printers we will now compare the forms considered above with those found in subsequent editions of the *Canterbury Tales* printed by Wynkyn de Worde and Richard Pynson. The following table presents a comparison of these same items in Wy and Pn.

---

[2] A number of Chancery and other government documents are edited in Fisher, Richardson and Fisher 1984.
[3] For further explanation of colourless language see Samuels 1988e. For a discussion of Caxton's use of 'ony' see p. 88. Further discussion of colourless usage may be found in the 'General Introduction' to *LALME*, and Benskin 1992.

	Wy	Pn
MANY	many	many
NOT	not	nat, ((not))
ANY	ony	any
SUCH	suche	suche
THOUGH	though	though
THEIR	her, ((theyr))	their(e)
HER	her	her
THEM	hem, ((them))	them
THESE	thise, thyse	these
MUCH	moche	moche

An examination of the above table demonstrates that de Worde followed many of the spelling practices used by Caxton and made little effort to introduce further changes in the direction of Type IV. Thus a number of idiosyncratic forms identified in Caxton's repertoire are also found in de Worde's text, e.g. 'ony'. Similarly Caxton's tendency to preserve a number of distinctively Chaucerian spellings was continued by de Worde, as is shown by the appearance of the pronouns 'her', 'hem'. However de Worde's text does reveal the introduction of standardised spellings not recorded in Caxton, as demonstrated by the appearance of a single occurrence of the Chancery form 'theyr' at line III.381. Other examples show the complete replacement of the 'Chaucerian' form with standardised usage as exemplified by de Worde's use of the spelling 'moche' rather than the form 'muche' adopted by Caxton.

Richard Pynson shows a completely different attitude towards the orthography of his copytext, and his edition replaced many of the oddities of Caxton's spelling habits with spellings common to Type IV documents. For example the form used for THEM in Pn is consistently the Type IV spelling 'them', and there are no occurrences of the Chaucerian spelling 'hem'. Another example of Pynson's regularisation is shown by the wholesale removal of the earlier form 'thise' which is replaced by the Type IV spelling 'these' in all instances. The idiosyncratic forms found in the editions of Caxton and de Worde such as the form 'ony' have also been replaced by Type IV spellings, such as 'any'. There is however a single instance of a change made by Pynson away from Type IV in his introduction of the Type III spelling 'nat' which is regular throughout. There is also a single relict spelling of the Caxton and Type IV spelling 'not' thus confirming that this was the spelling found in Pynson's copytext.

In general Caxton's spelling practice does show some correspondence with Type IV, although the consistent appearance of a number of 'colourless' features such as 'ony' seems to contradict Fisher's view that Caxton modelled his habits closely on that of Type IV. A degree of correspondence between both editions of the *Canterbury Tales* and editions of Caxton's own prose, and other works analysed by Gómez-Soliño demonstrates that

Caxton was reasonably consistent in his habits (1984: 448–80). However the presence of a number of Type III spellings in both editions of the *Canterbury Tales* suggests that Caxton deliberately preserved a number of forms which he considered to be Chaucerian. This suggests that Caxton accorded a degree of authority to the spellings of Chaucer's text, not accorded to other authors. Such a situation provides some evidence to counterbalance the view that Caxton's interest in Chaucer's works was purely commercial rather than literary (Blake 1991d). It seems that Caxton was interested in the orthographic details of his editions, although his concern was not necessarily to enforce regularity and consistency upon the English spelling system. Caxton's successor, Wynkyn de Worde, made few changes to Caxton's practice and his spelling system is largely that of Caxton with slight modifications in the direction of the standard.

However it is with the edition of Richard Pynson that we see a more conscious move towards the consistent replacement of Chaucerian and colourless features with those of Type IV.[4] While Pynson's edition replaces most of the non-standard features of Caxton's earlier editions with Type IV forms, certain changes represent a move away from Type IV; shown by Pynson's consistent replacement of 'not' with 'nat'. While much work remains to be done on the importance of printing in the standardisation of written English, this survey of early printed editions of the *Canterbury Tales* suggests that the role of Pynson in this process should be given greater consideration. The motivation behind Pynson's decision not to adopt the language of the earlier printed editions and to make a decisive move towards greater standardisation remains unclear. However it does seem possible an answer lies in the type of works being printed by Pynson in the late fifteenth and early sixteenth centuries. It is during this period that we see the publication of the first grammar books and a revival of interest in the use of the vernacular in the Tudor education system (Nelson 1952). The publication of Latin-English grammars, such as the *Vulgaria* of William Hormon, published by Pynson in 1519 (James 1926), increased the prestige of the vernacular and promoted an interest in correct usage both in writing and speech. Pynson was also associated with John Palsgrave and the publication of his French grammar, *Lesclarcissement de la Langue Francoyse* (1530), as is recorded in the surviving contract between the author and the printer. This work is one of the earliest foreign language grammars and contains detailed phonetic description of both French and English, representing 'the first example of phonetic writing by an Englishman' (Dobson 1968: I, 7–10). Pynson's publication of translations of classical works, printed in parallel text editions for use in classrooms is also likely to be a contributing factor to his interest in adopting a standardised spelling system. Works like the Latin-English version of the *Acolastus* translated

---

[4] A similar shift towards a more standardised system is also observed by Hellinga in Pynson's editions of Nicholas Love's *Mirror*. See Hellinga 1997, esp. p. 156. For Pynson's usage in a number of other works see Gómez-Soliño 1984: 494-501.

by John Palsgrave are indicative of a higher status accorded to the vernacular, and an increased sense of the desirability of the standardisation of its use. In his preface to this work, directed to Henry VIII, Palsgrave addressed the question of standardisation, the 'great aduantage to waxe vniforme', and the possibility that the 'englysshe tonge . . . shulde by this occasion remayne more stedy and parmanent in his endurance . . . and by that meanes longe to be preserued' (Carver 1937: 10).

This survey of the spellings used in the fifteenth-century printed editions of Chaucer's *Canterbury Tales* suggests that the early printers were concerned with the orthographic details of the texts they printed, but that their concern was not simply to employ the spellings associated with the incipient standard. The spelling systems employed by these printers appear to represent a much more individualistic response to the perceived authority of the work being printed. Where a writer was considered to be of a particular status certain distinctive features of his orthography were preserved and reproduced in early printed editions. Such a situation shows that while the advent of the printing press was an important factor for the standardisation of written English, this was a gradual process which even by the close of the fifteenth century still remained unfinished.[5]

Printed Editions from Pynson to Benson

The next printed edition of Chaucer to appear was William Thynne's edition of the *Workes of Geffray Chaucer*, published in 1532. While Thynne's edition presents a considerable number of modifications to Chaucer's language, it also retains certain of the marked Chaucerian linguistic forms identified above. For instance Thynne's sole spelling of the item SUCH is 'suche' and there are no instances of Chaucerian 'swich'. Similarly the sole form of THOUGH is the standard spelling 'though'. In some instances the Type IV form is introduced alongside the Chaucerian equivalent, as is exemplified in the use of the two spellings of NOT, 'nat' and 'not'. A similar situation is found in the spellings of the noun GIFT and the verb GIVE, which are both found in spellings showing initial ⟨y-⟩ and ⟨g-⟩, e.g. 'gift, yafe, yeue, gyue'. An example of a modernisation not recorded in the fifteenth-century printed editions is the use of the ⟨ea⟩ graph in words like 'great', 'eate', 'please'. These forms may be compared with the Chaucerian equivalents 'grete', 'ete', 'plese'. Despite these examples of Thynne's tendency to update Chaucer's language there are a number of instances of Chaucerian forms which have been consistently retained. For example the third person plural pronouns are consistently those of

---

[5] For a similar conclusion and the suggestion that 'the initial result of the introduction of the printing press was to provoke variety in spelling rather than to promote uniformity', see Blake 1991c.

Chaucer's system, 'they', 'hem', 'her', rather than the Type IV paradigm 'they', 'them', 'their'. Thynne's edition also preserves the archaic forms of the verb BE, those derived from OE 'beon' used by Chaucer, e.g. 'ben'. Thynne is also careful to preserve the archaic ⟨y-⟩ prefix in past participles, another feature of Chaucer's English which was obsolete by the sixteenth century. In order to allow a comparison of some of the common linguistic features of Thynne's edition with those of his fifteenth-century predecessors, the following table compares Wy and Pn with equivalent data from Thynne's edition:

	Wy	Pn	Thynne
MANY	many	many	many
NOT	not	nat, ((not))	nat, not
ANY	ony	any	any
SUCH	suche	suche	suche
THOUGH	though	though	though
THEIR	her, ((theyr))	their(e)	her
HER	her	her	her
THEM	hem, ((them))	them	hem
THESE	thise, thyse	these	these
MUCH	moche	moche	moche

It is interesting to note that in certain features, particularly in the forms of the third person pronoun, Thynne's edition is more archaic than those of de Worde and Pynson. This situation suggests that by the sixteenth century the status of these forms had become increasingly marked and therefore they were deliberately retained by editors. The discovery of printer's marks on certain manuscript copies of Chaucerian texts has enabled the identification of copytexts for certain works included in Thynne's edition. These identifications enabled James Blodgett (1984) to compare certain linguistic details of Thynne's edition with those of the immediate copytext where this has been identified. Blodgett notes that Thynne made a series of consistent emendations to the language of his copytexts in order to restore archaic, authorial readings. One of the most common and consistent of these changes concerns the restoration of the Chaucerian third person plural pronoun paradigm, 'they', 'hem', 'her'. Blodgett writes of this change: 'the consistency with which this change occurs suggests that Thynne gave the printer general instructions always to make the change' (p. 47). Other consistent archaisms noted by Blodgett include the use of the ⟨-(e)n⟩ infinitive inflexion and the addition of the ⟨y-⟩ prefix in past participles.

That Chaucer's English had become regarded as increasingly old-fashioned in the sixteenth century is demonstrated by another edition published during this period, that of Thomas Speght printed in 1598. Speght's edition of the works of Chaucer is the first to include a glossary which explains the meaning of old and obscure words. This glossary consists of a list of approximately 2000 words accompanied by single-word synonyms, arranged in a somewhat chaotic attempt at alphabetical order. The disorderly arrangement of the glossary gives the appearance of hasty assembly, an impression which is further conveyed by the fact that some words lack synonyms and other words make appearances in several places, with different synonyms.[6] Speght's glossary contains a wide range of vocabulary including both learned, technical words and relatively common words, e.g. 'swich'. The definitions are generally limited to a single word although certain words are given more elaborate explanations. For example 'moile' is described as 'a dish made of marrow and grated bread'. In fact Speght seems to have been particularly interested in explaining culinary terms which he often does at length and in detail. For example 'mortreis' is glossed as 'a meat made of boiled hens, crummed bread, yolkes of egs and saffron, all boiled together'. Other definitions are much more vague, as may be demonstrated by Speght's explanation of 'perse' as 'skie colour'. Speght's glossary was much revised and expanded in his second edition of 1602, partly as a result of suggestions made by Francis Thynne, son of William, in his *Animadversions* (Kingsley 1865). However despite Speght's generous acknowledgement of Francis Thynne's assistance in the production of the revised glossary and of the edition itself, it is apparent that Thynne's help was not always beneficial.[7] The differences between the two glossaries are substantial, with the second edition comprising an additional 600 words. In addition to the extra words the glossary of the second edition also omits 200 words included in the previous edition and merges the synonyms for 100 homographs which were listed separately in the first edition. The revised glossary presented a much fuller treatment of Chaucer's "hard words" and formed an important source for lexicographers of the seventeenth century. Speght's treatment of the language of the text itself in both editions is very similar to that of Thynne and there are few major differences in their representations of Chaucer's language. Speght shows the same mixture of Chaucerian and standard forms of NOT, 'nat', 'not' and of the words GIVE and GIFT, 'yafe', 'yeue', 'gift' etc. Speght also used the standard spellings 'though' and 'such', although sporadic examples of the non-standard 'soch' do also appear. Speght's forms of the third person plural pronouns are those of Thynne, while he also regularly retained the ⟨y-, i-⟩ prefix in past participles. Speght's forms of the item MUCH, both 'much' and 'moch', show a slightly increased influence of standardisation in his text over that of Thynne.

We will now turn to the eighteenth century and focus on the work of the

---

[6] For a more detailed discussion of the layout and content of the glossary, and a consideration of its place within the early lexicographical tradition see Kerling 1979.

[7] For an assessment of Francis Thynne's contribution to Speght's second edition see Pearsall 1984. Pearsall writes of Francis Thynne that 'Even for his day he is not a very good scholar, and certainly no Chaucerian. His judgment is poor, his understanding of context unsound, and he lacks all sense of the difference between important and trivial matters' (p. 84).

most important editor of Chaucer of this period, Thomas Tyrwhitt. Tyrwhitt prefaced his edition of the works of Chaucer, published in five volumes between 1775 and 1778, with an essay on the language and versification of Chaucer. In this essay Tyrwhitt attempted to situate Chaucer's language within the variety of Middle English used by his contemporaries and to place this language within the historical development of the English language more generally. By contextualising Chaucer's language in this way, Tyrwhitt aimed to resolve the debate concerning the proportion of French words which made up Chaucer's vocabulary. Tyrwhitt's reasoned discussion of the importance of the French language during the Middle English period concluded that 'the English language must have imbibed a strong tincture of the French, long before the age of Chaucer, and consequently that he ought not to be charged as the importer of words and phrases, which he only used after the example of his predecessors and in common with his contemporaries' (p. xxiii). The second part of this essay provided a discussion of Chaucer's grammar in which Tyrwhitt charted the linguistic changes which had occurred since the Old English period. Tyrwhitt's grammar is a thorough account of the significant differences between Old and Middle English, stressing the similarities between Chaucer's grammar and that of his contemporaries. There are however a number of problems in Tyrwhitt's account of the developments from Old to Middle English. For instance in his discussion of the process of inflexional loss that characterises the move from the more synthetic Old English to an increasingly analytical Middle English, Tyrwhitt claimed that in Chaucer's English adjectives were no longer inflected. However the preservation of the final ⟨-e⟩ inflexion in weak adjectives and as a marker of plurality is an important feature of Chaucer's grammar, with significance for an understanding of Chaucer's metre (see chapter 6 below, p. 97). Tyrwhitt's lack of understanding of the function of adjectival final ⟨-e⟩ is clear from even a brief consideration of his use of ⟨-e⟩ in his text of Chaucer's poems. This may be shown by a comparison of the following readings from Tyrwhitt's text of the *General Prologue* with that of the Hg manuscript. In both instances the adjectives are used indefinitely and therefore belong to the strong declension which remained unmarked in Chaucer's practice. However in both instances Tyrwhitt's edition includes adjectival final ⟨-e⟩, demonstrating the lack of understanding of the weak/strong distinction:

Hg 79   With hym ther was his sone a yong Squyer
T   With hym ther was his sone a yonge Squyer

Hg 174 By cause þat it was oold and som deel streyt
T   By cause that it was olde, and som deel streyt

One of the major shortcomings of Tyrwhitt's account is his complete omission of the impact of the Old Norse language upon English. The Viking invasions and settlements are not mentioned in his historical account and Tyrwhitt seems totally unaware of the importance of Old Norse in explaining certain changes in the development of English. For instance in his description of Chaucer's pronominal system Tyrwhitt charts the gradual adoption of the ON third person plural pronouns, THEY, THEIR, THEM. Tyrwhitt's account of Chaucer's use of these forms is accurate, although he is clearly unaware of the origins of the innovative forms:

> It is very difficult to say from whence, or why, the Pronouns, *They*, *Them*, and *Their*, were introduced into our language. The Saxon pronouns, *Hi*, *Hem*, and *Hir*, seem to have been in constant use in the time of Robert of Gloucester. Sir John Mandeville and Chaucer use *They*, for *Hi*; but never, as I remember, (in the MSS. of authority) *Them*, or *Their*. (p. xxv)

Tyrwhitt's treatment of the language of his edition remains reasonably faithful to the variety of Middle English contemporary with that of Chaucer. He does however include a number of modernisations which are not typical of the language of the earliest and most accurate Chaucer manuscripts. For instance he regularly uses the forms 'not' and 'give' as opposed to the Hg forms 'nat' and 'yeue', thereby giving his text a slightly more modern appearance. In some instances Tyrwhitt appears to have preferred to preserve a deliberately archaic appearance to his text. For instance Tyrwhitt's treatment of past participles reveals a distinct preference for forms with the ⟨i-⟩ prefix derived from OE ⟨ge-⟩, despite his recognition that its use was variable in Chaucer's language.

Tyrwhitt also added a glossary to his edition in which he provided definitions for a large proportion of Chaucer's vocabulary, accompanied by a note of each word's etymology and some line references. These etymologies are generally accurate although they do employ an amount of morally-loaded terminology. For example Chaucer's 'swich' is described as a 'corruption of Saxon *swilke*'. Tyrwhitt's lack of knowledge of the Old Norse language is again evident in the glossary where a number of Norse words are incorrectly derived from Old English etymons. This is most apparent in Tyrwhitt's discussion of the dialect forms in the speech of the undergraduates in the *Reeve's Tale*. Tyrwhitt recognised that the language used by the students represents a Northern dialect of ME although he described many of the ON-derived dialect words as 'obsolete Saxon forms', e.g. 'slike' (ON 'slíkr') which Tyrwhitt claimed is derived from OE 'swilk'. Tyrwhitt's philological integrity and desire for accuracy is further demonstrated by his list of 53 'words and phrases not understood' which stands at the end of his glossary. This list consists largely of rare lexical items or obscure idiomatic phrases. Some of these words are specialised terms which are not recorded elsewhere in ME, such as 'popper' whose appearance in the *Reeve's Tale* is the only citation of this word in the *Middle English Dictionary* [*MED*]. A similar example is the word 'pavade' which is a misreading of 'panade', a word which appears twice in the *Reeve's Tale*. The word 'panade', denoting a type of dagger, is only recorded elsewhere in

MED in two Latin documents. Similarly the use of the word 'gnof' in the *Miller's Tale* is the only appearance of this word in the ME record. Its etymology still remains obscure and it clearly presented difficulty for fifteenth-century scribes, some of whom provided interesting misreadings, e.g. 'guffe', 'chuf', or substituted an easier equivalent, e.g. 'chorle'. An example of a rather obscure idiomatic phrase is the expression 'to turne coppes' used in the *Reeve's Tale*. This phrase is glossed in the *Riverside Chaucer* as 'to turn up the cups (?), play a drinking game' (Benson 1987: 78), demonstrating that the meaning is no less obscure to modern scholars. Tyrwhitt's edition is therefore characterised by his wide knowledge of Middle English and of the development of the English language generally. Tyrwhitt had a vast philological knowledge, which included classical and many European languages, and he rigorously applied this to the editing and interpretation of Chaucer's text.

The nineteenth century is characterised by Thomas Wright's edition of 1847–51 which formed the basis of all subsequent editions until Skeat's *Clarendon Chaucer*. Unlike the eclectic text produced by Tyrwhitt, based on readings from a number of manuscripts, Wright's edition was a best-text edition based upon a single witness. This manuscript, British Library MS Harley 7334 [Ha^4], played an important part in Tyrwhitt's edition, although its readings were treated with some caution. Wright castigated Tyrwhitt for his eclectic approach which he described as the 'most absurd plan which it is possible to conceive' (p. 14). Wright blamed Tyrwhitt's apparent misuse of the manuscript evidence on his total lack of the necessary philological and palaeographical skills, and on his 'entire ignorance of the grammar of the language of Chaucer' (p. 14). By relying on the text of a single, early copy of the poem Wright was convinced that his was a much more faithful record of Chaucer's language and text. As well as claiming that the Harley manuscript contains an early and accurate text, Wright argued that its language had little or no appearance of local dialect forms. By using this manuscript as his base Wright therefore offered his text as presenting Chaucer 'in his own language' (p. 17). However despite its early date and general degree of accuracy, the Harley manuscript contains an idiosyncratic text copied by a scribe whose native dialect was that of the West Midlands. Jeremy Smith's analysis (1985, 1988b) of all of the many manuscripts copied by the Harley copyist, Scribe D, has shown that Scribe D introduced a layer of West Midland dialect features into each of the manuscripts he copied. In addition to the large number of West Midland forms the Harley manuscript also contains a layer of Northern dialect features not found in other manuscripts copied by Scribe D. Therefore far from presenting an accurate record of Chaucer's own linguistic practices, the Harley manuscript contains a blend of provincial West Midland, Northern and Chaucerian linguistic features. That Wright was unaware of the high degree of dialectal variation found in the Harley manuscript is clear from his lack of attempts to regularise or remove such variation. For instance the opening folios of the manuscript show a consistent use of the West Midlands inflexion ⟨-ud⟩ in preterite verb forms, e.g. 'bathud', 'enspirud', 'esud'. However in the *Knight's Tale* these forms are suddenly replaced by the more widespread ⟨-ed⟩ inflexion, e.g. 'wered', 'chaunged' etc. Wright made no attempt to explain or regularise this clear shift in linguistic practice and he simply included both the ⟨-ud⟩ and ⟨-ed⟩ inflexions as he found them in his base text. Another indication of Wright's lack of knowledge of Middle English dialectology is provided by his cursory treatment of the Northern dialect in the *Reeve's Tale*. Having located the students' home town of Strother in the West Riding of Yorkshire, Wright added that 'I am informed that the dialect of this district may be recognized in the phraseology of Chaucer's "scoleres tuo"' (p. 117). It seems that despite his criticism of Tyrwhitt's philology Wright's edition is marked by a lack of understanding of Chaucer's language and of dialect variation in Middle English more generally. In spite of his condemnation of Tyrwhitt, Wright relied heavily on his edition, reproducing many of his learned annotations and quoting wholesale Tyrwhitt's history of the printed editions of Chaucer's *Canterbury Tales*.

Skeat's edition of *The Complete Works of Geoffrey Chaucer* appeared in six volumes between 1894 and 1895. His text of the *Canterbury Tales* used El as a base manuscript, as a result of a collation of its readings with the other manuscripts printed as part of Furnivall's 'splendid "Six-text" Edition' (IV, p. vii). Skeat stressed the importance of the orthographical and grammatical regularity of this manuscript. While Skeat did rely principally on important manuscripts, they are only a small proportion of the large number of complete manuscripts that have survived. He may be further criticised for his frequent assertions that certain manuscripts are better than others: assertions which seldom receive any justification. His editorial practice received close scrutiny from Eleanor Hammond in *Chaucer: A Bibliographical Manual*, from which she concluded that 'his editorial procedure . . . is guided by the erroneous supposition that the true Chaucerian readings may be picked out intuitively, instead of by the laborious and impartial comparison of all the authorities' (Hammond 1908: 146). Despite his claim to have 'refrained from all emendation', Skeat introduced many alterations, particularly with regard to orthography and metre, which have led to the incorporation of a body of unrecorded and purely subjective material into the text. A.S.G. Edwards writes: 'Skeat's dexterity as emender has served to interpose a layer of editorial conjecture between manuscript and printed text that is not easy to penetrate, given the vagaries of Skeat's printed variants' (Edwards 1984: 184). Skeat saw the spelling of the text as of paramount importance, particularly for its evidence regarding the pronunciation of the text. Of his own edition he claimed that it was the first text of Chaucer to have been 'tested by phonetic considera-tion'. He was particularly impressed by the language of El and the orthographic and phonetic regularity of its text, which he felt was a clear and accurate guide to the pronunciation of the text: 'the spelling of the

Ellesmere MS. is phonetic in a very high degree. Pronounce the words *as they are spelt*, but with the Italian vowel sounds and the German final *e*, and you come very near the truth' (V, p. xxv; cited in Edwards 1984: 185).

Skeat's strong belief in the importance of the language and text of the Ellesmere manuscript is largely upheld throughout much of the twentieth century. During the twentieth century a number of major editions of the poem appeared. The first of these is F.N. Robinson's edition of 1933 which was later followed by a second edition in 1957. The second edition of *The Works of Geoffrey Chaucer* was produced in order to incorporate any revisions made necessary by the appearance of the Manly-Rickert findings published in 1940. Robinson retained almost the entire text of his first edition of 1933, which was based upon El. While Robinson recognised the new evidence in support of the Hg text, he was never convinced by the arguments discrediting the El readings as editorial, which he described as 'Manly's argument, if not demonstration, that readings peculiar to the Ellesmere group of manuscripts are often due to emendation' (Robinson 1957: vii). Robinson adopted nearly all the readings of his first edition, which was based upon a complete collation of the eight manuscripts published by the Chaucer Society and the two extra manuscripts Cn and Mg. He did however include 160 variant readings, although his acceptance of Manly-Rickert readings is far outnumbered by instances of its rejection. G.F. Reinecke, having compared the readings in the *Miller's Tale* and the *Manciple's Tale*, describes Robinson's attitude to the Manly-Rickert text: 'It would seem that he treated their findings in an aesthetic way; his choices are those of a learned literary critic' (Reinecke 1984: 250). Thus with Robinson's second edition El retained its claim to represent the finest witness to the text, order and language of the *Canterbury Tales*.

The next major landmark in this period was the publication in 1980 of the *Canterbury Tales* edited from the Hg manuscript by N.F. Blake. Blake's attitude towards Hg demonstrates a more radical stance than seen previously, although his view represents a development of the work of Manly-Rickert (1940), Tatlock (1935) and Dempster (1948, 1949). Blake's edition follows the text of Hg, varying from it only when readings can be shown to be the result of scribal sophistication or errors in the copytext. The number of such emendations is relatively small and an important aspect of the editor's policy was to present 'a "plain" text to remind us of what is actually in the best manuscript so that we can reformulate our ideas about Chaucer's language and metre' (Blake 1980: 12). The edition is also unique for its use of the Hg order, where most editors follow that of El or a variation of it. Blake presents the poem in 12 separate sections which are reproduced according to the Hg order, altered only in the restoration of part III, containing the tales of the Monk, Nun's Priest and Manciple, to its intended place before misbinding. Blake also sticks rigidly to Hg in deciding the contents of his edition, a decision which results in the excision of the *Canon's Yeoman's Prologue* and *Tale, Man of Law's Endlink* and the

Merchant's Prologue. He varies from Hg only in the relegation of the spurious Squire-Merchant and Merchant-Franklin links to the appendix, and in the restoration of the final 528 lines of the *Parson's Tale* and the *Retraction* edited from El, missing from Hg due to loss of leaves. Despite its controversial approach towards the contents and arrangement of the poem, Blake's edition presented the *Canterbury Tales* in the manuscript version which best preserves Chaucer's linguistic practices. Blake makes no attempt to regularise the linguistic variation found in the Hg manuscript, thus presenting a text which appears to be closer to Chaucer's own language than that of El. Despite the fact that Blake's edition presents a more appropriate basis for study of Chaucer's language, his edition is not frequently cited in the literature and was largely replaced by the subsequent publication of the *Riverside Chaucer* in 1987.

The *Riverside* edition does not represent a fundamentally new edition, and its primary significance lies in its widespread adoption as the principal reference work by Chaucer scholars. The editors mainly reprinted the text of Robinson's second edition, correcting some readings and adding very little that was new. The major difference between this edition and that of Robinson lies in the greater scepticism with which the editors treated readings unique to El, although the editors state clearly that they were 'especially chary of deserting El completely because we remain unconvinced . . . by Manly and Rickert's argument that El represents a text "editorially sophisticated"' (1120). The textual notes also record the editors' particularly critical attitude towards Robinson's frequent tendency to select metrically smoother lines on the dubious evidence of later manuscripts. However the adoption of much of Robinson's language and text has ensured that the language of the El manuscript has remained the basis for critical discussions of Chaucer's work. Despite the reservations about its textual and linguistic accuracy that have been voiced by scholars, the language of El has come to be considered synonymous with Chaucer's language.

6

Chaucer's Grammar

In previous chapters we have looked principally at aspects of Chaucerian spelling practices and to some extent at the way these reflect phonology. However as well as their phonological significance spelling systems are important for their reflection of grammar, particularly through the representation of inflexional morphology. In this chapter we will focus on aspects of Chaucer's grammar and specifically on the area of morphology in order to observe the ways in which Chaucerian morphology was transmitted across the fifteenth-century manuscript tradition. A large number of morphological changes were ongoing in London English in the fourteenth and fifteenth centuries and Chaucer frequently exploited such variation for metrical and rhyming purposes. The gradual obscuration and loss of grammatical inflexions which characterises the shift from the more synthetic Old English to an increasingly analytic Middle English had important implications for the understanding of both Chaucerian grammar and metre. Many of the grammatical inflexions employed by Chaucer were lost from both the spoken and written language in the century following his death. The loss of these inflexions therefore carried severe implications for the transmission of Chaucerian verse and the understanding of its metre. Chaucer was aware of these problems in his own lifetime and he expressed his anxieties regarding linguistic variation and change and their implications for his metre at the end of *Troilus and Criseyde*.[1] In this chapter I will examine a number of grammatical features of Chaucer's language in order to consider how Chaucer exploited variation within the London dialect and how later scribes treated these grammatical features. This analysis will allow us to see how scribes responded to these grammatical variants and the extent to which scribes were aware of their metrical significance. There have been a number of important discussions of scribal attitudes to Chaucerian metre such as those by Pearsall and Solopova. Solopova (1997) has examined the way in which scribes edited Chaucer's metre, although her study focuses only on the earliest manuscripts and does not treat grammatical features. Pearsall's most recent work on Chaucer's metre has concentrated on the use of the weak adjective inflexion and its importance for our understanding of Chaucer's verse (Pearsall 1999). Pearsall's study is

---

[1] *Troilus and Criseyde*, lines 1793–6.

largely restricted to the Hg and El manuscripts although like Solopova he does include some of the earliest manuscripts. In this chapter I will concentrate on grammatical features which have significance for both metre and rhyme, and will trace the treatment of these features across the entire manuscript tradition rather than focusing purely on the earliest manuscripts. Such a study will enable us to observe the processes of linguistic change, as inflexional endings became increasingly obscured and lost, and the ways in which scribes understood Chaucer's verse within the context of such changes. I will begin by examining adjectival inflexion in Chaucer's language as this was a feature of major metrical significance for Chaucer's verse.

This adjectival ⟨-e⟩ inflexion was used in Chaucerian Middle English as a marker of definiteness and plurality. This grammatical feature has been much discussed and its significance for Chaucer's metre is well-known. However the fifteenth century witnessed the complete loss of adjectival inflexion and as a result scribes were presented with a number of difficulties in their treatment of this feature in copying Chaucer's verse. There has been no thorough study of scribal treatment of this feature, despite its significance for our understanding of linguistic change in this period and of scribal responses to Chaucer's metre. I will begin by rehearsing the rules concerning the use of the adjectical final ⟨-e⟩ as it is found in the Hg manuscript of the *Canterbury Tales*. When modifying singular headwords the ⟨-e⟩ is added when the adjective is preceded by a definite article, a demonstrative, or a possessive pronoun. These uses may be demonstrated by the following examples taken from the *Wife of Bath's Prologue*:

42   The firste nyght hadde many a murye fit
18   And that ilke man which that now hath thee
708   Of venus werkes worth his olde sho

In addition to these uses the final ⟨-e⟩ inflexion is also found where an adjective is modifying a proper noun, or forms part of a vocative expression. This use may be demonstrated as follows:

235   Sire olde kaynard is this thyn array

In addition to these uses concerning singular adjectives, the final ⟨-e⟩ inflexion is also added to adjectives modifying a headword in the plural:

187   And techeth vs yonge men of youre praktyke

It has been shown that the Hg manuscript is extremely regular in its use of the final ⟨–e⟩ inflexion (Burnley 1982). However throughout the late fourteenth and early fifteenth centuries adjectival final ⟨-e⟩ ceased to function as a grammatical marker. As this inflexion ceased to be pronounced in the spoken language it also began to disappear in the written language. As this process of loss became more widespread scribes began to add ⟨-e⟩ in unhistorical environments, thereby demonstrating that the grammatical system was no longer understood. Despite the consistency in the treatment of adjectival final ⟨-e⟩ in the Hg manuscript there are a number of instances where ⟨-e⟩ is omitted in environments where it is required by the grammar. For example line 431 of the *Wife of Bath's Prologue* reads as follows in Hg:

> Thanne wolde I seye good lief taak keep

Here the use of a vocative expression demands a final ⟨-e⟩ on 'good' which is absent in both Hg and El. The omission of ⟨-e⟩ in vocatives in Hg is possibly a reflection of the process of loss of ⟨-e⟩ in the spoken language. Such expressions are probably closest to the spoken language and common in the speech of contemporary Londoners. As the loss of final ⟨-e⟩ must have been more advanced in the spoken language than in the more conservative written language, it seems likely that the loss of ⟨-e⟩ in such expressions in Hg is indicative of this process of change. David Burnley (1982) has shown that the adjective 'hey', 'heigh' is frequently written without ⟨-e⟩ in Hg in positions where the grammar demands it. Burnley explains this situation as indicative of its regular appearance in vocative expressions and forms of address such as 'youre hey lordshipe', which must have been in frequent usage in the spoken London dialect. It is also interesting to note that this expression appears twice in the *Tale of Melibee* where the final ⟨-e⟩ serves no metrical function. Other examples of forms of address lacking final ⟨-e⟩ include the phrases 'youre good name' which also appears in the *Tale of Melibee* (VII.1862).[2] Therefore although the Hg manuscript is extremely regular in its use of final ⟨-e⟩ there are instances of its omission. These omissions appear to reflect the ongoing process of inflexional loss in the London dialect. By the copying of the El manuscript this process seems to have advanced further. The El manuscript contains many of the same omissions of ⟨-e⟩ identified in the Hg manuscript. But in addition El also contains instances of ⟨-e⟩ in unhistorical environments suggesting that the grammatical function of this inflexion was no longer fully understood.[3]

During the fifteenth century this process of loss of final ⟨-e⟩ advanced considerably and scribes were increasingly erratic in their treatment of this grammatical feature, which is frequently omitted where it is grammatically required or added in unhistorical environments. The purpose of the first section of this chapter is to survey the treatment of final ⟨-e⟩ in the manuscripts of the Chaucer's work in order to observe scribal treatments of this feature. In order to consider the treatment of final ⟨-e⟩ throughout

---

[2] In the *Tale of Melibee* El also has two examples of the phrase 'his good name' (lines VII.1843, 1844).

[3] See also the discussion of the El treatment of final ⟨-e⟩ in the Northern dialect in the *Reeve's Tale* in chapter 3.

the fifteenth century as a whole I will focus on a single text, the *Wife of Bath's Prologue* [WBP], in all its manuscript copies. The WBP survives in fifty-four manuscript and four pre-1500 printed versions, produced throughout the fifteenth century. In addition to the wide diachronic spread presented by this group of texts, many were copied in different dialects of Middle English thus providing a diatopic dimension to our study (see chapter 4 and appendix 1). In order to carry out this study I have grouped the fifty-eight witnesses according to their date of copying. Manuscripts are assigned to groups of twenty-five years as listed in appendix 2. In what follows I will survey the treatment of adjectival inflexion in a number of different grammatical environments, as outlined above. The first such environment concerns the treatment of adjectives following a definite article. In order to exemplify scribal treatment of final ⟨-e⟩ following the definite article I shall consider the following three lines in Hg and their representation across the manuscript tradition:

21   But þat I axe why þat the fifthe man
42   The firste nyght hadde many a murye fit
608   I hadde the beste quonyam myghte be

The following table shows the number of instances of the loss and preservation of adjectival final ⟨-e⟩ in these three examples throughout the fifteenth century, divided into periods of twenty-five years.[4]

	⟨-ø⟩	⟨-e⟩
1400–1425	4	14
1425–1450	14	19
1450–1475	28	38
1475–1500	18	13

The above table shows that in the first quarter of the fifteenth century the majority of instances show final ⟨-e⟩ in its correct grammatical environment. However these examples are mostly the work of two scribes, Scribes B and D, who copied four of the manuscripts in this group. Two other manuscripts, La and Dd, show a greater tendency towards loss of ⟨-e⟩ in this position, with both manuscripts adding ⟨-e⟩ in only one such instance. Throughout the remainder of the century there is a gradual increase in the proportion of examples of loss of ⟨-e⟩ as compared with the inclusion of ⟨-e⟩. However it is only in the final quarter of the century that we see the number of instances of ⟨-ø⟩ appear greater than the number of occurrences of ⟨-e⟩. The period 1425–75 shows a much greater appearance of random variation at the level of individual manuscripts than in the first twenty-five years. Most scribes appear to fluctuate considerably in their use of the inflexion

---

[4] Some manuscripts replace 'fifthe' and 'firste' with numerals and are therefore not included in the following table. Where a particular manuscript is out or has a variant reading in this and subsequent tables, it must also be excluded from the figures presented.

with few scribes showing a consistent use of ⟨-ø⟩ or ⟨-e⟩. An interesting exception to this is the scribe of Dl, copied between 1450 and 1475, who is consistent in his use of ⟨-e⟩ in this position. This rare tendency may be explained by the fact that the Dl scribe wrote in the conservative Kentish dialect, which preserved inflexional endings longer than other dialects.[5] One significant exception to the general pattern discussed with reference to the above table occurs with the adjective 'wys'. This adjective is recorded with final ⟨-e⟩ in every manuscript of WBP except for La which has the following reading: 'Loke here þe wisman kinge Salomon'. If we compare this data with that for the use of the adjective 'wys' indefinitely we find that the majority of manuscripts also include final ⟨-e⟩ in strong position. This may be exemplified by a consideration of line 209: 'A wys womman wol bisye hir euere in oon'. The form of the adjective with final ⟨-e⟩ is found in forty-five manuscripts. It seems therefore that despite the distinction between 'wys' and 'wyse' observed in Hg, most other manuscripts spell this word 'wyse' irrespective of its use.

Clearly the loss of final ⟨-e⟩ in these positions causes problems for the metrical regularity of the lines, although most scribes seem unconcerned by such details. The Dd scribe for example makes no efforts to repair the metrical damage caused by his omission of final ⟨-e⟩. It could be argued that the La scribe was aware that his lack of ⟨-e⟩ has left the line metrically deficient, as in each case an extra syllable is added elsewhere in the line as follows:

Hg 21   But þat I axe why þat the fifthe man
La   Wele Bot þat I ax whi þe fift mane

Hg 42   The firste nyght hadde many a murye fit
La   þe first nyht he hadde mony a mery fitt

Hg 608 I hadde the beste quonyam myghte be
La   I hadde þe best quoniam þat myht be

However the metrical regularity of Chaucer's verse is not dependent purely on syllable count, but more importantly on the alternation of stressed and unstressed syllables. While Chaucer's verse is regularly pentameter it is sufficiently flexible to allow a degree of variation in the number of syllables. The regularity of the alternation of stressed and unstressed syllables is a more important feature and it is precisely this aspect of Chaucer's metre that is disrupted in the Lansdowne readings quoted above. In fact it seems likely that the scribe had little understanding of the technical aspects of Chaucer's verse-form and the alterations made above represent common scribal tendencies towards a more prosaic syntax through the introduction of pleonastic 'that' and personal pronouns.

---

[5] See for instance Pamela Gradon's (1979) discussion of this feature in the Kentish text *Ayenbite of Inwyt*.

The pattern for the omission of final ⟨-e⟩ following demonstratives is similar to that outlined above concerning definite articles. However there is a significant exception to this pattern concerning the adjective 'ilk'. The figures for the use of final ⟨-e⟩ in 'ilk' in the following line are as follows:

18   And that ilke man which that now hath thee

	⟨-ø⟩	⟨-e⟩
1400–1425	0	5
1425–1450	4	8
1450–1475	5	20
1475–1500	0	12

This example demonstrates that the treatment of 'ilk' is quite different to that of other weak adjectives. In this case only a handful of manuscripts omit final ⟨-e⟩ while the majority of manuscripts preserve ⟨-e⟩ throughout the fifteenth century. It is particularly striking that all manuscripts copied in the final quarter of the century preserve final ⟨-e⟩ in this instance. A possible explanation for this situation is that unlike other adjectives 'ilk' can only be used in weak positions, following a determiner or a demonstrative. As a result scribes were accustomed to writing 'ilk' with final ⟨-e⟩ and this practice was preserved longer than with other adjectives.

In order to allow comparison with the treatment of ⟨-e⟩ after the definite article, the following table presents the treatment of final ⟨-e⟩ after possessive pronouns in line 708 of the WBP:

708   Of venus werkes worth his olde sho

	⟨-ø⟩	⟨-e⟩
1400–1425	0	6
1425–1450	4	9
1450–1475	6	20
1475–1500	5	7

This table shows a broadly similar situation to the use of ⟨-e⟩ following the definite article. The tendency to preserve ⟨-e⟩ remains relatively stable throughout the period 1400–1475 while the number of instances of ⟨-ø⟩ gradually increases during this period. It is only in the final twenty-five years that we see the number of occurrences of ⟨-ø⟩ approach the number of instances of ⟨-e⟩.

In vocative expressions there is a greater tendency for scribes to omit the adjectival inflexion than demonstrated following determiners. We have already observed this tendency in the Hg manuscript above in the following line:

431   Thanne wolde I seye good lief taak keep

We explained the omission of the final ⟨-e⟩ in this expression as a reflection of the advanced process of loss in the spoken language, and we would therefore expect a corresponding increased tendency towards ⟨-ø⟩ in the scribal copies of this line. The following table represents a summary of the treatment of this line across the manuscript tradition:

	⟨-ø⟩	⟨-e⟩
1400–1425	3	4
1425–1450	8	4
1450–1475	15	11
1475–1500	10	2

This table shows a clear increase in the instances of loss of ⟨-e⟩ as compared with the examples considered above. Here the number of occurrences of ⟨-ø⟩ exceed the instances of ⟨-e⟩ as early as 1425–50. The proportion of instances of ⟨-ø⟩ compared to instances of ⟨-e⟩ continues to increase throughout the century until there is a substantial difference in the final twenty-five years. This evidence would appear therefore to support the view that inflexional loss was accelerated in vocative expressions.

If we turn to the use of final ⟨-e⟩ to mark plurality in adjectives we find the following distribution of ⟨-e⟩ and ⟨-ø⟩ across the following line in the WBP:

187   And techeth vs yonge men of youre praktyke

	⟨-ø⟩	⟨-e⟩
1400–1425	0	6
1425–1450	3	9
1450–1475	11	15
1475–1500	10	2

This table shows that the retention of ⟨-e⟩ in plurals was greater than in weak adjectives in the singular. However by the period 1475–1500 the number of instances of unmarked plural adjectives is significantly greater than the number of adjectives with ⟨-e⟩. A completely contrasting scenario is found where such adjectives appear in rhyming position. In such instances scribes were careful to preserve the ⟨-e⟩ throughout the century, as may be demonstrated by the following couplet:

121   Of vryne and oure bothe thynges smale
122   Was eek to knowe a femelle from a male

The plural form of the adjective 'smale' is found with final ⟨-e⟩ in every fifteenth century copy of the line, suggesting that scribes paid greater attention to such details in rhyme words than elsewhere within the line.

Another feature of plural concord found in the Hg manuscript concerns the frequent use of final ⟨-e⟩ in possessive pronouns to mark agreement with a plural noun. This feature was a purely written device and was not reflected in pronunciation. As a result it is employed in a particularly erratic way in both the Hg and El manuscripts, although El has a slightly more regular treatment of this feature. For instance a comparison of the use of final ⟨-e⟩ to mark plural concord in the masculine possessive pronoun in the Hg and El copies of the *Clerk's Tale* shows a greater consistency in El. The following is a list of every instance of a masculine possessive pronoun preceding a plural noun in the *Clerk's Tale* in both Hg and El:

28	Hg	As proued by his wordes and his werk
	El	As preued by his wordes and his werk
65	Hg	As were his worthy eldres hym bifore
	El	As were hise worthy eldres hym bifore
67	Hg	Were alle his liges bothe lasse and moore
	El	Were alle his liges bothe lasse and moore
70	Hg	Bothe of his lordes and of his commune
	El	Bothe of hise lordes and of his commune
85	Hg	Oonly that point his peple bar so soore
	El	Oonly that point his peple bar so soore
89	Hg	That he sholde telle hym what his peple mente
	El	That he sholde telle hym what his peple mente
190	Hg	And her vp on he to his officers
	El	And heer vp on he to hise officeres
192	Hg	And to his pryuee knyghtes and Squyers
	El	And to hise priuee knyghtes and Squieres
237	Hg	Hise eyen caste on hir but in sad wyse
	El	Hise eyen caste on hir but in sad wyse
669	Hg	Hise eyen two and wondreth þat she may
	El	Hise eyen two and wondreth þat she may
682	Hg	His tendre lymes delicat to sighte
	El	His tendre lymes delicaat to sighte
725	Hg	Hath mordred bothe his children pryuely
	El	Hath mordred bothe his children priuely
729	Hg	For which wher as his peple ther bifore
	El	For which wher as his peple ther bifore
741	Hg	How þat the pope as for his peples reste
	El	How þat the pope as for his peples reste
748	Hg	Bitwix his peple and hym thus seyde the bulle
	El	Bitwixe his peple and hym thus seyde the bulle
766	Hg	To bryngen hom agayn his children two
	El	To bryngen hoom agayn hise children two
1016	Hg	With so glad cheere his gestes she receyueth
	El	With so glad chiere his gestes she receyueth

Comparison of the treatment of the possessive pronoun in these two manuscripts in these examples reveals that El is more consistent in its use of final ⟨-e⟩ which is found in 7 occurrences, while Hg only adds the ⟨-e⟩ inflexion in 2 instances. However it is striking that there are a further 10 occurrences in which neither manuscript shows agreement. Five of these occurrences are found where the pronoun precedes the noun 'peple' and it may be that this noun could be treated either as plural or singular. Certainly mass nouns of this kind were frequently not subjected to the same rules of concord as other nouns.[6] In contrast to the number of scribes who retain ⟨-e⟩ in plural adjectives there are very few examples of the preservation of this system in later manuscripts. For instance the use of the final ⟨-e⟩ in the possessive pronoun in the following line in Hg is also found in just three other manuscripts: El, Dd, Gl:

39　　Which yifte of god hadde he for alle hise wyuys

We may now compare the above examples with instances of adjectives where a final ⟨-e⟩ is not required grammatically. For example the following table records the treatment of a strong adjective where ⟨-e⟩ is not found in Hg:

281　What eyleth swich an old man for to chide

	⟨-ø⟩	⟨-e⟩
1400–1425	4	3
1425–1450	3	9
1450–1475	5	19
1475–1500	3	9

In the scribal treatment of this line we see a quite different trend to that demonstrated above. Here the number of instances of ⟨-ø⟩ is greater in the first quarter of the century while in the period 1425–50 the number of occurrences of ⟨-e⟩ is greater than of ⟨-ø⟩ and this situation is then maintained throughout the remainder of the century. Evidently the loss of the distinction between weak and strong adjectives resulted in the frequent use of ⟨-e⟩ in unhistorical environments, rather than in the complete loss of the ⟨-e⟩ inflexion.

Having considered the treatment of adjectival inflexion I will now turn to consider some features of nominal inflexion, and will start by looking at the treatment of plural inflexion in nouns. In Chaucer's Middle English there were three principal markers of plurality: ⟨-es⟩, ⟨-en⟩, ⟨-ø⟩. The ⟨-es⟩ inflexion, derived from the OE strong noun declension was by far the most common and had become generalised to most OE weak nouns. However a number of nouns retained the ⟨-en⟩ inflexion derived from the OE weak noun declension, while some nouns are found used with both ⟨-es⟩ and ⟨-en⟩ inflexions. For instance the Hg manuscript has examples of the following plural forms showing both the ⟨-es⟩ and the ⟨-en⟩ inflexions: 'toon', 'toos', 'shoon', 'shoos', 'been', 'bees'.[7] Other nouns remained

---

[6] Burnley 1982 discusses the uncertainty in adjective concord found in the Hg manuscript concerning the number of corporate nouns.

[7] For further examples and a discussion of Chaucer's lack of exploitation of such variation for rhyming purposes see Burnley 1983: 118–19.

endingless in the plural, e.g. 'folk'. An example of each of these three types of plural forms can be found in the following line from the *Wife of Bath's Prologue*:

285   Thow seist þat Oxen Asses hors and houndes

It is interesting that every scribal copy of this line preserves the weak plural inflexion in 'oxen' despite the fact that this ending was recessive during this period. In fact in addition to preserving the ⟨-en⟩ inflexion in 'oxen' 20 scribes transfer the same ending to the noun 'asses'. The endingless plural 'hors' is apparently less favoured by these same scribes and 11 manuscripts introduce a form with the strong plural, 'horses', while 5 manuscripts add the ending ⟨-e⟩. Where the ⟨-en⟩ plural inflexion appears in rhyme every scribe preserves this ending as is demonstrated by the consistent preservation of the ⟨-en⟩ ending of word 'eyen' in the following instances in Hg:

315   That oon thow shalt forgo maugree thyn eyen
358   Thogh thow preye Argus *with* his hundred eyen
723   Thurgh which tresoun loste he bothe hise eyen

Further variation in the spelling of noun plurals is found in the representation of the unstressed vowel in the inflexion of the strong ending which may be written ⟨-es, -ys, -is⟩. The most common form in Chaucer is the ⟨-es⟩ form although the other spellings appear both within the line and, most importantly, in rhyme. The use of the ⟨-ys, -is⟩ spellings in rhyme demonstrate that these forms represent a different phonetic realisation to that of the ⟨-es⟩ spelling. For instance the ⟨-is⟩ plural inflexion in 'talis' in line 319 is deliberately used to indicate a raised variant of the ⟨-es⟩ inflexion and thereby allowing a rhyme with the final unstressed syllable of 'Alis':

Taak youre disport I nyl leue no talis
I knowe yow for a trewe wyf Dame Alis

Despite the care with which this rhyme is represented in the spelling of the plural inflexion in the Hg manuscript, many scribes disturb this exact rhyme in their representation of the inflexion. A total of 32 scribes substitute the more common inflexion ⟨-es⟩ in line 319 thereby creating an inexact rhyme. However 11 of these scribes appear to have recognised the resulting problem with maintaining the rhyme scheme and therefore introduce the spelling 'Ales' in line 320. A similar example may be found at line 39 where the Hg manuscript has the ⟨-ys⟩ plural inflexion in rhyme, thereby representing a closer realisation of the unstressed vowel for rhyming purposes:

Which yifte of god hadde he for alle hise wyuys
No man hath swich that in this world alyue is

In this example 44 scribes replace the ⟨-ys⟩ inflexion with the more widespread ⟨-es⟩ form and thereby spoil the rhyme with 'is'. David Burnley

(1989) has shown the care with which early scribes preserved exact rhymes in their spelling of rhyme words. However it appears that in the representation of noun plurals these scribes were unconcerned to retain ⟨-ys, -is⟩ inflexions despite their significance for the rhyme. In addition to the plural inflexion nouns also add inflexions to represent the genitive case and, in some prepositional phrases, to mark the use of the dative. The dative inflexion, although no longer a living part of the spoken language, is preserved in certain fossilised inflexions such as 'on/in honde'. This phrase is frequently found in rhyming position and the dative inflexion ⟨-e⟩ is therefore often crucial in maintaining the rhyme scheme. This may be exemplified by the following couplet (lines 327–8):

> That rekketh nat who hath the world in honde
> By this *prouer*be thow shalt vnderstonde

Despite the fact that the dative inflexion no longer served any grammatical function in the spoken language most scribes recognise its importance to the rhyme in this example, and only 14 scribes omit the ⟨-e⟩ inflexion. A similar rhyme is found at lines 379–80 and here a similar scribal response is recorded, with 13 scribes omitting the inflexional ⟨-e⟩:

> Lordynges right thus as ye han vnderstonde
> Bar I stifly myne olde housbondes on honde

A very different scenario is presented by the treatment of an inflexional ⟨-e⟩ in the expression 'by nyghte' which is found in rhyme at lines 397–8 in Hg as follows:

> I swoor that my walkyng out by nyghte
> Was for to espye wenches that he dighte

In this example the majority of scribes clearly did not recognise the function of the final ⟨-e⟩ and simply omitted it and only 13 include the inflexional ⟨-e⟩, although a further 11 have a flourish on the final ⟨t⟩ which may be indicative of an inflexion.

One further type of inflexion which may be added to nouns is the ⟨-es⟩ ending which converts a noun into an adverb. This was a common feature of Middle English and is commonly found in Chaucer's language, e.g. 'hennes', 'amyddes', 'unnethes'. The treatment of this inflexion is not always consistent in the Hg manuscript which has an example of the adverbial form 'unnethe' at line 394:

394   Whan that for syk they myghte vnnethe stonde

A further 24 manuscripts agree with the Hg reading with the ⟨-e⟩ inflexion while 16 scribes include the ⟨-es⟩ inflexion. However 15 scribes omit the inflexion entirely thereby removing an unstressed syllables and consequently disrupting the metre.

Having dealt with inflexion in nouns I will now turn to verbal morphology, and will begin by examining forms of the infinitive. There are two principal forms of the infinitive in Hg, marked by the inflexions ⟨-e⟩ and ⟨-(e)n⟩, thus allowing variation for metrical effect. The use of an infinitive with final ⟨-e⟩ would allow elision with a following vowel or ⟨h⟩, while the form with final ⟨-en⟩ would remove this possibility. For instance the metre of the following line depends upon the ⟨-en⟩ inflexion to prevent elision with the following vowel: 'Poul dorste nat comanden at the leeste' (WBP line 73). Throughout the fifteenth century the ⟨-(e)n⟩ inflexion was gradually lost and most infinitives had the ⟨-e⟩ inflexion or were unmarked. It is therefore interesting to observe the extent to which scribes retained the ⟨-en⟩ inflexion where it serves a metrical function. The following table indicates the treatment of the infinitive in line 73 across the fifteenth-century manuscript tradition:

	⟨-(e)n⟩	⟨-e⟩/⟨-ø⟩
1400–1425	5	1
1425–1450	6	6
1450–1475	8	15
1475–1500	3	9

It seems from the above table that scribes were increasingly less aware of the importance of infinitive inflexions throughout the course of the fifteenth century. A large number of scribes omit the final ⟨-n⟩ thereby allowing elision with the following vowel and causing the line to be metrically deficient. Few scribes attempt to repair the resulting metrical damage although there are some variants which could represent attempts to restore regularity. For instance the Ha[4] scribe adds a further negative particle thereby adding a further unstressed syllable: 'Poul ne dorst not comaunde atte lest'. The scribes of Py, Ne, and Nl also have variants which effect the metre, adding 'it' in place of the missing unstressed syllable: 'Paul durst nat comaunde it at the leste'. It is however likely that this reading was introduced not as a result of an awareness of the metrical problems but rather to supply a dummy object: a frequent scribal tendency (see Windeatt 1979). The scribe of Ii supplies a similar solution although he introduces the phrase 'it no thyng', producing a regular iambic line but with an extra metrical foot: 'Paule durst not commaunde it in no thing at the leste'. The Ii reading may perhaps be linked with that of Ha[4] as demonstrating a common tendency to make the sense more explicit: in this case by increasing the negation.

The next example I shall consider concerns the use of the infinitive inflexion in the word 'vsen' in order to prevent elision with a following ⟨h⟩: 'To goon and vsen hem in engendrure' (line 137). The treatment of this inflexion across the manuscript tradition may be summarised by the following table:

	⟨-(e)n⟩	⟨-e⟩/⟨-ø⟩
1400–1425	6	1
1425–1450	8	4
1450–1475	17	8
1475–1500	5	6

Several scribes make certain alterations to the line which may be attempts to restore metrical regularity. For instance the Gg scribe, the only scribe in the period 1400–1425 to omit the ⟨-n⟩, adds a further unstressed syllable in his spelling of 'engendrure': 'To gon & vse hem in engenderure'. One other reading, shared by Cn, Ph[2], Pn, may represent an attempt to prevent elision by adopting the ON-derived form of the third person pronoun 'them': 'To go and vse them in engendrure'. However it is probably more likely that the introduction of the ON-derived pronoun here is simply a result of the processes of linguistic change which saw these pronouns become increasingly acceptable throughout the fifteenth century. Each of these three manuscripts was copied after 1450, while Pn was produced in 1492, by which time these pronouns were widely accepted. Each of these three texts shows the influence of Type IV language and these pronouns are also part of this linguistic variety. We should therefore probably view the use of the 'them' pronoun in this example as not motivated by metrical considerations.

In addition to variation in the treatment of the inflexion in infinitives Chaucer also exploited the possibility of using the plain form of the infinitive or preceding it with the prepositions 'to' or 'for to'. An example of the latter usage is found in the following line from the WBP:

28   God bad vs for to wexe and multiplye

In this instance only 20 scribes retain both prepositions thereby preserving a metrically regular line. 7 scribes retain only the 'to' thereby producing a metrically deficient line, although certain copyists may attempt to remedy this lack. For instance the scribes of Ld[2], Ln, Ry[2] add an extra syllable by adding a final ⟨-n⟩ to the first of the infinitives, thereby preventing elision with the following vowel: 'God bad vs to wexen & multiplie'. However as noted above this does not restore metrical regularity according to the demands of Chaucer's stress based system. A total of 29 scribes omit both prepositions producing an octosyllabic line, although an additional syllable is added in 6 manuscripts as follows: 'That God bad vs wex and multeple' (He, Ii, Ne, Pn, Tc[2], Wy). In this instance we are probably dealing once again with a common scribal tendency towards a more explicit syntax rather than a concern for metrical regularity. Where the single preposition 'to' appears alone scribes are apparently more concerned to preserve this feature. For instance in the following line in Hg all subsequent copyists preserve the 'to', while 2 scribes add the preposition 'for' (Fi, Ha[4]):

443   What eyleth yow to grucche thus and grone

However it is perhaps unlikely that the widespread tendency to preserve the 'to' in this example is due to a recognition of its metrical value, as 7 scribes also omit the inflexional ⟨-e⟩ in the following infinitive form 'grucche'. It is perhaps more likely that scribes perceived the 'to' as part of an infinitive construction while 'for to' was not such an inherent part of the construction.

Having considered the treatment of infinitives I now want to turn to consider forms of the present tense, and specifically the third person singular and plural present indicative inflexions. Chaucer's dominant form of the third person singular present tense was the Southern inflexion ⟨-(e)th⟩ which is the sole form recorded in his later work. As discussed in chapter 2 the Northern variant ending in ⟨-(e)s⟩ is found in rhymes in some earlier verse, but in later poetry Chaucer only used this form in the Northern dialect dialogue in the *Reeve's Tale*. However during the fifteenth century the Northern variant became more acceptable in the London dialect and was adopted more widely than in the previous century. The process of acceptance was however comparatively slow and the ⟨-(e)th⟩ form was that adopted by Type IV, thereby guaranteeing it a longer lifespan. Despite this longer preservation of the ⟨-(e)th⟩ ending the ⟨-(e)s⟩ form gathered considerable ground during the fifteenth century and we would expect to see its influence in the manuscript copies of the *Wife of Bath's Prologue*. However a comparison of the following line in Hg across the entire manuscript tradition reveals that every witness preserves a variant of the ⟨-eth⟩ ending, ⟨-eth, -ith, -yth⟩:

102   God clepeth folk to hym in sondry wyse

A similar tendency to preserve the ⟨-(e)th⟩ ending is also observed in line 64 where most scribes use variants of this same inflexion:

64   Thapostle whan he speketh of maydenhede

8 manuscripts include the verb in the preterite, giving the form 'spak', which removes an unstressed syllable from the line. The two related manuscripts, Bo[1] and Ph[2], both have the unmarked form 'speke'. Only one manuscript, Ps, has the form 'spekis' which is no doubt a result of the scribe's Lincolnshire origins. Further variation is also possible in Chaucer's language in the use of contracted and syncopated forms of the third person present tense. Examples of these forms may be exemplified by the following line:

389   Who so that first to Mille comth first grynt

The metre of this line relies upon the preservation of the contracted form 'comth' rather than the more common form 'cometh'. Despite the importance of this form for the metre only 9 scribes have a contracted form of the verb, while 46 scribes have uncontracted forms with an additional unstressed vowel. We might compare this situation with the consistent scribal tendency to preserve this feature of Gower's language (Smith 1988c). The third person present form 'grynt' also found in this line exemplifies a regular tendency for verbs with a stem ending in a dental consonant to undergo phonetic attrition. The form 'grynt' is found in every single manuscript of WBP apart from a single exception, Ry[1], which has 'Who so Firste to þe Mylle comeþe Firste gryndeþe'. However we have observed elsewhere that scribes were careful not to adjust spellings in rhyme and it is therefore likely that their treatment of 'grynt' was constrained by its appearance in rhyme with 'stynt'. If we compare this treatment with an occurrence of a similar form within the line we find a much more various scribal response. For instance line 826 of WBP reads as follows in Hg:

826   I pray to god that sit in magestee

Here the form 'sit' is a third person singular present tense form which has undergone a similar process of phonetic modification. Despite the importance of this form for the metre only 31 manuscripts contain this spelling with 22 scribes introducing the disyllabic form 'sitteth' and one scribe (Ps) having a similarly hypermetrical form 'syttys'.

The majority of Chaucer's third person singular forms falls into the above categories, although there remain a number of uses of the subjunctive mood which retain a distinct form. However the gradual obscuration and loss of unstressed syllables meant that the subjunctive ending, ⟨-e⟩, became increasingly indistinct and its function increasingly replaced by modal verbs.[8] However despite the confusion concerning the form and function of the subjunctive in the fifteenth century, Chaucer's scribes appear to have recognised such forms and preserved them with consistency and accuracy. For example a consideration of the following line across all its manuscript copies reveals that every scribe preserves the subjunctive ending in ⟨-e⟩ rather than the indicative equivalent ⟨-eth⟩:

268   Til that she fynde some man hir to chepe

There is however a greater tendency to replace the use of the subjunctive forms of the verb 'to be' with their indicative equivalents, as may be demonstrated in the following line:

490   For which I hope his soule be in glorie

In this line 50 scribes preserve the subjunctive form of the verb 'be' while 8 scribes replace it with the indicative form 'is'.

The forms of the imperative found in Chaucer's language display an amount of important variation. The singular form of the inflexion is commonly found without an ending, while the plural form generally

---

[8] See further the discussion in Smith 1996: 151–3.

adopts the ⟨-eth⟩ inflexion. However when a speaker addresses a single individual either form of the imperative may be adopted, representing a stylistic distinction similar to that displayed in the use of second person pronouns, as discussed below. Often the variation in the use of the two forms may have no such significance and may be purely motivated by metrical considerations, as in the following example where the Pardoner addresses the Wife of Bath:

186 Telle forth youre tale spareth for no man
187 And techeth vs yonge men of youre praktyke

Here both singular and plural forms are adopted within the same line and the motivation appears to be metrical rather than stylistic. Scribal treatments of this line reveal a strong preference for the endingless form in addressing a single individual. 40 scribes preserve the endingless form 'telle' as opposed to 17 instances of the form 'telleth', which could be explained as the careful preservation of the Hg form. However the treatment of 'spareth' shows that 28 scribes prefer the form 'spare' thereby suggesting that the preservation of 'telle' has a similar motivation. Certainly few scribes show any concern for the corresponding metrical problems such changes cause.

The endings used to mark third person plural present indicative forms in Chaucer are similar to those found in infinitives, where the verb may end either ⟨-e⟩ or ⟨-(e)n⟩. As with the infinitive endings Chaucer manipulated this variation for metrical effect by using the ⟨-n⟩ to prevent elision with a following vowel or ⟨h⟩ as in the following line:

257 Thow seyst som folk desiren vs for richesse

Here the metre depends upon the use of the form of the present plural with final ⟨-n⟩ in order to prevent elision with the following vowel. However during the fifteenth century the final ⟨-n⟩ was gradually lost in this position and many scribes employed forms of the present plural without ⟨-n⟩. The following table demonstrates the treatment of this grammatical feature in the above example across the fifteenth-century manuscript tradition:

	⟨-(e)n⟩	⟨-e⟩/⟨-ø⟩
1400–1425	4	3
1425–1450	1	12
1450–1475	5	16
1475–1500	3	9

The above table shows that the use of the ⟨-en⟩ inflexion was rare throughout the fifteenth century, although the majority of scribes in the period 1400–1425 do preserve it. In addition to these variants three manuscripts in the period 1450–75, Ra[2], Ra[3], Tc[1], use the restricted Southern ending ⟨-eth⟩. Ra[3] and Tc[1] were both copied by the 'hooked g' scribe, a scribe working in London but with Kentish origins (see appendix 1).

Presumably the introduction of this conservative feature is due to the influence of his Kentish upbringing. Few scribes seem to have understood the metrical significance of the ⟨-en⟩ inflexion and few make any attempt to repair the resulting metrical damage. However a number of scribes do add an inflexional ⟨-e⟩ to 'folk' thereby adding a further unstressed syllable elsewhere in the line, although this may simply represent a clumsy attempt to make the noun plural. Another example of a line where the form of the present plural inflexion has metrical significance is line 381:

381   That thus they seyden in hir dronkenesse

A comparison of the form of the present plural in this line across the manuscript tradition shows a very different treatment of the inflexion than in the example considered above. The following table illustrates the differing scribal treatments of this inflexion:

	⟨-(e)n⟩	⟨-e⟩/⟨-ø⟩
1400–1425	6	1
1425–1450	8	3
1450–1475	18	6
1475–1500	8	2

The difference between the two examples is striking with the above example showing a much more consistent scribal tendency to preserve the ⟨-(e)n⟩ inflexion throughout the entire century. It is possible that the difference in treatment of the two examples may be explained by a confusion concerning the plural subject. It is possible that some scribes were unsure whether to treat 'folk' as a a plural noun, whereas the immediately preceding third person plural pronoun, 'they', is unambiguous in its demand for a plural form of the verb.

   The final feature of verbal morphology which I will examine concerns the forms of the past participle, and specifically the use of the prefix ⟨y-⟩. This prefix is a reduced form of the OE ⟨ge-⟩ and in Chaucer's ME it represented a variant form of the past participle. Chaucer was able to exploit this grammatical variation for metrical effect and as a result his use of the prefix is crucial for maintaining metrical regularity, as in the following line:

17   Thow hast yhad fyue housbondes quod he

The treatment of this feature in this same line by later scribes may be demonstrated by the following table:

	⟨y-⟩	⟨ø-⟩
1400–1425	6	0
1425–1450	6	6
1450–1475	12	12
1475–1500	3	7

The above table shows that in the early period of the fifteenth century all scribes were careful to preserve the ⟨y-⟩ prefix. Instances of its omission increase throughout the century although it is not until the period 1475–1500 that the number of omissions is greater than the number of instances of its preservation. Few scribes are concerned about the impact the omission of this prefix has on the metre and most simply copy the line with a missing unstressed syllable. However some scribes omit the past participle completely thereby creating a regular iambic line, but one which lacks a complete foot (Ad[1], Ds, En[3]). A number of other scribes spell the past participle 'hadde' which might suggest a disyllabic pronunciation, thereby creating a further syllable in order to compensate for the loss of the prefix (Hk, Ht, Ii, Ma). Another example of a line where the ⟨y-⟩ prefix is of metrical importance is line 71 of the WBP which in Hg reads:

71   And certes if ther were no seed ysowe

The treatment of the ⟨y-⟩ prefix across the fifteenth-century manuscript tradition may be demonstrated by the following table:

	⟨y-⟩	⟨ø-⟩
1400–1425	6	0
1425–1450	8	3
1450–1475	22	2
1475–1500	10	2

This table shows that in this instance there was a strong movement towards the preservation of the ⟨y-⟩ prefix, with very few manuscripts omitting it. Three of the seven manuscripts which do omit the prefix have the plural form of the noun 'sedes' thereby adding an extra unstressed syllable as compensation: 'And certis if þer were no sedys sowe' (Bo[2,] Ii, Ps). An even stronger tendency to preserve the prefix is found at line 117 which in Hg reads as follows: 'And of so *parfit* wys a wight ywroght'. Only 3 manuscripts fail to include the prefix: Ln, Ps, Ra[2]. Both Ln and Ra[2] were copied after 1450 while Ps was copied by a scribe using the Lincolnshire dialect which might explain the loss of the prefix in these three manuscripts alone. The scribe of Ra[2] seems not to have been aware of any corresponding metrical problems and no attempt is made to restore the missing syllable. However the Ps scribe does include an extra unstressed syllable with the inclusion of the word 'is': 'and of parfyte wyse a wyght is wrought'. However again this change appears to correlate with tendencies noted above and elsewhere towards a more explicit syntax. The Ln scribe may also have attempted to remedy the metrical deficiencies caused by the missing unstressed syllable, by introducing the pronoun 'it': 'And of so parfit & so wijs a wriȝt It wrouȝte'. However this reading is more likely caused by the scribal tendency to introduce pronouns in order to make the meaning more clear.

In the final section of this chapter I will turn to a consideration of the use of second person pronouns in the *Wife of Bath's Prologue*, to see how Chaucer's usage is treated by later scribes. In this section I will be considering both grammatical and stylistic factors and this will lead to a discussion of forms of address in the prologue more generally. This broader discussion will lead to a consideration of how scribal treatment of these features can provide important insights into how Chaucer's first readers responded to the depiction of the Wife of Bath.

The significance of variation in use of singular and plural forms of the second person pronoun in Middle English is well-known. When addressing a group of individuals the plural pronoun 'ye' is used. When addressing a single individual either of the singular or plural forms is possible, depending on certain pragmatic rather than grammatical factors. Where a socially inferior individual is being addressed the singular form is employed, whereas the plural form is required to express deference when addressing a social superior. Within courtly relationships husband and wife refer to each other using the plural form, reserving the singular form for moments of emotional intensity or intimacy. This is perhaps best indicated by Criseyde's dramatic switch to the singular pronoun in addressing Troilus: 'For I am thyn, by God and by my trouthe!' (III.1512). The singular pronoun may also be used to show a lack of respect or even contempt to an addressee.[9]

It is generally assumed that in non-courtly contexts these rules are not observed although the distinction between courtly and non-courtly contexts has not been clearly defined. A close examination of the forms of address used in the *Wife of Bath's Prologue* reveals that these pragmatic rules are deliberately maintained and undermined for specific effects. Much of the Wife's prologue is concerned with her pursuit of domination over her husbands, and especially in her more complex union with Jankin, whom she 'took for loue and no rychesse' (526). This complex power struggle is further enacted in the forms of address which are exchanged between the wife and her husbands throughout the prologue. In addition to a study of Chaucer's use of forms of address we may also observe the treatment of such forms by the fifteenth-century scribes who copied the prologue. A consideration of the treatment of forms of address by these many fifteenth-century scribes gives us access to a variety of different responses made by Chaucer's first generation of readers.

In her prologue the Wife of Bath frequently makes direct reference to her husbands, whom she addresses using the singular (T) form of the personal pronoun, 'thow' etc. The use of this form seems to be a deliberate attempt to reject or subvert the language of courtly love and its expectation of male dominance and feminine subservience. Alison's use of T forms suggests at

---

[9] A useful description of the contextual factors which condition the use of second person pronouns, accompanied by a flow-chart, may be found in Burnley 1983: 17–22. For an important discussion of the sociolinguistics of such usage in present-day language varieties see Brown and Gilman 1960.

the least an equality between husband and wife, and is perhaps symbolic of her assumed superiority or contempt for her husbands. This contempt is further demonstrated in the consistent use of derogatory titles in her reference to her husbands, whom she addresses as 'Sire olde kaynard', or 'Sire olde lecchour' which also suggest a deliberately ironic mocking of the language of respect due to a husband from his wife.[10] In addition to Alison's addresses to her husbands, her prologue also contains an example of Alison addressing herself in her husband's voice:

> Thow sholdest seye wyf go wher thee liste
> Taak youre disport I nyl leue no talis
> I knowe yow for a trewe wyf Dame Alis   (III.318–20)

In these lines Alison instructs her husbands how they should treat her with complete trust and allow her complete freedom in her actions. In adopting a male voice Alison also adopts the V form of the second person pronoun, in order to highlight the subservient status of the husband. These lines are also significant for the forms of address Alison uses in referring to herself. At line 320 she adopts a respectful and loving tone and addresses herself as 'Dame Alis', a title reserved for ladies of refined and elevated character in Chaucer's works. The use of the title 'Dame' in conjunction with the first name is particularly rare in the *Canterbury Tales*, and is only used with reference to Custance, Hermengyld, Pertelote and Prudence. Indeed the use of the phrase 'trewe wyf' is a conventional address in the language of courtly love. Thus it seems that while Alison is content to ignore such conventions in addressing her husbands, she expects them to show her the respect appropriate to a courtly relationship.

However this situation seems to be contradicted by line 318 in which Alison addresses herself in a manner that appears dramatically inappropriate in such a context. For as Alison has her husbands invest her with total freedom, she uses forms of address which simultaneously imply an assumption of male authority and lack of respect, thereby undermining the gesture of equality. The use of the T form of the second person pronoun is stylistically marked in this context and is especially evident given the adoption of plural (V) forms in the following lines. In addition to this the direct use of the word 'wyf' as a form of address represents an aggressive and dominant gesture on the part of the husband. The use of this word as a form of address, stripped of all adjectival embellishments such as found in line 320, is rare in Chaucer's poetry and frequently used as an assertion of male 'maistrie'. Derek Pearsall (1995) has argued that Arveragus' use of this form of address at line 1472 of the *Franklin's Tale* indicates a resumption of male sovereignity and authority over Dorigen that he had previously promised to revoke. Similar examples of the use of this vocative form may be found in relationships where the male assumes an authority over the

---

[10] See the discussion of the use and connotations of the title 'Sir' in Burrow 1984: 69–74.

wife. In the *Clerk's Tale* Walter frequently refers to Griselda as 'wyf', thereby clearly demonstrating her inferior status. A similar effect is achieved in the patronising tone with which the merchant addresses his wife in the *Shipman's Tale*:

> Wyf quod this man litel kanstow deuyne
> The curious bisynesse that we haue.   (VII.224–5)

When the word 'wyf' is used in direct address in a courtly context in Chaucer's poetry it is typically couched in possessive pronouns and flattering adjectives, as in Palamon's final address to Emily in the *Knight's Tale*:

> Allas myn hertes queene allas my wif
> Myn hertes lady, ender of my lyf   (I.2775–6)

Further evidence that the use of the simple vocative 'wyf' and the use of the T form of the personal pronoun in this context in this line in the WBP seems inappropriate, is provided by its treatment by fifteenth-century scribes. Twenty manuscripts have the V form of the pronoun, 'you' or 'ye', rather than the T form. In addition to this change twelve scribes add the adjective 'good' before 'wyf', while two other manuscripts read 'faire wyf'. Therefore it would seem that the very words in which Alison describes her husband's submission of authority undermine that process by assuming a position of male power and superiority.

Other important evidence of the power struggle between the Wife and her husbands is found in two speeches towards the end of the prologue, where Jankin relinquishes sovereignty and hands over the authority to Alison. In the first of these addresses Jankin apologises for hitting his wife and asks her forgiveness:

> And neer he cam and kneled faire adown
> And seyde deere suster Alisoun,   ·
> That I haue doon it is thy self to wyte
> Foryeue it me and that I thee biseke   (III.803–7)

Here Jankin addresses Alison using T forms of the pronoun and there is no scribal variation in the forms of the pronoun used. Evidently Chaucer's scribes considered the use of the T pronoun, expressing equality, to be appropriate to such a context. Jankin also uses a form of address couched in terms of intimacy and familiarity, which provoked a number of scribes to increase the terms of affection. So for instance the manuscripts show the following variants: 'dere hert myn owne A.' (Bo[1]), 'dere suster swete A.' (Cx[2], He, Pn, Se, Tc[2], Wy), 'dere spouse A.' (Gl, Ra[3], Tc[1]), 'myn dere sistyr A.' (Gg, Ph[2]), 'sustyr swete A.' (Ii, Ne), 'dere wyf A.' (Fi, Mc).

Jankin's final address to the wife, and the terms in which he hands over his 'maistre' and 'soveraynetee' to Alison were also subjected to scribal alteration. In the Hengwrt manuscript these lines read:

> myn owene trewe wyf
> Do as thee lust the te*r*me of al thy lyf
> Keep thyn honour and keep eek myn estaat   (III.819–22)

However the fifteenth-century copyists of the work seem to have felt the use of the T form of the personal pronoun inappropriate in this context, where marital sovereignty is being relinquished. As a result a number of scribes replaced the T pronoun with the V form indicating the respect and authority with which Jankin must subsequently treat his wife.

In conclusion it seems that forms of address and second person pronouns in the *Wife of Bath's Prologue* are important markers of the power struggle between Alison and her husbands. Variation in the use of these stylistic markers in crucial passages in the prologue seems to undermine both the Wife's own request for sovereignty at line 318, and Jankin's own submission and handing over of authority at 819–22. This discussion has also highlighted that forms of address and personal pronouns are important in non-courtly contexts, as well as in more familiar courtly environments. Indeed the deliberate undermining and ridiculing of courtly language is often a feature of Chaucer's non-courtly tales. In addition to this the evidence of the treatment of these features of the text by fifteenth-century copyists demonstrates that scribes were aware of these pragmatic conventions and their significance as discourse markers. This is therefore further evidence of the importance of scribal responses as evidence of fifteenth-century readers of Chaucer's verse. This examination of the treatment of personal pronouns in the *Wife of Bath's Prologue* has also suggested that the use of these pronouns is not simply a question of obeying a series of grammatical rules, but rather it represents a complex pragmatic code, which in turn reflects the shifting and unstable nature of personal and social relationships in the fourteenth and fifteenth centuries.

7

The Influence of Chaucer's Language

In this final chapter we will turn from our consideration of scribal attitudes towards and treatment of Chaucer's language to consider the influence of Chaucer's language on the poetry of his fifteenth- and sixteenth-century followers. The fifteenth century witnessed the work of a number of poets writing in a Chaucerian style, and I intend to focus here on the two most important of these, Thomas Hoccleve and John Lydgate. In chapter 1 I included quotations from both of these poets which demonstrate their overt dependence on the model established by Chaucer. However in the following discussion I want to consider the extent to which the language of these two poets shows the direct influence of that of Chaucer, setting aside other stylistic, thematic influences which have been treated in detail elsewhere.

Thomas Hoccleve

I shall begin my discussion with Thomas Hoccleve. Study of Hoccleve's language is greatly facilitated by the survival of three manuscript collections of his verse in the poet's own hand.[1] The following discussion will therefore be based upon study of the language of these three important codices. As noted in chapter 2 the language of Thomas Hoccleve's holograph manuscripts belongs to Type III London language, also recorded in the Hg and El manuscripts. This association of Hoccleve's language with that of the Chaucer manuscripts is potentially surprising given that Hoccleve was a generation younger than Chaucer. Furthermore Hoccleve was employed as a professional scribe in the Privy Seal and we might therefore have expected him to have had early contact with the new administrative language, Type IV. All that survives of Hoccleve's professional copying is a Formulary copied in French and Latin, and we are therefore unable to compare his literary language with any professional use of the vernacular.[2] However the survival of three manuscripts of Hoccleve's verse in the poet's own hand allows us a rare glimpse of an author's own language, without the interference of scribal intermediaries. Despite the very few examples of

---

[1] For a complete list of manuscripts of Hoccleve's works see Burrow 1984: 50–4.
[2] For a discussion of the contents and function of Hoccleve's Formulary see Thompson 2000.

extant authorial holographs in Middle English Hoccleve's language has not been studied in detail since 1899 (Vollmer 1899). In this section we will examine the language of Hoccleve's holographs and situate this within the London language of the early fifteenth century. In particular we will compare this language to that of Scribe B as recorded in the Hg and El manuscripts. In addition to the language of the poet's own holographs we may also consider the language of Hoccleve's contribution to the Trinity Gower manuscript; a manuscript in which he collaborated with Scribes B and D (Doyle and Parkes 1978). This comparison will enable us to consider whether Hoccleve's linguistic practices varied depending on whether he was copying his own works or those of another poet such as Gower. I will begin my analysis by considering Hoccleve's spellings for a number of common items as follows:

	Scribe B	Hoccleve holographs	Hoccleve Trinity MS
THOUGH	thogh, though	thogh	thogh
SUCH	swich	swich	swich
WHICH	which	which	which
NOT	nat, noght	nat, noght, naght	nat ((noght, not))
BUT	but	but	but
THROUGH	thurgh	thurgh	thurgh
THEY	they	they	they
THEIR	hir(e)	hir(e)	hir(e)
THEM	hem	hem	hem
ARE	be(e)n ((arn))	been ((arn))	ben
MUCH	muche(l)	moche, muchil	mochil
GAVE	yaf, ((gaf))	yaf	yaf
SAW (vb.)	saw, saugh (say, seigh)	sy	—

It is clear from the above table that Hoccleve's spelling system remained consistent whether he was copying his own verse or that of John Gower. Furthermore it is apparent that Hoccleve's spelling system bears a striking similarity to that of Scribe B as recorded in the Hg and El manuscripts. In the majority of the forms compared in the above table Hoccleve and Scribe B are in complete agreement, although there are a few minor differences. For instance Hoccleve's stint on the Trinity Gower manuscript records the minor variant 'not', a Type IV spelling feature not found in Hg, El or in the Hoccleve holographs. However the apppearance of this form may be explained as a relict Gowerian form, rather than as a part of Hoccleve's active repertoire. An important difference between the language of Hoccleve and Scribe B is found in the preterite forms of the verb SAW. Scribe B displays an equal preference for the forms 'saw' and 'saugh', although there are a number of occurrences of 'say' and 'seigh' as well. Much of this variation is found within the line and it is not frequently exploited by Chaucer for rhyming purposes. In fact the only one of these variants to appear in rhyme position in the *Canterbury Tales* is the form 'seigh' in the following two examples only:

> I.1065   Was risen and romed in a chambre anheigh
> I.1066   In which he al the noble Citee seigh

> V.849   Hir to disporte vp on the bank anheigh
> V.850   Wher as she many a Ship and Barge seigh

However despite the two occurrences of the form 'seigh' in rhyme it was evidently less favoured by Scribe B in copying the El manuscript than when he copied Hg. In El the form 'seigh' appears in only one additional instance, other than those where it is demanded by the rhyme above, at line 193 of the *General Prologue*. The appearance of this sole instance within the line at this early position in the manuscript is best explained by the concept of "working-in" (Benskin and Laing 1981). It seems that the scribe has erroneously introduced a form early in his work which he otherwise suppressed throughout the remainder of his copying of El. The form preferred by Scribe B in his work on El is 'saugh' which appears much more frequently in this manuscript than it does in Hg. However Hoccleve used neither of these forms and his dominant spelling for this form of the verb is the rare 'sy'. In addition to this form a second much less frequent form, 'say', does also appear in rhyme as in the following example:

> 18.9[3]   Thynkynge thus / byfore me I say
>   A crois depeynted with a fair ymage.
>   I thoghte I nas but asshes and foul clay:

Hoccleve's dominant form 'sy' is extremely rare in Middle English. As a singular form of the preterite tense it is recorded in only three other linguistic profiles listed in *LALME*: LP 7052 (Gloucestershire), LP 4686 and LP 7890 (Warwickshire). As a plural form it is found in just two *LALME* Linguistic Profiles: LP 9580 (Gloucestershire) and LP 699 (Warwickshire).[4] Interestingly this form does appear just once in the whole of Chaucer's work in the *Canon's Yeoman's Tale*; a tale not found in the Hg manuscript. Here the single occurrence of 'sy' is used for rhyming purposes as follows:

---

[3] Line references refer to the numbering and lineation system used in Furnivall 1970.

[4] See *LALME* IV, item 211 SEE, pp. 244–8. M.L. Samuels and J.J. Smith note the common appearance of the similar form 'syh' in Gower's language which they claim is also found in Hoccleve's language. They explain the appearance of this form in Hoccleve's language as the result of his imitating Gower's usage. However the form 'syh' does not appear at all in Hoccleve who consistently adopts the distinct form 'sy', a form never employed by Gower. The only occurrence of this form in London English outside Hoccleve's poetry is the single instance in the *Canon's Yeoman's Tale* discussed here. See Samuels and Smith 1988, esp. p. 17 and n. 17.

VIII.1380   Quod the Chanoun and farwel grant mercy
VIII.1381   He wente his wey and neuer the preest hym sy

Despite the rarity of Hoccleve's form, which appears to have a Western or Central Midlands origin, it was evidently known to Chaucer and must therefore have had some currency in London English in this period.

Another difference between the language of Hoccleve and that of Scribe B, not represented in the above table, concerns the representation of OE *y*. As noted in chapter 2 Chaucer exploited the different realisations of this vowel for rhyming purposes, and considerable variation is recorded in its representation in both Hg and El. However comparison of the treatment of this vowel in Hg and El in chapter 3 showed that El shows a greater tendency to regularise this practice within the line. It seems that the status of these variants had changed in the intervening period and that in copying El Scribe B favoured the use of ⟨i, y⟩ to represent this vowel. This preference is also reflected in Hoccleve's spelling practices which show a consistent tendency to reflect this vowel as ⟨i, y⟩. For instance the following forms are the only recorded spellings for these common words, and there are no examples of variant spellings with ⟨u, e⟩: 'synne', 'bisy', 'biry', 'chirche', 'mirthe', 'miry'. A similar preference is displayed in Hoccleve's use of these variants in his rhymes where he rhymes most frequently on forms with ⟨i, y⟩.[5] In fact Hoccleve's preference for these forms even stretches to his use in rhyme of the rare form of the verb SHUT 'shit' (OE 'scyttan'), a form which was commonly avoided on account of the homonymic clash with the taboo noun SHIT:[6]

2.149   Is al to feeble to despute of it!
         To Clerkes grete / apparteneth þat aart
         The knowleche of þat, god hath fro yow shit;

However there are some rare instances of rhymes dependent upon the Eastern and Kentish reflection ⟨e⟩, as in the following example which depends upon the form 'asterte' (OE 'astyrian') with OE *y* reflected in ⟨e⟩:

2.258   And mo shuln be / thow shalt it nat asterte;
         Thow art nat wys / ageyn god to debate!
         The flood of pryde / caste out of thyn herte!

The representation of long vowels in Hoccleve's orthography shows a considerable overlap with that of the Hg manuscript, although Hoccleve's practice reveals a slightly greater preference for vowel doubling than that of Hg. For instance the representation of /aː/ before a consonant may be spelled as follows:

---

[5] For a list of examples see Vollmer 1899: 205–6.
[6] The form 'shit' is never used by Chaucer.

MADE	Hoccleve	Hg
maad	7	34
made	12	118
maade	0	4

Here we see that the use of both ⟨aa⟩ and ⟨aCe⟩, where C represents any consonant, is found in both texts and that the preference for ⟨aCe⟩ is also common to both. However, setting aside the greater number of occurrences in Hg, the proportion of spellings with ⟨aa⟩ is greater in Hoccleve than in Hg. The four occurrences of the form 'maade' in Hg, not recorded in Hoccleve, are all found in the *General Prologue*, and may therefore represent inherited exemplar forms rather than part of the scribe's active repertoire.[7] The representation of /o:/ as ⟨oo⟩ and ⟨o⟩ in Hg, e.g. 'hom', 'hoom' is found only as ⟨oo⟩ in Hoccleve, 'hoom'. The representation of ⟨a/o⟩ before nasal consonants, e.g. 'hand', 'land', shows considerable variation in both Hoccleve and Hg and the two spellings appear to be in free distribution.

Treatment of consonants shows several further resemblances between the practices of Hoccleve and those of Hg. For instance the Hg scribe's tendency to use ⟨k⟩ in initial position before a back vowel to represent the velar plosive [k], e.g. 'kan', 'konne', 'koude' is also found in Hoccleve's practice although Hoccleve prefers 'can', 'konne', 'kowde'. Initially /ʃ/ is represented by ⟨sh⟩ in both Hoccleve and Hg, e.g. 'shal', 'she', 'shyne', while before morpheme boundaries both have ⟨ssh⟩, e.g. 'fressh', 'englissh'. Both texts represent /tʃ/ as ⟨cch⟩ as in words such as 'cacche'. The reflex of OE /hw/ is written ⟨wh⟩ in both texts as is exemplified by the following forms: 'which', 'what', 'where'.

At the level of morphology Hoccleve shows both similarities and contrasts with Chaucer's own practices. The consistent use of adjectival final ⟨-e⟩ which we observed in Chaucerian language in the previous chapter is maintained in some environments and not in others in Hoccleve's language. Despite the appearance of certain apparent exceptions the distinction between weak and strong singular adjectives found in Chaucer's language is not always preserved by Hoccleve. For instance the following examples show instances where a final ⟨-e⟩ is expected but is not found in the spelling.

2.285   Which yee han leid on his good old knygthode,
12.10   Be my good lord / and now to stynte / I gesse

In his recent edition of the *Complaint* and *Dialogue* John Burrow (1999) notes that the holograph section of the *Dialogue* does preserve two examples of adjectives with the weak singular inflexion, as follows:

555   In al this wyde world / lord is ther noon
731   Thogh his wyf do to him þat selue same.

---

[7] This form is recorded at the following lines of the *General Prologue* in Hg: 33, 387, 427, 513.

While both these adjectives are indeed subject to the weak/strong distinction in Chaucer's language, these two isolated examples could be understood as fossilised expressions where the ⟨-e⟩ inflexion has been preserved due to its prosodic rather than grammatical function. It is perhaps also worth noting that there are no examples of the uninflected forms of either adjectives elsewhere in Hoccleve's verse. However despite the uncertainty concerning the weak/strong distinction in singular adjectives, Hoccleve's language does clearly retain the inflexional ⟨-e⟩ as a marker of plurality, and this grammatical ending is consistently applied. The following line provides an example of Hoccleve's use of this grammatical feature:

2.412   Of thoghtes goode / and causen men honure

The Chaucerian distinction between singular and plural forms of the demonstrative and possessive pronouns is also maintained in Hoccleve's written practice, despite the fact that this feature appears to have served a purely written function. For instance in a survey of 65 occurrences of the form 'this' only 1 occurrence was found of an uninflected form modifying a plural head:

10.60   For sorwe of him, ran by this cheekes doun!

Similarly all instances of the inflected form 'thise' were found to be in agreement with a plural headword, as shown in the following example:

2.202   To thise stories sit it thee to goon:

Another grammatical feature of Chaucer's language which is maintained in Hoccleve's practice concerns the endings found in third person plural forms of the present tense. We noted in the previous chapter that Chaucer used the inflexion ⟨-e(n)⟩ in these forms and that he drew on the optional ⟨-n⟩ for metrical purposes. A similar variation is also found in Hoccleve's verse and his use of this variation has a similar metrical function. Where such forms appear before a consonant the ⟨-en⟩ inflexion is favoured. However where these forms are followed by a vowel or ⟨h-⟩, ie. where there is the possibility of elision, there is variation between ⟨-e⟩ and ⟨-en⟩ according to the metre.[8] For instance consider the following examples:

2.387   As yee diden late in this contree heere,
16.27   How wel þat yee doon / & how soone also,

Similar exploitation of grammatical variants is found in Hoccleve's treatment of past participles, which are found with or without the ⟨y-⟩ prefix and/or a final ⟨-n⟩ according to metrical necessity. Similarly infinitive forms may

---

[8] For a fuller discussion of this practice with more detailed consideration of Hoccleve's metrical practice see Jefferson 1987.

terminate in ⟨-e⟩ or ⟨-en⟩ and Hoccleve also varies his use of 'for to', 'to', and 'ø' according to the metre.[9]

As suggested in chapter 2, it is perhaps not surprising that Scribe B and Thomas Hoccleve should have similar spelling systems given that they were both involved in the professional production of copies of vernacular verse. However it seems unlikely that the shared linguistic habits derives from shared training. Doyle and Parkes' analysis of the hand of Scribe B concluded that his use of the anglicana formata book hand was relatively old-fashioned in the early fifteenth century and that he probably received his training in the late fourteenth century (1978: 172). Hoccleve's manuscripts, mostly dated to around 1420, are copied in a more modern Secretary hand which was likely the result of professional training in the Privy Seal office. Perhaps the most likely explanation for the close relationship between Hoccleve's and Chaucer's linguistic practices is that Hoccleve deliberately modelled his practice upon that of Chaucer. Given the many references made by Hoccleve to his dependence upon his mentor and poetic father it seems perfectly possible that this influence stretched to details of orthography and morphology. It is perhaps not surprising that Hoccleve should choose to exploit many of the same features of phonological and morphological variation as Chaucer, as these would have provided him with greater flexibility in his metrical and rhyming practices. In this context it is therefore striking that Hoccleve does not consistently preserve the weak/strong adjectival distinction that is such a consistent feature of Chaucer's verse. Perhaps the reason is that it was no longer a living feature of the London language, even in the more conservative written register. We observed in the last chapter the process by which this feature was progressively omitted and confused across the scribal tradition of the *Canterbury Tales*, and Hoccleve's practice provides further primary evidence for the loss of this feature in the London dialect early in the fifteenth century.

It is perhaps more surprising that Hoccleve should use an orthographic system that is so similar to that of Chaucer, particularly where such details do not affect rhyme or metre. For instance why should Hoccleve consistently use the 'swich' spelling of SUCH when the innovative Type IV form 'such' was already current in London English? Here it is difficult to posit any explanation other than direct Chaucerian influence. We know from the work of Doyle and Parkes (1978) that Hoccleve had worked with Scribe B and that he had contact with the language being used for the production of major literary compositions in the early fifteenth century. Despite Doyle and Parkes' warnings of the ad hoc nature of the relationship between the scribes who produced the Trinity Gower, it seems likely that there must have been some contact between these scribes. Doyle and Parkes' findings show that the production of some of the major Chaucerian, Gowerian and Langlandian codices in this period are the work of a small group of

[9] See further Jefferson 1987.

professional scribes and it is difficult to imagine that there was no contact between this small unit of copyists. It therefore seems likely that Hoccleve's adoption of this spelling system is a deliberate decision to model his orthography on that of Chaucer, as it has been transmitted by Scribe B.

John Lydgate

Having considered Hoccleve's language, we will now examine the language of another major writer of the fifteenth century whose work also reveals the influence of Chaucer. John Lydgate was born in the Suffolk village of Lidgate in 1373 and spent much of his life as a monk at the Benedictine abbey of Bury St Edmunds. He did however spend an amount of time out of the cloister during his career as a Lancastrian propagandist poet. His considerable literary output survives in many manuscripts although, unlike the case of Thomas Hoccleve, none of these is in the author's own hand. However there is an extant presentation copy of Lydgate's *Life of Saint Edmund and Saint Fremund*, British Library MS Harley 2278, which was made at Bury presumably under Lydgate's supervision for presentation to Henry VI during his visit to the abbey in 1433 (Pearsall 1970: 26–7). This manuscript is therefore likely to preserve the poet's own language and text and will form the basis of the following discussion. I shall also draw upon the evidence of the earliest and most accurate copy of Lydgate's continuation of the *Canterbury Tales*, the *Siege of Thebes*. The overt link with Chaucer provided by this work and its survival in an early and accurate manuscript, British Library MS Arundel 119, make it a useful comparison with the Harley manuscript. There are also interesting connections between the Arundel manuscript itself and the Chaucer family. The manuscript contains the coat of arms of the Duke of Suffolk, William de la Pole, second husband of Alice Chaucer, grand-daughter of the poet. It seems likely that the manuscript was commissioned by de la Pole and that it was produced in Suffolk, possibly even at Bury. Hanna and Edwards (1996) have also noted the presence of the gloss 'Phoebus in ariete' in the margin of the Arundel manuscript alongside the prologue in which Lydgate imitates Chaucer. The presence of this gloss recalls a similar gloss, '*id est* sol in ariete', at line 8 of the *General Prologue* in the Ellesmere manuscript, the only manuscript to include such a gloss. The link with the Ellesmere manuscript further strengthens the Suffolk connections, as Ellesmere can also be located in Suffolk early in its history.[10] The scribe of the Arundel manuscript has been credited with the copying of a number of other Middle English productions and it will be useful to reconsider these attributions in the context of a linguistic examination of the scribe's work on Arundel. These attributions

---

[10] For the early provenance of the Ellesmere manuscript see Manly and Rickert 1940: I, 152–9 and Hanna and Edwards 1996. Hanna and Edwards also note the similarities in the ordinatio of Arundel and Ellesmere as further evidence of a close relationship between the two manuscripts. For further discussion of the early history of the El manuscript see chapter 4.

have been based entirely upon palaeographical similarities between the various manuscripts and no attempts have hitherto been made to supplement these conclusions with a linguistic study. Jeremy Griffiths claimed that the Arundel scribe was responsible for the following three other manuscripts, and these attributions are also noted by Hanna and Edwards: Takamiya MS 54, a copy of the *South English Legendary*, Pembroke College, Cambridge, MS 307, Gower's *Confessio Amantis*, and Schøyen Collection, Oslo, MS 615, Walton's *Boethius*. In his description of the Petworth manuscript of the *Canterbury Tales*, Dan Mosser (1996) cites a private communication from Ian Doyle attributing folio 196v to the end of the Lichfield copy of the *Canterbury Tales* to the same scribe. Mosser further notes that both Doyle and Griffiths find close correspondences between this hand and the following manuscripts: Pembroke 307, Takamiya 54 and Arundel 119. It appears that a large corpus of manuscripts has been attributed to a single hand, although there is evidently a degree of hesitancy on the part of the palaeographers. In fact the linguistic evidence does not support the identification of all the above manuscripts to a single scribal hand. Jeremy Smith (1985) has analysed the language of the Pembroke Gower which he assigns to the Gloucestershire/Worcestershire border. In a further article on the language of the Waseda manuscript of Nicholas Love's *Mirror of the Blessed Life of Jesus Christ*, Smith (1997b) provides confirmation that the scribe of the Pembroke Gower also copied the Waseda manuscript and a further copy of the *Mirror*, preserved in Edinburgh University Library MS Advocates 18.1.7. The linguistic evidence of these manuscripts also confirms the identification of their common scribe with that of the Petworth manuscript, localised in appendix 1 below to 'the borders of South-West Worcestershire and Gloucestershire'. Therefore it seems likely that a single scribe, whose native dialect is that of the Worcestershire/Gloucestershire border, was responsible for copying the following group of manuscripts: Pembroke 307, Petworth 7, Lichfield MS 2, folios 196–294, and the Advocates and Waseda manuscripts of Nicholas Love. We must now consider whether this same scribe was responsible for copying Arundel 119. In appendix 1 I have identified several linguistic features of the Petworth manuscript which are indicative of the South-West Midlands localisation, and therefore characteristic of this scribe. The following table presents a comparison of these same diagnostic features with the equivalent forms in the Arundel manuscript:

	Petworth	Arundel
MANY	mony	many
FIRST	furst	first
HER	hur(e)	her
THEM	hem, ham	hem
IF	if, ʒif	if, ʒif

It is clear from the above table that, with the exception of the spelling 'ȝif', none of these characteristic forms is recorded in Arundel, and it seems therefore unlikely that the Arundel scribe may be identified with that of the Petworth group of manuscripts. For the purposes of identification we would expect to see a combination of all or most of these features, while the absence of almost all of these criteria from the Arundel manuscript suggests that the Arundel manuscript was copied by a separate scribe.

Having discussed the nature of the evidence for a study of Lydgate's language I will now turn to the nature of that language itself. Lydgate's language has been accorded little attention despite the huge volume of his output, the large number of surviving witnesses, and the close connection of the Harley and Arundel manuscripts with the poet. One of the most detailed considerations of Lydgate's language is provided by H.C. Wyld in his *A History of Modern Colloquial English*. Wyld's summary of Lydgate's usage suggests that, despite his Suffolk origins, Lydgate's language is 'hardly distinguishable from his contemporary Hoccleve, or from the official London Eng. of the period, except for the occurrence of rather more *e*-forms for O.E. *y*' (Wyld 1920: 82). In order to consider this claim the following table presents a comparison of a number of common items across the Hengwrt manuscript and Arundel 119 and Harley 2278.

	Hg	Arundel 119	Harley 2278
SUCH	swich	swich, such	such
THOUGH	thogh, though	thogh, thouh, al thoh	thouh
THROUGH	thorgh	thorgh, thurgh	thoruh
THEY	they	they, thei, þei	thei
THEIR	her	her ((their))	ther, her
THEM	hem	hem	them, hem
BUT	but	but, ((bot))	but
ANY	any	eny	any
HIGH	heigh	hegh, high, hih	hih
NOT	nat, noght	nat, noght, not	nat, ((not))

Comparison of the Hengwrt and Arundel manuscripts reveals a number of common features which are suggestive of imitation by Lydgate of Chaucerian forms. For example Arundel includes the following Chaucerian spellings: 'swich', 'thogh', 'thorgh'. However if we compare these forms with the equivalent spellings in Harley it appears that these forms are scribal rather than authorial. For instance where Arundel has both 'swich' and 'such' the Harley manuscript has only 'such', suggesting that this is the authorial form and that 'swich' is the spelling of the Arundel scribe. Similarly the spelling 'thogh' is found only in Arundel while the form 'thouh' is common to both Arundel and Harley, suggesting that this is Lydgate's form. In some instances both manuscripts contain two forms, suggesting that both forms were found in Lydgate's repertoire. For example both Arundel and Harley have the Type III and Type IV spellings 'her', 'their', 'ther' and it seems likely that Lydgate used both forms. In this case the use of the 'her' form does indeed provide a link with the London variety associated with Chaucer and Hoccleve, while the 'their', 'ther' forms suggest a link with the administrative London variety.

If we consider the spellings showing the reflection of OE *y* we find a quite different treatment to that observed in Chaucer's variety of London English. Where Type III London language tolerated a variety of different spellings, which were frequently exploited by Chaucer in rhyme, Lydgate's language contains much less variation. For example the following words are found only in the following spellings: 'first', 'firy', 'myrth', 'synne', 'brigge', 'gilt'. In addition to these forms showing OE *y* consistently reflected in ⟨y, i⟩ there are a handful of forms recording OE *y* reflected in ⟨e⟩ or ⟨u⟩, although these are often used alongside variants with ⟨y, i⟩, e.g. 'busy', 'bysy'. Lydgate makes little use of this variation in rhyme and there are only a handful of instances of words showing OE *y* in ⟨e⟩ in rhyming position, e.g. 'seie: dreye' (*Siege of Thebes* [ST] 163–4). This example may be compared with the appearance of the spelling 'drye' rhyming with 'malencolye' at ST lines 2553–4, and 'drie' rhyming with 'remedie' and 'malladie' in Harley. The consistent apperance of forms of the verb SHUT with ⟨e⟩, 'shet, 'shette', both in rhyme and within the line may be explained as deliberate avoidance of the homonymic clash with the form 'shit', a form found in Hoccleve but not common elsewhere. It appears that Lydgate's language was much less tolerant of variants showing OE *y* reflected in ⟨e⟩ or ⟨u⟩ than Chaucer's London dialect. In fact Lydgate's language demonstrates the continuing process of standardisation observed above in Hoccleve's language by which variants with ⟨i, y⟩ were selected in preference to the more provincial alternatives. The lack of acceptance of variants with ⟨e⟩ is particularly marked in Lydgate's language as this form was common in East Anglia and continued to appear in written documents from that area throughout the fifteenth century. Perhaps Lydgate was aware that despite the continued existence of this variable in the spoken and written language of his native dialect, it was however increasingly stigmatised in the more prestigious language of London and he therefore avoided it where possible. It seems that while we might expect H.C. Wyld's claim that Lydgate's language shows more examples of ⟨e⟩ than Chaucer to be true, the reality is in fact the reverse of this.

Despite the signs of increasing standardisation in Lydgate's language over that of Chaucer, there is evidence of dialect features which appear to derive from the poet's own idiolect. For instance we noted above that the form 'thoruh' was likely to derive from the poet's repertoire, and to this form we may add 'thouh' and 'hih' and a number of other spellings with the velar fricative /x/ spelled ⟨h⟩, e.g. 'bryht', 'riht'. These spellings are indicative of the Suffolk dialect during this period and therefore are likely to belong to Lydgate's own spelling practices. However it remains difficult to determine the degree to which Lydgate's language was typical of the Suffolk dialect during this period, and the extent to which it was influenced by the incipient London standard. In order to begin to answer this question we may compare these features with the linguistic profiles of local Bury documents included in *LALME*.[11] A comparison of Lydgate's language with contemporary local documents reveals that Bury usage during this period contains a number of more distinctively dialectal features than those identified in Lydgate's language. For instance a copy of a will in the Bury Register (*LALME* LP 8460) records the following forms which may be compared with those in Lydgate's language discussed above: 'suyche', 'ony', 'mekyl', 'mygth', although these appear alongside the more widespread equivalents: 'such(e)', 'any', 'moche' In addition to these forms there are a number of spellings showing the reflection of OE *y* in ⟨e⟩, e.g. 'feer', 'beryed'. So it seems that while Lydgate's language does preserve some traces of his Suffolk dialect, his language has also been influenced by the process of standardisation which was ongoing in the London language during this period.

As regards morphology Lydgate's practice shows a number of similarities to that of Chaucer and the London language. For instance Lydgate's regular form of the third person singular tense ends ⟨-(e)th⟩, although there are several examples of ⟨-es⟩ inflexion in rhyme, e.g. 'lerys: banerys' (ST 1547–8), 'specifies: fantasies' (ST 1507–8). The preference for the ⟨-eth⟩ inflexion with the retention of the ⟨-es⟩ variant for rhyming purposes mirrors the situation in Chaucer's poetry, although as we saw in chapter 2, Chaucer only used the ⟨-es⟩ ending early in his career. The dominant plural form of all nouns is with the strong inflexion ⟨-es⟩, also spelled ⟨-is, -ys⟩ in Lydgate. However as in Chaucer there are several examples of plural forms with the inflexion derived from the OE weak declension, e.g. 'foon', 'doghtren'. The dative singular inflexion is also preserved in some fossilised prepositional phrases, as also found in Chaucer, such as 'on honde'. Lydgate's treatment of adjectival final ⟨-e⟩ also frequently mirrors Chaucer's practice as demonstrated in the following examples from Arundel 119 where ⟨-e⟩ is found marking weak adjectives:

214   Cler expownyng this derke poysye
500   And felly mused in his owne thouȝt

There are also instances of its use in genitive expressions and as a marker of plurality, especially in adjectives in rhyming position:

187   Bylt and begonne of olde antiquite
205   Be vertue only of the werbles sharpe

---

[11] For linguistic profiles of Suffolk manuscripts see *LALME* III, 474–92.

However alongside these instances of the regular application of these grammatical rules, there are frequent occasions where ⟨-e⟩ is missing. Whether the lack of ⟨-e⟩ is due to scribal error rather than a feature of Lydgate's language is difficult to determine, although the metre suggests that the loss of ⟨-e⟩ is frequently scribal. For instance, in his edition of the *Siege of Thebes* Axel Erdmann restores ⟨-e⟩ in each of the following examples of its omission in the Arundel manuscript:

295   Seyn that Cadmvs the famous old man
372   The silf houre of his natyvyte
376   On Augrym stoones and on whit caartes
457   This ȝong chylde to foster and to kepe

Therefore despite Lydgate's use of adjectival final ⟨-e⟩ the scribes of Lydgate's poetry did not preserve this feature in all expected environments. Its preservation appears to be most regular in plural adjectives and especially those in rhyming position. We have noted in the previous chapters that Chaucer's scribes were most careful to preserve inflexions in rhyming environments and this same motivation may explain the distribution of ⟨-e⟩ in the Arundel manuscript.

In summary we may observe that Lydgate's language preserves a number of linguistic features which recall aspects of Chaucerian language, although his spelling system shows a closer relationship with the incipient Type IV. In this way Lydgate's language differs considerably from the much more closely imitative language of his contemporary Chaucerian poet Thomas Hoccleve. Lydgate's language also reveals certain dialect traces which reveal his Suffolk origins, although these are considerably less marked than contemporary local dialect as used in Bury records. It is in fact striking how few Suffolk features appear in Lydgate's dialect, suggesting that the poet may have consciously modelled his language on that of the emerging London standard. However unlike his contemporary Thomas Hoccleve, Lydgate's linguistic model is not Chaucer but rather the incipient administrative standardised language, Type IV.

Chaucer in Scotland

Having discussed the influence of Chaucer's language upon the English Chaucerian poets Thomas Hoccleve and John Lydgate, I now want to turn to consider the impact of this language north of the border, in Scotland. The language of Chaucer's poetry was an important influence upon the verse of the fifteenth- and sixteenth-century Scots poets. Scots writers of this period frequently refer to Chaucer in their works, often employing the same conventional phrases employed by their English contemporaries. William Dunbar for example praises Chaucer's rhetorical eloquence in lines 253–61 of his poem *The Golden Targe*:

> O reverend Chaucere, rose of rethoris all,
> As in oure tong ane flour imperiall
> That raise in Britane ewir, quho redis rycht,
> Thou beris of makaris the tryumph riall;
> Thy fresch anamilit termes celicall
> This mater coud illumynit haue full brycht:
> Was thou noucht of oure Inglisch all the lycht,
> Surmounting ewiry tong terrestriall
> Alls fer as Mayes morow dois mydnycht?

A similar attitude is expressed by Gavin Douglas in his translation of Virgil's *Aeneid*, *Eneydos*, published in 1513. Douglas refers to Chaucer as 'venerabill Chauser, principal poet but peir', emphasising that Chaucer stands alone at the head of English literary tradition. Despite the profound effect Chaucer's language and style had on the Middle Scots poets, little is known about the way in which Chaucer's works were circulated and read in medieval Scotland. Despite the survival of large numbers of manuscript and early printed copies of Chaucer's works, few of these can be associated with a Scottish provenance with any certainty. The survival of a manuscript containing copies of several of Chaucer's poems, which can be localised in Scotland early in its history is therefore of great importance to an understanding of Chaucerian reception in Scotland. This manuscript, Bodleian Library MS Arch. Selden B.24, is best known as the unique surviving witness to the *Kingis Quair*, attributed in a scribal colophon to James I of Scotland. However in addition to this work the manuscript contains copies of Chaucer's *Troilus and Criseyde*, *Parliament of Fowls* and several of his minor poems. A number of poems by the English Chaucerians, Thomas Hoccleve and John Lydgate, are also included, several of which are erroneously attributed to Chaucer himself. The manuscript was copied in the late fifteenth or early sixteenth century probably for Henry, Lord Sinclair, whose arms appear in the manuscript with a note of ownership: 'liber Henrici domini Sinclar'. The Selden manuscript may be divided into two principal sections: the first containing Chaucerian verse and the second containing Scots verse (see Boffey and Edwards 1997). The process of anthologising both Chaucerian and Scots verse within the same manuscript is an act of both literary and linguistic significance. That Henry Sinclair was interested in asserting the use of the Scots language as a vehicle for literary expression is made clear by his patronage of Gavin Douglas' translation of Virgil's *Aeneid*, which was completed in 1513. In addition to providing a Scots translation of a classical text, Douglas' work is significant for its explicit reference to the use of the Scots language rather than the more common term 'Inglis', used by Douglas' contemporaries (for a discussion see Corbett 1999).

> Quat so it be, this buke I dedicait,
> Writtin in the langage of the Scottis natioun.   (I. Pro. 102–3)

The Selden manuscript is frequently viewed as a collection of English poems "translated" into Scots, although there has been little detailed consideration of the language of the English texts it contains. For instance Kratzmann describes Selden as the 'largest single source of such works, in which Scots words and forms are substituted for southern ones'. However Kratzmann subsequently qualifies his use of the word 'translation', adding that 'all of these poems contain a large number of distinctively English features' (Kratzmann 1980: 14).

Despite the significance of this manuscript for an assessment of the place of Chaucer within fifteenth-century Scottish literary tradition, the Chaucerian texts it contains have received relatively little attention. One exception is Fradenburg's study 'The Scottish Chaucer', which draws upon the evidence of the Selden manuscript in an attempt to consider the influence of Chaucer upon the Middle Scots poets. Fradenburg places much emphasis on a stanza which appears at the end of the *Troilus*, which she states was written by the scribe of Selden, James Gray, as a 'commentary' on the poem. However this stanza was certainly not composed by the Selden scribe, who was incidentally not James Gray, as it is the first stanza of a poem titled 'Greneacres A Lenvoye vpon John Bochas' which appears at the end of a manuscript of Lydgate's *Fall of Princes*.[12] Fradenburg links her interpretation of this stanza with the placement of Chaucer's *Truth* immediately afterwards: 'It is therefore no accident that Gray should have chosen to place, after his own stanza of lamentation, Chaucer's "Truth" – with its rhetoric of urgent exhortation and its message of consolation' (173). Fradenburg's sense of the appropriateness of this placement is centered upon her reading of the Envoy to this poem, with its urgent and direct appeal to Vache mirroring the palinode in the *Troilus*. However this analysis ignores the fact that the Envoy to *Truth* is not found in the Selden manuscript; it is in fact only recorded in a single extant copy of the poem, British Library MS Additional 10340.

In the following discussion we will consider the evidence this manuscript provides concerning the treatment of Chaucerian language by a scribe copying in Scotland for a Scottish readership. In order to assess this we will compare the treatment of language in the Chaucerian texts with another manuscript in the hand of the first scribe of the Selden manuscript. The first scribe of Selden has been identified in three other manuscripts, including National Library of Scotland MS Acc. 9253, a copy of the Gilbert de la Haye's translations into Scots of French works, such as *The Buke of the Law of Armys*, *The Buke of Knychthede*, and *The Government of Princes*. These texts were translated in the middle of the fifteenth century at the request of William, Lord Sinclair, grandfather to the owner of the Selden manuscript, and represent the earliest literary prose translations into Scots.

---

[12] For details of the scribes and the contents of the Selden manuscript see the introduction to Boffey and Edwards 1997 and references there cited.

The identification of this manuscript in the same scribal hand as Selden has significance for a study of the scribe's treatment of language in his work on the Selden manuscript. By comparing the language and spelling of the Selden manuscript with another manuscript in the scribe's hand we may observe the scribe's treatment of Chaucerian language as compared with that of a text known to have been composed in Scots. The following table presents a comparison of a number of linguistic features found in the Hengwrt, Selden and Haye manuscripts.

	Hg	Selden	Haye MS
MANY	many	many	mony
NOT	nat	nat	nocht
ANY	any	any	ony
SUCH	swich	suich	sik
THROUGH	thurgh	throu	throu
THEY	they	thai	thai
THEIR	hire	thair	thair
THEM	hem	thame	thame, thaim
MUCH	muche	muche	mekle
SHALL	shall	schall	sal
SHOULD	shuld	schuld	suld
ALSO	also	also	alssua, alsa
IF	if	gif	gif

The table shows that the language of Selden presents a blend of both Chaucerian and Scots features. In certain words the Scots form is found, e.g. 'gif', 'throu', while in others the Selden scribe retains a form more characteristic of Chaucerian usage, e.g. 'suich', 'nat'. It seems that in copying the Chaucerian texts the Selden scribe's linguistic behaviour was constrained by the language of his copytext. It seems that in copying the Chaucerian texts the scribe considered certain features of the language to be worthy of retention and he therefore adjusted his repertoire accordingly, employing a number of Chaucerian forms rather than his own native Scots forms, as found in the Haye manuscript. In addition to the features set out in figure 1 a similar process may be observed in other features of the language of these manuscripts. For instance at the level of phonology the Haye manuscript shows a number of Scots features, where the Selden manuscript preserves Southern equivalents. For example the Haye manuscript preserves the unrounded vowel as a reflex of OE $\bar{a}$, e.g. 'haly', 'amang', 'na', 'mare', 'wrang', 'warld'. The Selden manuscript has the rounded vowel ⟨o⟩ in this position, common to Southern dialects like Chaucer's during this period, e.g. 'lore', 'more', 'told', 'long', 'fro', 'old', 'owne', 'mo'. However the Selden manuscript does contain a scattering of spellings showing the unrounded vowel, e.g. 'ȝa', 'ilkane', 'amang'. The Haye manuscript has the characteristic Northern ME and Scots reflection of OE ⟨hw-⟩ in ⟨quh-⟩ as found in the following examples: 'quhilk', 'quhat', 'quhare', 'quhen', 'quheythir'. These same spellings are also found in the Selden MS, e.g. 'quhat', 'quherfore', 'quhere', 'quhich', 'quhill', 'quhoso', 'quhois', 'quho' although the spelling 'quhich' shows the Southernised ⟨ch⟩ ending rather than the Scots ⟨-lk⟩. Another phonological difference in the two manuscripts is shown in a comparison of spellings showing the reflex of OE /oː/: e.g. Haye 'buke', 'gude' and Selden 'book', 'good'. In Older Scots OE /oː/ was fronted creating a long vowel /øː/, representing one of the major differences between the vowel systems of Older Scots and Middle English (See McClure 1994: 47). Thus where the Haye manuscript has the Scots vowel the Selden manuscript preserves that of Chaucer's Middle English.

These same spellings also indicate a difference in the conventions of orthography adopted in these manuscripts. This is a difference concerning the marking of long vowels, as may be shown by a comparison of the following: 'gude' (Haye), 'good' (Selden). Older Scots adopted two methods of marking long vowels; the use of a silent final ⟨-e⟩ as a diacritic as found in present-day English 'stone', 'wise' etc., and the use of ⟨i⟩ as a diacritic, when placed immediately after the vowel in question, e.g. 'deid' DEED, 'guid' GOOD. The practice found in the Haye manuscript is the former of these as found in words like 'gude', 'buke'. However in Chaucer's English final ⟨-e⟩ continued to function as a living part of the linguistic system, as a grammatical marker indicating definiteness and plurality (see chapter 6 p. 97). This usage, which was a relic of the Old English weak declension, was no longer observed in Northern dialects as a result of the earlier simplification and loss of the OE inflexional system in the north of the country. As a result the final ⟨-e⟩ was no longer a part of the spoken system and thus was available as a silent diacritic, an innovation not possible in Chaucer's more conservative system. The Selden manuscript preserves the Chaucerian system in marking long vowels by doubling vowels as found in the following: 'book', 'good'.

In addition to these differences in the orthography and phonology of these two manuscripts, there are a number of differences in morphology. For instance the third person singular form of the present indicative in the Haye manuscript is the ⟨-es, -is⟩ inflexion common to the Northern ME and Scots dialects during this period. However the Selden manuscript preserves a number of forms with the Southern form with ⟨-th⟩, e.g. 'commyth', 'semyth' found in Southern dialects such as Chaucer's. In addition to these forms the Selden manuscript contains several forms with the Scots equivalent, such as 'dois', 'dansis'. Another difference in the verbal morphology of these manuscripts is evident in the forms of the present participle. The Haye manuscript uses the Northern ME and Scots inflexion ⟨-and⟩, 'pertenand', 'langand', 'displesand', 'doand', while the Selden manuscript has the Southern form as found in the Hengwrt manuscript ⟨-ing, -yng⟩, 'furthering', 'sitting', 'preying'.

Certain aspects of the treatment of lexis in these two manuscripts reveal a similar procedure as found at other linguistic levels. So, for instance, where the Haye manuscript employs a number of Old Norse derived words typical of Scots these words are generally found in their Southern, OE derived, forms in Selden. This may be exemplified by the use of the ON words 'till', 'kirk', 'ar' in Haye, as compared with the OE words 'to', 'chirche', 'ben' in Selden. However Selden does contain some examples of Scots dialect vocabulary, as for instance in the use of the Scots adjective 'sterny', from ON 'stjarna' alongside the OE 'sterris', from OE 'steorra'.[13]

It is apparent from the above comparison that the language of the Selden manuscript preserves a number of the same linguistic features which in previous chapters we have identified as being peculiarly Chaucerian. However there are a number of Scots features introduced into Chaucer's text in the Selden language, giving the text a Scottish appearance. However it is important to distinguish between written features which have a purely orthographic significance and those written features which may affect the pronunciation of the text. The majority of the Scottish features introduced into the Selden manuscript are of a purely graphemic significance and do not affect the pronunciation of the text. Examples of such features are 'suich', 'schall', 'thai' for Chaucerian 'swich', 'shall', 'they'. However comparison of the language of Selden with the same scribe's treatment of the Haye manuscript shows the avoidance of forms showing aspects of Scots phonology, such as the fronted reflex of ME /o:/, the unrounded reflex of OE *a*, and the unpalatalised reflex of Germanic /k/ e.g. 'gud', 'warld', 'quhilk'. The blend of ME and Scots features found in Selden therefore combines to lend its texts a Scottish appearance while retaining the sound of their Middle English originals. The presentation of a text which has a Scottish appearance but retains a ME sound is further underlined by the general avoidance of aspects of Scots lexis. The avoidance of Scots lexical items in Selden is highlighted by the appearance of a number of peculiarly Scots words in the unique conclusion to the *Parliament of Fowls* which appears to have been composed for inclusion in Selden.[14]

The language of these genuine and pseudo-Chaucerian works may be compared with the language of contemporary verse composed in Scots also found in the Selden manuscript. The influence of Chaucerian themes and style was not limited to south of the border and Chaucer's work was also influential in the development of fifteenth- and sixteenth-century verse in Scots. This influence is found in other Scots verse preserved in the Selden manuscript, and in poems found elsewhere such as the *Lancelot of the Laik* and the *Quare of Ielusy*. The *Lancelot of the Laik* may also show another link with the Selden manuscript as some scholars have suggested that the second scribe of Selden, responsible for copying all of the Scots verse in the anthology, was also the scribe of the manuscript which contains the

---

[13] For a map indicating the distribution of these lexical items see McIntosh 1989.
[14] For a discussion of the Scottish vocabulary in the unique conclusion to the *Parliament of Fowls* in Selden see Boffey and Edwards 1999.

Lancelot of the Laik, and signed his name V. de F. This manuscript, CUL MS Kk.I.5, has another link with Selden as it contains a copy of Chaucer's *Truth*: a poem also found in Selden and other Scots verse anthologies. In order to demonstrate the use of a language containing both ME and Scots forms for works composed in Scots, I will briefly examine the language of a single Scots text found in the Selden manuscript, the *Quare of Jelusy*. At the level of phonology we may observe a mixture of Southern and Northern features, such as OE *a* reflected as ⟨a⟩ and ⟨o⟩, e.g. 'world', 'warld', 'more', 'mare'. Another example may be seen in the reflection of ME /o:/ as /o:/ and /ø:/ in spellings like: 'sodaynly', 'sudaynly'. Other mixed forms are the following spellings for WHICH: 'quhilk', 'quhich' and SHALL: 'schall', 'sall'. In this instance the ME spelling with ⟨sch⟩ is dominant and the Scots form with ⟨s⟩ only appears once. For the item SUCH the two recorded forms are both ME spellings: 'suche', 'suich', with the 'suich' form showing a close relationship with the Chaucerian spelling 'swich'. At the level of verbal morphology we find some instances of past participles with the ⟨y-⟩ prefix characteristic of Southern dialects, although its use is sporadic, e.g. 'take', 'ytake'. There is evidence that its use in past participles was not understood by the scribe or the author, as is suggested by its unhistorical appearance in some present participles, e.g. 'ysuffering'. In addition to these ME forms there are appearances of Scots lexical items within the poem, such as 'ane', 'euerilkone', 'mene', 'syse'. The appearance of this last form in rhyming position at line 181/2: 'syse: dispise' demonstrates that this is the poet's own form rather than that of the scribe.

A similar type of mixture of English and Scots forms is attested in the *Lancelot of the Laik*, which has been argued to be by the same author as the *Quare of Ielusy*. For example this poem also shows OE *a* in both rounded and unrounded reflexes: 'knaw', 'know', OE /hw/ reflected as ⟨quh, qwh, qu, wh, w⟩, and has Scots and ME forms of the third person feminine singular pronoun, 'sche', 'scho'. In addition to these mixed forms there are also further examples of confusion in the adoption of ME forms, for example in the adoption of the Southern ⟨-ing⟩ inflexion for both the present participle and the infinitive.

Alongside an assertion of the use of the Scots language is the persistent and continued use of a language which contains a mixture of Middle English and Middle Scots forms. This language is not just found in copies of Chaucerian poetry in Scots, but is also used in literary texts composed in Scots, such as for example the the works of Gavin Douglas. Douglas' language shows a number of Southern features, including forms which were archaic for Southern English dialects by this time. The most common of such features are the use of 'bene' BE, the use of the ⟨-en, -ing⟩ inflexion in verbs, most commonly in infinitives and third person plural indicative forms, and the retention of the prefix ⟨y-, i-⟩ in past participles. This last feature was derived from the OE ⟨ge-⟩ prefix and even by the end of the fourteenth century in England it survived largely as a metrical device.

Douglas added this prefix frequently to verbs of both native and Romance origins and, as with the ⟨-en, -ing⟩ inflexions, exploited its metrical potential. The following examples from the *Palice of Honour* give an indication of Douglas' exploitation of Southern ME grammatical features for metrical effects:

357 As dois ane Catiue yrunkin in sleip
753 The wife of Loth Ichangit sair did weip
666 Me tyl accusyng as of a dedly cryme
824 Thay fast approching to the place weill neir

Douglas' use of these Southern inflexions is often unhistorical, such as the use of the ⟨-ing, -yng⟩ inflexion in the infinitive and third person plural forms of the verbs found above. However Douglas adopted these forms for metrical purposes irrespective of their grammatical functions. It is also possible that Douglas' use of these Southern grammatical features was an attempt to retain a flavour of the Chaucerian idiom which we have observed in the works of other Scots writers above. It is clear that Chaucer's language was influential in Scotland throughout the fifteenth and sixteenth centuries and that poets and scribes continued to adopt aspects of this language both in copies of Chaucerian verse, and in verse composed in Scots throughout this period.

In summary therefore we have seen that fifteenth and sixteenth-century poets in both England and Scotland frequently employed linguistic features which are characteristic of Chaucer's own variety of Middle English. In the case of Thomas Hoccleve the influence appears to be more direct and to be more comprehensive, while Lydgate's language appears to be influenced more by the emerging London variety which subsequently replaced that of Chaucer. In Scotland we see both poets and scribes deliberately accommodating their linguistic practices when copying and composing Chaucerian verse in order to reflect the linguistic habits of their Southern models. Linguistic behaviour of this kind is familiar to us from the scribal habits we have already encountered in the manuscript tradition of the *Canterbury Tales*, and it appears that the authority of certain distinctively Chaucerian forms persisted throughout the fifteenth and into the sixteenth century.

8

Conclusion

In this conclusion I will summarise the principal findings of this book and highlight areas in which traditional theories are in need of fresh assessment and modification in the light of this study. There is clearly a need for a reconsideration of the development of the London dialect as a whole, taking account of its intra- and extra-linguistic histories. The availability of electronic texts, sophisticated search facilities and major diachronic corpora will greatly facilitate such a study.[1] My preliminary study has revealed that textual register is an important factor in the development of the London dialect in the late fourteenth and early fifteenth centuries and this consideration should be extended to both earlier and subsequent stages in the development of the language of London. The use of diachronic corpora allows the data to be classified in a number of different ways and therefore further studies may take account of other external factors such as script type and ordinatio in assessing a scribe's linguistic choices. Electronic texts also enable scholars to consider larger amounts of text with greater accuracy. Searches of this kind have revealed greater linguistic variation in the corpus of London texts than previous scholars have recognised. The presence of this variation has forced us to look for new explanations for the evolution of the London dialect in this critical period. This methodology has also permitted the distribution of scribal variation across a text or a corpus of texts to be taken into account in ways that have not previously been possible. Analysis of the distribution of such variation across manuscript copies of the same text provides insights into the origins of variants. Where minor variants are found to cluster in specific sections of a text, or to appear in the same positions in more than one witness, these are likely to derive from the authorial copytext. This methodology has enabled us to identify certain variants which are likely to derive from Chaucer's own copytext and are therefore probably Chaucerian forms. The presence of a number of such forms which appear to derive from Chaucer's language suggests that Scribe B did not translate his copytext into his own language, but rather that he carefully preserved certain minor details of this copytext in both Hg and El.

[1] A number of electronic corpora of Middle English are available or in preparation. These include the *Helsinki Corpus: Diachronic and Dialectal*. The Middle English Grammar Project is also constructing a diachronic and diatopic corpus of Middle English which is described in Horobin and Smith 1999.

This calls into question the relationship between the language of Scribe B and Chaucer himself. It seems likely that Scribe B's practice was to preserve details of the language of his exemplar and therefore it is possible that the language of Hg and El is much closer to Chaucer than previously accepted. One major objection to this suggestion is the fact that Scribe B employed a similar language when copying the Trinity Gower, thereby endorsing the conclusion that the common language is that of the scribe, rather than Chaucer. However given the close connection of the Hg and El manuscripts with Chaucer's own papers, and the possibility that Hg was produced during the poet's lifetime, it is possible that Scribe B worked under Chaucer's supervision. It may be that Scribe B learned his spelling habits from Chaucer himself and subsequently transferred these same habits to his stint on the Trinity Gower. Or perhaps if Hg and El were both posthumous productions it may be concluded that Scribe B's spelling habits derive from his copying of large amounts of Chaucerian verse. In addition to Hg and El Scribe B was responsible for the Cecil Fragment of the *Troilus and Criseyde*, a manuscript that was presumably once complete, and possibly also a further copy of the *Canterbury Tales*, now the fragmentary CUL MS Kk.I.3/20 (See Doyle 1997). This large amount of copying of Chaucerian texts may have led to the scribe's adoption of Chaucerian linguistic features. A similar process of adoption of characteristic Gowerian spelling features has been demonstrated as resulting from Scribe D's lengthy encounter with the text of the *Confessio Amantis* (Smith 1985, 1988b).

The identification of certain forms as Chaucerian has also called into question the attribution of the text of the *Equatorie of the Planetis* to Chaucer. The spelling evidence presented by Samuels in favour of Chaucerian authorship has been highly influential in the debate over the authority of this work. However it seems that the spellings identified by Samuels as Chaucerian are simply variants which existed alongside other similar forms in Chaucer's repertoire. We must therefore conclude that the linguistic evidence of the *Equatorie* does not point to Chaucerian authorship as Samuels has suggested.[2] In fact the evidence of the variety of Chaucer's language and the greater degree of variation found within the London dialect during this period may force us to reconsider certain other traditional conclusions concerning Chaucerian authorship. For instance only the first section of the ME translation of the *Roman de la Rose* preserved in Glasgow University Library MS Hunter 409 is traditionally ascribed to Chaucer. The reasons for the exclusion of the other two sections from the Chaucer canon include the evidence of certain rhymes which are considered to belong to the Northern dialect. It is therefore assumed that the author(s) of Fragments B and C were Northerners. However the findings of this study

---

[2] A similar conclusion is reached in Stephen Partridge's (1992) study of the vocabulary of the *Equatorie* which shows that many of the words which have been considered to be distinctively Chaucerian are in fact found in a number of other contemporary scientific treatises.

suggest that we should rethink these conclusions. The evidence of Chaucer's use of third person singular forms of the present tense demonstrate the way in which a typically "Northern" dialect feature was available to a London poet. Chaucer's use of this inflexion for rhymes early in his career and his avoidance of the feature in later works demonstrates the changing status of such variants within the poet's lifetime. Given the scholarly consensus that Chaucer translated the *Romaunt* early in his career it is quite possible that he should draw upon London variants in rhyme which he later rejected as their status changed and his confidence and skill as a poet grew. Since Skeat first rejected Fragments B and C from the canon on the basis of their Northern rhymes it has been shown that certain of these Northern features were also found in the London dialect in the generation before Chaucer. For instance Skeat cited the use of the ⟨-and⟩ inflexion of the present participle in rhyme as evidence of Northern authorship. This may be exemplified by the following couplet taken from Fragment B of the *Romaunt*:

> Poyntis and sleves be wel sittand,
> Right and streght on the hand.   (2263-4)

While this inflexion is indeed a Northern feature it is also common in the London dialect in the fourteenth century and is frequently found in texts preserved in the Auchinleck manuscript.[3] It is therefore possible that Chaucer adopted the form for rhyming purposes early in his career and subsequently rejected it as it became increasingly stigmatised. The identification in chapter 3 of a particularly unusual non-Chaucerian form in rhyming position in Fragment A of the *Romaunt* further highlights the need for a more inclusive view of Chaucer's language, particularly early in his career and early in the development of London English. The presence of this form 'shittyng' in rhyme serves as a reminder that the London dialect in this period permitted greater variation, and forms which were later stigmatised were as yet unmarked by such sociolinguistic connotations. This is not the place to attempt a thorough reassessment of the language of the text of the *Romaunt of the Rose* but this study has clearly indicated that such a reconsideration is necessary.[4]

In addition to the evidence it provides for the study of Chaucer's own linguistic habits, comparison of the linguistic details of the Hg and El manuscripts has revealed a number of differences which have wider implications for the study of Chaucer's text. For instance differences in the treatment of certain phonological and grammatical features in the two manuscripts suggest that there may have been a considerable time interval

---

[3] For a discussion of the distribution of this feature in place-names in Northampton and Cambridge and in the London dialect see Macrae-Gibson 1971.

[4] A fresh assessment of the authorship of the *Romaunt* will be aided by the publication of an electronic edition of the Glasgow manuscript alongside the edition printed by William Thynne, edited by Graham Caie.

between the copying of the two witnesses. Scribe B's treatment of features such as the reflexes of OE *y* and the adjectival final ⟨-e⟩ inflexion suggests that considerable changes had occurred in the London dialect and in the scribe's own idiolect in the intervening period between the copying of Hg and El. Samuels has suggested an interval of a decade based upon certain orthographic differences such as vowel doubling, ⟨y⟩ and ⟨i⟩ variation etc. (Samuels 1988c). Linguistic differences between Hg and El considered in this study reinforce Samuels' suggested time difference. This possibility has further implications for the reliability and authority of the El text. A ten-year time difference between the production of the two manuscripts would also force us to reconsider the dating of the two manuscripts. Kathleen Scott (1997) has recently proposed an earlier date for the illumination of El, suggesting a date of composition of c. 1400-1405. This antedating would therefore force us to reconsider the possibility that the Hg manuscript was copied during Chaucer's own lifetime. This suggestion chimes with recent codicological research into the Hg manuscript which has argued that the manuscript was copied under the poet's supervision (Stubbs 2000). Stubbs has also suggested that the Hg and El manuscripts were produced concurrently, a theory which would contradict the linguistic evidence which appears to suggest a time gap between the copying of the two manuscripts. However it may be that the linguistic differences should be accounted for by differences in the perceived functions of the books rather than chronology, with El representing a more polished, standardised production in which linguistic variation has also been regularised. In contrast Hg shows more signs of improvisation and hesitancy in its codicology and less concern with regularity and standardisation in its treatment of orthography.

Linguistic differences between the two manuscripts may also have relevance for study of the textual differences between Hg and El and therefore have further implications for the editing of the *Canterbury Tales*. For instance M.L. Samuels (1991) has analysed spelling variation in the Hg copies of the Squire-Merchant, Merchant-Franklin links. These links are late additions to the Hg manuscript, copied onto leaves which were left blank in order to accommodate linking passages at a later date. However the order adopted by the Hg scribe for these tales, Squire-Merchant-Franklin, contradicted the arrangement demanded by the links when they were subsequently supplied. These links assume the ordering of these tales adopted in El, that is Merchant-Squire-Franklin. Most scholars accept that the text of the links in Hg represents the scribe's own attempt to solve this problem by adapting the links to suit his ordering of the tales.[5] A different solution has been proposed by Blake (1985) who argues that the Hg links are scribal and were composed to link the tales in the present order when no

---

[5] This explanation of the nature of the links for these tales as found in Hg is that generally accepted by scholars. See for instance Doyle and Parkes 1979 and Cooper 1997.

genuine links were forthcoming. The question of the authenticity of these links is therefore central to the question of the ordering of these tales in the Hg and El manuscripts. Samuels' analysis of spelling variation in these linking passages led him to suggest that these unique versions of the links may have been received by the Hg scribe on separate sheets and may derive directly from Chaucer's papers. This claim has major editorial implications as it contradicts Blake's argument that the links are scribal additions. The scribal origin of these links is central to Blake's hypothesis concerning the genesis of the Hg manuscript: if these links are genuine then they are testimonies to the piecemeal acquisition of parts of the poem, a theory which Blake firmly rejects. Samuels' 'hint' is based upon the spellings of the word YET in these links which Samuels argues deviate from the scribe's typical practice. Samuels argues that the scribe's usual spelling for this item is 'yet' and that 'yit' is found only in rhyming position. However in these links the spelling 'yit' is found twice within the line. The coincidence of this form with the main form in the manuscript of the *Equatorie of the Planetis* identifies this as a Chaucerian form and thereby confirms that these links are indeed genuine. There are however a number of factors which have arisen in this study which cast doubt on this conclusion. We have seen that the Hg manuscript shows a greater tolerance of spelling variation than El and there are in fact a number of further instances of 'yit' within the line in Hg. The presence of both forms 'yet' and 'yit' in rhyming positions and within the line suggests that both forms derive from Chaucer's own repertoire and that the presence of these forms in the Hg links does not provide any information concerning the authority of the links. Furthermore the evidence of these spellings may not be used as evidence for the piecemeal acquisition of parts in the making of Hg. Both these instances of 'yit' cited by Samuels are spelled 'yet' in El and this manuscript has no instances of 'yit' outside rhyming environments. This situation is indicative of the consistent regularisation of spelling variation found in the El manuscript noted above. In copying El Scribe B was much less tolerant of such variation and tended to retain minor variants only where they are required by the rhyme. The removal of minor variation of this kind thereby reduces the amount of information concerning authorial spelling habits and the genetic relationship between manuscripts. As such we cannot draw any firm conclusions concerning the origins or the relationship between the two sets of links in the two manuscripts on the basis of spelling evidence. We have also seen that Samuels' conclusion that the manuscript copy of the *Equatorie of the Planetis* is a Chaucerian holograph is in need of qualification and therefore the presence of the spelling 'yit' in this text does not allow us to make any conclusions concerning authorship. It seems most likely that the two spellings 'yit' and 'yet' both derive from Chaucer's repertoire, and that he was able to draw upon either both in rhyme and within the line.

The distribution of certain linguistic features across the manuscript tradition is also suggestive of genetic relationships between manuscripts, and therefore of further importance for the editing of Chaucer's text. We have seen that certain minor linguistic variants cluster in certain parts of the poem in Hg, and that these same forms appear at the same positions in a number of other manuscripts. This situation suggests that these manuscripts had access to the same copytext used by the Hg scribe with these spellings in these same positions. The theory that many of the early manuscripts of the *Canterbury Tales* were copied from a single copytext has been voiced most strongly by N.F. Blake. Working on the assumption that circulation of individual tales would have been in the form of tales without links, Blake argues that such circulation would have resulted in the breaking up of the order of constant groups of tales in subsequent collected manuscripts. As the constant groups in our extant manuscripts show complete stability in their positioning of individual tales, such a process can be discredited. Pursuing the issue of the poem's incompleteness, Blake argues that at the time of Chaucer's death there must have been a working-draft of the poem among his own papers. It therefore seems most likely that the early editors of the poem would turn to this authorised copy, which would contain all the fragments Chaucer had composed, rather than attempt to obtain various separate parts from a number of dispersed sources. Such a suggestion renders the theory of prior circulation of parts of the poem unnecessary, and draws the discussion of the early textual scene back to the author's copytext, and the notion of a single archetype. Blake argues that the text and arrangement of the early manuscripts can be seen as developments of those aspects in Hg; which in turn suggests that these scribes were aware of these other early manuscripts. As none of these texts recreates the excellence of that of Hg, this situation is best explained by the collective use of the Hg exemplars. These scribes made many rearrangements and alterations of these exemplars, some of which would have been added to the copytext itself. Over this period of early copying extra lines were added to the authorial text, and tales and links were added on extra sheets attached to the copytext. The copytext would therefore become progressively more difficult to read, and a greater variety of interpretations would become available. The resulting state of this draft exemplar would encourage freedom in the handling of the text, while simultaneously offering many varied possibilities. This scenario has been criticised by subsequent scholars, particularly by C.A. Owen who argued strongly for the circulation of individual parts of the poem during Chaucer's lifetime, which subsequently formed the basis of complete collections of the text.[6] However the identification of these spelling variants at specific positions in these manuscripts supports the view that, for these parts of the poem at least, these manuscripts shared a common ancestor. It is interesting to note

[6] See Owen's review of Blake 1985 in which he writes: 'The possibility of a tale circulating without its links and at the same time remaining in Chaucer's possession firmly in place in its section does not occur to him' (1987: 186). For an account of Owen's theory of prior circulation of individual tales and the genesis of the manuscript tradition of the *Canterbury Tales* see Owen 1991.

that it is not simply the earliest manuscripts that preserve such features. In chapter 2 I noted the appearance of 'theigh' type spellings of THOUGH which are found at the exact same positions in a number of late fifteenth-century manuscripts as well as in the earliest copies. This situation suggests that the Hg copytext that was used for the earliest copies of the poem remained intact and available throughout the fifteenth century and was copied by certain scribes, such as that of the Ch manuscript copied late in the century. This possibility is further supported by Peter Robinson's (1997) cladistic analysis of the manuscripts of the *Wife of Bath's Prologue* which has identified a group of manuscripts, including the Ch manuscript, which appear to share an exemplar with the Hg manuscript for this portion of the text. So it would appear that both the linguistic and textual evidence supports the view that the Hg copytext remained intact throughout the fifteenth century and was available to scribes of a number of manuscripts, both in the early period and in the final quarter of the century.

These linguistic differences between Hg and El also point to differences in their functions as books. For instance Hg is more consistent in its treatment of adjectival final ⟨-e⟩ and is as such likely to be closer to Chaucer's own usage for this feature. El however is less regular in its preservation of this grammatical feature, a situation which has implications for the treatment of Chaucer's metre in the two manuscripts. However we have also noticed that El is much more regular in its treatment of spelling and there is much less variation of a purely orthographic significance in this manuscript. This difference suggests that the production team(s) conceived of the function of these books differently. The Hg manuscript demonstrates greater consistency and regularity with regard to features which affect the pronunciation of the text, while the El manuscript appears to be more concerned with regularising the appearance of the text. Such a distinction may be suggestive of the function of the books themselves. Perhaps Hg was designed for reading the text aloud while El was produced for silent reading? This suggestion may be further supported by the treatment of plural concord in possessive pronouns and demonstratives, discussed in chapter 6. This was a purely written feature which performed a deictic function, providing cohesion and coherence within the text. The treatment of this inflexion is more haphazard in Hg than in El, where it is more regularly applied. Its purely graphemic significance, and its more consistent employment in El therefore appears to support the possibility that this was a manuscript designed for the reader rather than the listener.

This study has also demonstrated that fifteenth-century copyists of Chaucer's works were careful to preserve certain details of his language despite the pressures of linguistic change. While the fifteenth century was a period of increasing linguistic standardisation, copyists of Chaucer's works retained certain linguistic features despite their archaistic and dialectal status. This represents a collective response to the importance of linguistic details to Chaucer's works and a perception of the authority of Chaucer's works similar to that of Gower.[7] These findings have further implications for studies of the dissemination of the incipient standard language in the fifteenth century. It is clear that the adoption of this standardised language in Chaucerian manuscripts was constrained by an equal or even greater pressure exerted by the language of the Chaucerian tradition. Therefore studies of the dissemination and adoption of the standard must take further account of genre and textual tradition in charting the rise of the written standard during this period. The role of the printing press in the dissemination of the standard language must also be reconsidered in a similar way. It is apparent that printed editions of Chaucer in the late fifteenth and early sixteenth centuries were similarly influenced by the language of the Chaucer tradition and that, in some instances, later editions were more archaic than their predecessors. The *Canterbury Tales* was one of the earliest and most frequently published books in this period, and its rejection of the standard language in favour of Type III equivalents must have had an impact on the dissemination of the standard.

Finally this study has demonstrated the importance of studying the primary data provided by the manuscripts themselves, rather than relying on texts which are the result of the modern editorial process. Such studies must take into account the evidence provided by all the manuscripts of the *Canterbury Tales* tradition, not just a few of the earliest ones as has become traditional. We must learn to accept that not only is the *Riverside Chaucer* not the *Canterbury Tales*, but neither is Hg nor El.

---

[7] For the argument that scribes preserved Gowerian spellings as a response to the authority of the work see Smith 1988c.

Appendix 1
Notes on the Language of *Canterbury Tales* Manuscripts

British Library MS Additional 5140 [Ad¹]

This manuscript was copied by the same scribe as BL Egerton 2864. These two manuscripts form LP 8301, localised by *LALME* to Suffolk. Characteristic features include the use of ⟨h⟩ to represent /x/ e.g. 'throuh', 'thoruh' THROUGH, 'thouh' THOUGH. Other such features are the reflection of OE *y* in ⟨e⟩, e.g. 'feere' FIRE, 'cherche', and the use of ⟨-eng⟩ in present participles. Both manuscripts also show the influence of Type IV in some items, e.g. 'suche'. However a number of Chaucerian spelling features are preserved in both manuscripts despite their late date, e.g. 'nat', 'hem', 'hir'. Despite the fact that these manuscripts were copied by the same scribe from closely affiliated exemplars, there are a small number of differences in the language of these manuscripts. These differences reveal a slightly greater proportion of dialect spellings in En³, suggesting that this is the earlier of the two manuscripts. For instance for the item NOT both manuscripts favour the Type III spelling 'nat', although both also have instances of Type IV 'not'. However Ad¹ has a greater number of examples of 'not' than En³, and En³ also has a single example of the spelling 'nawht'. A similar situation is found in the spellings of IF in these two manuscripts. Ad¹ favours the standardised spellings 'if/yf', alongside a small number of examples of 'yif'. However En³ has a greater number of 'yif' spellings, in addition to a scattering of 'yiff' forms, as well as some examples of the Type IV form 'yf'.

British Library MS Additional 35286 [Ad³]

Many of the central features of the Ad³ orthography correspond to either Type III or Type IV usage. For instance Ad³ has both Type III and Type IV spellings of SUCH: 'swich' and 'such', and of NOT: 'nat', 'noght', 'not'. It seems that while Type IV did exert a degree of influence on the language of Ad³, the spellings associated with Hg and the Chaucerian tradition continued to dominate even in words most likely to display influences of standardisation. However there remain a number of forms which cannot be explained in this way, and which appear to make up a distinct linguistic layer which must be considered separately. The clearest indicators of this layer are the following spellings of THOUGH and NOT: 'thagh', 'thaugh', 'naght', 'nought'. Both spellings of NOT are predominantly Midlands forms, covering both West and East Midlands, with some Southern examples (see *LALME* I maps 276 and 283). Despite the wide distribution of these forms, the evidence of 'thaugh', 'thagh' allows us to be more specific in our localisation. 'Thaugh' is a distinctly West Midland form with little currency outside an area along the Gloucestershire and Herefordshire borders, while 'thagh' is also limited to this area, with a minor number of uses in the North-West Midlands (see *LALME* I maps 195 and 198). Thus it can be shown that these dialect forms cohere in a specific area of the South-West Midlands: specifically that of the borders of Gloucestershire and Herefordshire. The clustering of these forms in the opening folios suggests that these forms belong to the Ad^3 exemplar, carried over into Ad^3 by a process of *literatim* copying. The appearance of a number of further West Midland dialect features in these opening folios seems to confirm this suggestion. These forms include 'mon', 'mony', showing the rounding of vowels before nasal consonants characteristic of the West Midlands, the spellings 'seluer', 'ferst' and single occurrences of 'sheo' and 'iffe'.

Bodleian Library MS Bodley 414 [Bo^1]

This manuscript is closely related to that of Ph^2 and some scholars believe that they were copied by the same scribe. The language of the two manuscripts is similar although there are some significant differences. Both contain a mixture of Type III features and Type IV spellings, with a scattering of dialectal forms not attributable to either of these incipient standards. Type III forms found include: 'though', 'nat', 'thurgh' and Type IV forms include 'such'. The major differences between the two manuscripts are differences in the ratio of Type III and Type IV forms. For instance the dominant spellings of the oblique forms of the third person plural pronoun in Bo^1 are 'hem', 'her', with several occurrences of 'their' and none of 'them'. In contrast Ph^2 has many more appearances of the Type IV 'their' alongside 'her', and a number of uses of 'them' alongside 'hem'. This situation is mirrored by the appearance of dialectal spellings in these manuscripts. For instance both manuscripts have the rare form 'hough' for HOW alongside 'hou'. However the spelling 'hough' is much more frequent in Bo^1 than in Ph^2. This suggests that Bo^1 is the earlier of the two manuscripts. Furthermore the close correspondences in these orthographic details suggests that these manuscripts were copied by the same scribe.

Bodleian Library MS Bodley 686 [Bo^2]

Bo^2 contains a number of dialectal forms which allow a fairly confident localisation in South Worcestershire. These forms include spellings showing the reflection of OE *y* in ⟨y, u⟩ showing the preservation of the OE rounded vowel broadly characteristic of West Midlands dialects, e.g. 'bury', 'yvel' (see *LALME* I maps 974, 978). In addition to this are the broadly West Midland forms 'mochel', 'no3t', and the retention of the conservative ⟨-en⟩

inflexion in third person plural forms of verbs, e.g. 'schenden', 'musten' (*LALME* I maps 103, 288). The spelling 'veire' FAIR shows the voicing of initial fricatives typical of the Western dialects, while the raised vowel represented in the forms 'hed', 'hedde' HAD allows a specific localisation in South Worcestershire (see *LALME* I maps 1180, 1012).

Bodleian Library MS Barlow 20 [Bw]

The language of Bw was localised by *LALME* to Worcs, although no linguistic profile was included. This localisation is confirmed by the occurrence of the following diagnostic features: 'cusse' KISS, 'bury', 'fury, fuyre' FIERY, FIRE, showing OE *y* reflected in ⟨u, uy⟩, a feature common to West Midland texts in this period (see *LALME* I map 412). The spelling 'mony' shows the rounding of vowels before nasals characteristic of Western dialects, while the spelling 'litul' LITTLE suggests North Gloucestershire or South Worcestershire (see *LALME* I map 464).

Christ Church College, Oxford, MS 152 [Ch]

Due to its late date this manuscript shows the impact of the process of standardisation, as evidenced by spellings such as 'but', 'which', 'suche'. Recent cladistic analysis of the manuscripts of the *Wife of Bath's Prologue* has shown that Ch preserves a text close to the Chaucerian archetype (P.M.W. Robinson 1997). This relationship is also evident in the language of this manuscript which contains a number of Type III spellings which must derive from this exemplar. Type III forms found in Ch are 'nat', 'sholde' and 'yaf' GAVE. There is also a single example of the Type II form 'theigh' THOUGH which corresponds with the use of this form in Hg, suggesting a close relationship between these two texts, and confirming the Ch's scribe tendency to preserve features of his copytext. Little is left for purposes of localisation, although several minor features are suggestive of a South-Western or West Midland provenance, e.g. 'hure' HEAR (see *LALME* I map 1016).

'Cardigan': University of Texas HRC MS 143 [Cn]

There are few dialectal features in the Cn language, with most forms belonging to the standardised variety of ME which emerged throughout the fifteenth century, e.g. 'not', 'such(e)', 'though', 'which'. However there are certain spellings which are suggestive of an Eastern provenance, such as 'berie' BURY, 'besy' BUSY, 'cherche' CHURCH, 'mery' MERRY, all showing OE *y* reflected in ⟨e⟩. The spelling 'eny' ANY may also belong to this same dialectal stratum. However the regular use of the spelling 'hur(e)' HER would seem rather to point to a Western localisation. However while this form is certainly dominant in the West it is recorded in several Eastern texts (see *LALME* I map 23). In fact the limited appearance of this form in the Eastern counties allows us to posit a reasonably exact localisation for the Cn language in South-East Suffolk or North Essex.

Corpus Christi College, Oxford, MS 198 [Cp]
See 'Scribe D' below, p. 162.

Cambridge University Library MS Dd. 4.24 [Dd]
Dd contains a number of forms which allow a fairly specific localisation of the scribal dialect. The Dd language contains forms which coincide with the Type III forms which lie at the heart of the *Canterbury Tales* tradition, and it is difficult to assess whether these are the scribe's own forms or constrained forms imported directly from the exemplar. These are spellings like 'swich', 'though', 'thurgh', 'which(e)'. Other forms are more clearly dialectal and are likely to derive from the scribe's own repertoire. The scribe's spellings of MUCH, 'meche', 'mechil' suggest a localisation in either the West or East Midlands (*LALME* I map 101). The evidence of other forms allows us to discard the Western counties in favour of East Anglia for the localisation of the language of the Dd scribe. The following spellings all point to East Anglia, and more specifically Cambridgeshire, as the home of the Dd scribe: 'theise' and OE *y* reflected in ⟨e⟩, e.g. 'bery', 'besy' (see *LALME* I maps 6, 972, 371).

'Delamere': Takamiya MS 32 [Dl]
This manuscript was localised by *LALME* to Kent (LP 5970).

'Devonshire': Takamiya MS 24 [Ds^1]
This manuscript was copied by the 'hooked g' scribe. See below for an analysis.

'Ellesmere': Huntington Library MS El. 26 C9 [El]
Copied by Scribe B. See chapters 2 and 3 for detailed analysis.

British Library MS Egerton 2726 [En^1]
This manuscript was localised by *LALME* to Essex (LP 6150).

British Library MS Egerton 2863 [En^2]
The language of En^2 contains a familiar mixture of Type III and Type IV forms, e.g. 'suche', 'whiche', 'thogh', 'but', 'nat', 'not'. However alongside these forms are a number of dialectal spellings. The spelling 'bot' is recorded in manuscripts copied in the West Midlands and Northern counties and in Norfolk (see *LALME* I map 375). The spelling 'mykel' MUCH indicates that the likely provenance of En^2 is Norfolk or the North Midlands (see *LALME* I map 106). The form 'eighen' EYES reduces the likely area further, suggesting that North Norfolk or Lincolnshire is the home of En^2 (see *LALME* I maps 751, 753).

British Library MS Egerton 2864 [En^3]
This manuscript was copied by the same scribe as BL Additional 5140. These two manuscripts form LP 8301, localised by *LALME* to Suffolk. See the entry for Ad^1.

Fitzwilliam Museum MS McLean 181 [Fi]
The language of Fi contains a mixture of Type IV features, such as 'though', 'but', 'such', 'not', and a number of Western dialectal features. The Western area is indicated by the reflection of OE *y* in ⟨u⟩, e.g. 'churche', 'furst', and the frequent use of the ⟨-ud⟩ inflexion in weak preterites and past participles, 'weddud', 'clepud', 'blessud', and the ⟨-us⟩ inflexion in plural forms of strong nouns, 'frerus' (see *LALME* I map 1199). The West Midlands area is further confirmed by the consistent appearance of 'hur' HER, and the use of 'mych' suggests Herefordshire as the likely provenance of Fi (see *LALME* I maps 23, 102).

Cambridge University Library MS Gg. 4.27 [Gg]
This manuscript was localised by *LALME* to Cambridgeshire.

Glasgow University Library MS Hunter 197 [Gl]
This manuscript is localised by the scribal colophon to Norwich, and was localised by *LALME* to the county of Norfolk. However there are few traces of Norfolk usage in the tranches selected for analysis. Comparison of Gl with its exemplar Mm shows that the main scribe of the manuscript, Geoffrey Spirleng, translated the language of the exemplar into his own usage. This usage is predominantly that of Type IV, as may be demonstrated by the presence of such prototypical Type IV forms as: 'suche' for Mm 'swich', 'gaf' for Mm 'ȝaf', 'though' for Mm 'þof'. However some changes do show the introduction of forms broadly typical of East Anglia, e.g. Gl 'fier' for Mm 'fir'. It is also interesting to note that in some instances Gl replaces a Type IV spelling in Mm with a Type III equivalent, e.g. Mm 'not' becomes Gl 'nat'.[1] The introduction of the minor variant 'nott' is also indicative of a Norfolk provenance (see *LALME* I map 286).

British Library MS Harley 1758 [Ha²]
The regular spellings of THOUGH in Ha² are 'though', 'thowȝ', although the single appearance of the spelling 'theigh' THOUGH suggests a West Midland or London provenance (see *LALME* I map 201). The West Midlands is supported by spellings showing the reflex of OE *y* in ⟨u⟩, e.g. 'burye', and spellings showing the rounding of vowels before nasals, e.g. 'mony'. However there are no forms which are sufficiently distinctive to allow more detailed localisation.

British Library MS Harley 7334 [Ha⁴]
See 'Scribe D' below, p. 162.

---

[1] For a more extensive comparison of the Gl manuscript with its exemplar see Beadle 1997b. Beadle 1997a discusses the context of the Gl manuscript and the career of Geoffrey Spirleng.

British Library MS Harley 7335 [Ha⁵]

The language of Ha⁵ retains certain archetypal spelling features, such as 'swich' SUCH, 'nat' NOT, 'hem' THEM, 'her' THEIR. In addition to these spellings are others which appear to form a separate dialectal layer, deriving from the scribe's own idiolect. This layer is represented by forms such as 'cherche' CHURCH, 'merthe' MIRTH, 'foer' FIRE, 'fery' FIERY which show OE *y* reflected in ⟨e⟩. These forms point to an Eastern provenance for the Ha⁵ scribe, and more specifically a South-Eastern or East Anglian localisation. An even more exact localisation is suggested by a number of spellings showing OE *eo* reflected in ⟨ie⟩, e.g. 'fierth', which is a characteristic of West Essex and West Kent. It is however possible that the Chaucerian forms identified above should also be considered as belonging to this Eastern layer, rather than as a separate linguistic layer. For instance the spelling 'swich' SUCH is common in East Anglia, and is also found in West Essex and West Kent (see *LALME* I map 74).

'Helmingham': Princeton University Library MS 100 [He]

This manuscript contains a number of dialect features which point to a localisation within Essex. Characteristic features are the use of ⟨v⟩ for ⟨w⟩ in certain contexts, e.g. 'vyvis' WIVES (see *LALME* I map 1182). The reflection of OE *y* in ⟨e⟩ is broadly characteristic of eastern areas of ME, specifically the East Anglian and Kentish counties; this feature is found in He in words like 'besy', and 'fier'. Another diagnostic feature of limited provenance in late ME is the spelling 'wordely', which appears in small pockets in far Eastern and Western regions. This spelling is again regular in He. The use of ⟨ij⟩ spellings in He, such as 'lijth', 'Alijs', 'crijd', 'storijs: orotorijs', shows a limited distribution in a few scattered Midlands texts from this period (*LALME* I map 1163). The form of the second person pronoun, 'ʒew(e)', is regular in He and is recorded in very few other texts (*LALME* I map 1155).

'Hengwrt': National Library of Wales MS Peniarth 392 D [Hg]

Copied by Scribe B. See chapters 2 and 3 for detailed analysis.

Holkham Hall MS 667 [Hk]

Hk contains a layer of dialectal forms which point to an Eastern provenance for this manuscript. These forms are 'nat' NOT, 'swich' SUCH and spellings showing OE *y* reflected in ⟨e⟩, e.g. 'beldeth' BUILDS, 'mery' MERRY. A more specific localisation is suggested by 'eny' ANY, 'seth' SINCE, 'werld' WORLD, 'worch' WORK, which are restricted to Norfolk, Suffolk and Essex in the East (see *LALME* I maps 98, 239, 296, 315). The combined weight of evidence points to the Essex/Suffolk border, although Norfolk is also a possible candidate. However alongside these are a number of forms showing OE *y* reflected in ⟨i, y⟩, e.g. 'synne' SIN, 'kissen' KISS. It is possible that these forms belong to a separate layer deriving from the exemplar, although it is perhaps more likely that the scribe's repertoire included both forms showing OE *y* reflected in ⟨y, i⟩ and in ⟨e⟩. Such a situation could be the result of the process of standardisation which saw regional spelling forms become progressively replaced by those in more widespread use. This possibility is reinforced by the presence of two spellings for the item SUCH in this manuscript: 'swich' and 'such'. The 'swich' spelling is a dialect form which only appears in a few occurrences in Hk, while the 'such' spelling, which is dominant in Hk, is the form found in the incipient standardised spelling system. Therefore it seems that the Hk scribe employed both Eastern dialect features and standardised features within his repertoire. A different scenario is also possible however. The spellings 'swich', 'nat' etc. are also the regular spellings for these items in the Hg manuscript and therefore their presence in Hk may be the result of the preservation of exemplar forms which ultimately derive from the archetype of the tradition.

Bodleian Library MS Hatton Donat. 1 [Ht]
Localised by *LALME* to Buckinghamshire (LP 6670).

Cambridge University Library MS Ii.3.26 [Ii]
The majority of the forms in the Ii language belong to Type IV London English, e.g. 'but', 'suche', 'which', 'not'. There are however a handful of forms which are suggestive of a separate Northern layer, e.g. 'agayne', 'gaf' GAVE, 'gyve' GIVE (see *LALME* I maps 220, 424). These forms could be accommodated within the Type IV layer already identified, although there are other dialectal features. The spelling 'mych(e)' is most common across the Midlands, and the appearance of this form with the Northern forms identified above suggests a localisation in the Northern Midlands (see *LALME* I map 102). The presence of the form 'nought' NOT, which is found in clusters in the West and North-East Midlands, allows us to posit the North-East Midlands as the likely provenance of Ii (see *LALME* I map 283). The suggested localisation of the language of the Ii scribe is therefore Southern Lincolnshire, or possibly North Norfolk.

British Library MS Lansdowne 851 [La]
The majority of the linguistic features of La point to a localisation in the South-West Midlands. For instance the dominant spelling of THOUGH is 'þouhe' which is recorded in a cluster of texts in the West Midlands as well as in a few texts scattered across the East Anglian counties. Alongside this form is a single occurrence of another spelling of this item 'theihe', a spelling whose heartland is also in the West Midlands with some occurrences in the South (see *LALME* I maps 201, 205). The use of both of these forms suggests a West Midland provenance for the La language. Other West Midlands features are the rounding of vowels before nasal consonants 'mony', 'londe', and some examples showing the retention of the rounded

reflex of OE *y*, e.g. 'yuel' (see *LALME* I map 978). Certain forms of the verb BE provide us with the most diagnostically useful spellings: 'bue', 'buen'. These forms are exclusive to a small area in the South-West Midlands, suggesting a specific localisation of La on the Gloucestershire/Worcestershire border (see *LALME* I map 127). The presence of the spellings 'world' and 'werldly' prompted Smith to suggest a possible influence from the Northern dialects upon the La language (Smith 1985: 225). These forms are however found in a handful of texts on the Gloucestershire/Herefordshire border and therefore belong to this same South-West Midlands layer (see *LALME* I map 296). The fact that these forms are comparatively rare for the West Midlands is helpful in the process of localisation, confirming the evidence of the 'bue(n)' spellings that the Gloucestershire/Worcestershire/Herefordshire border is the home of La.

Lichfield Cathedral Library MS 29 [Lc]

The Lichfield MS is in two hands. The *Wife of Bath's Prologue* is copied by the first scribe who copied folios 1–196. The second scribe copied folios 196–294 and is the same hand as that of the Petworth manuscript. See below for an analysis of the language of this scribe. The language of the first scribe presents a reasonably uncomplicated mixture of Type III and Type IV forms. Type III forms are 'nat', 'thurgh', 'though', 'thise', all of which are found in the Hg manuscript and other Type III texts. It seems likely that these forms are preserved from the scribe's exemplar. The Type IV forms recorded in this text are 'not', 'such', 'but', 'moche', 'agayn'. It is interesting that for certain items, for example the spellings 'nat', 'not', the scribe's repertoire consisted of both Type III and IV forms, although in these cases it is the Type IV form which is more common. There are 39 examples of the spelling 'not' in the WBP as compared with 9 instances of 'nat'. The mixture of Type III and Type IV features suggests that the scribe was working in London, and this is further supported by a number of spellings showing OE *y* reflected in both ⟨e⟩ and ⟨i⟩, e.g. 'mille', 'mery', 'chirche', 'brenne'. There are however a few examples of dialectal forms which might suggest that the scribe was not a native Londoner. For example in addition to the spellings 'nat', 'not' there are 9 occurrences of the provincial spelling 'nouȝt', which is recorded in a variety of ME dialects (see *LALME* I map 288). There are also several different spellings of the item THOUGH: 'þogh', 'þough', 'þouȝ' which might support a provincial origin for the Lc scribe. However these spellings may simply be different realisations of the 2 Type III spellings for this item, 'thogh', 'though'. Therefore while there are some hints of dialect forms in this text there is not enough to allow a localisation. It is however likely that the Lc scribe was working in London and that the Lc manuscript is a London production.

Bodleian Library MS Laud Misc. 600 [Ld[1]]

The majority of forms in Ld[1] may be understood as a mixture of Type III and Type IV London English. For example Type III forms found in Ld[1] are 'swich', 'nat', 'hem', while Type IV forms are 'suche', 'which', 'if', 'but'. The number of Type IV forms is much greater and where both Type III and IV spellings are recorded for an individual item the Type IV form is dominant. For example there are just 2 occurrences of the Type III spellings 'swich' and 'nat'. However in addition to these London forms there are hints of a dialectal layer. For example the spelling 'mykel' MUCH, which is a form found mostly in the North and North-East Midlands (see *LALME* I map 106). The scribe's spellings of the item YET, 'ʒitt', 'yett', 'yitt', are also suggestive of a dialectal origin (see *LALME* I map 249). The coincidence of these two dialectal forms suggests that the North-East Midlands may be the original provenance of this scribe, although there is not much evidence to support this tentative localisation. The single appearance of the spelling 'wisdam', showing the Northern and North-Eastern suffix ⟨-dam⟩ adds some further support to this suggested origin (see *LALME* I map 942). However the majority of forms point to a London provenance and it seems likely that the manuscript, if not the scribe, is of London origin.

Bodleian Library MS Laud Misc. 739 [Ld²]

The language of Ld² presents a mixture of Type III and Type IV forms with a number of dialectal forms. The Type III forms are few and often appear in only a few occurrences, e.g. 'swich' (1 occurrence), 'muche' (1), 'thurgh' (1). The Type IV spellings are much more common and are found in a greater number of occurrences, e.g. 'such(e)' (15), 'but' (56), 'many' (6). In addition to these forms are a number of dialectal spellings which appear to represent two separate layers. Diagnostic of the West are the reflection of OE y in ⟨u⟩, e.g. 'fust' FIST, 'burien', and spellings showing the rounding of vowels before nasals, e.g. 'mony', 'londe'. However in addition to this clear West Midland layer there are a number of features which suggest a Northern localisation for the Ld² scribe. This layer consists of features such as the use of the ⟨-ez⟩ inflexion in the third person singular of the present indicative, e.g. 'makez', 'faillez', and the spellings 'haith', 'caght' (See *LALME* I map 645). However this apparent contradiction may be resolved by reference to the textual history of the manuscript. Almost the entire text of Ld² was copied from Ry² and therefore we may compare the two manuscripts to see if either of these layers belongs to the Ry² scribe. It is apparent from a comparison of these two manuscripts that the Western features identified in Ld² do not belong to the Ld² scribe but are in fact inherited forms from Ry². This situation is determined by the appearance of the same Western features in Ry² at the same places in the text as found in Ld². So for instance the forms 'fust' and 'burien', 'mony', 'londe', discussed above, are all found in the same positions in Ry². However the Northern features identified in Ld², such as the use of the ⟨-ez⟩ inflexion in the third person singular of the present indicative, are not found in Ry². Therefore it seems likely that the Western forms in Ld² are inherited from the exemplar, while the Northern linguistic features belong to the scribe of Ld². Comparison of the two texts also allows us to attribute other spellings found in Ld^2 to the exemplar. For instance Ld^2 contains the two spellings 'ʒet', and 'ʒit' for the item YET. Comparison with Ry^2 reveals that the spelling 'ʒit' does not appear in this manuscript thereby confirming that this is the form introduced by the Ld^2 scribe. The spelling 'ʒet' appears throughout Ry^2 thereby confirming that its appearance in Ld^2 is as a relict from the exemplar. A similar method allows us to distinguish the spelling 'ʒiff' as that of the Ld^2 scribe, while the spelling 'ʒif' is inherited from the exemplar. The 'ʒiff' spelling with the geminate consonant thus provides further support for the Northern layer identified in the language of Ld^2 (see *LALME* I map 210). Certain other spellings reveal an overlap in the repertoires of the two scribes. For instance the spellings 'noʒt' and 'ʒif' both appear in the two manuscripts although they occur at different positions across the two texts. It may be that the introduction of these spellings in Ld^2 is a result of their use in Ry^2, despite their appearance in different positions. However both forms were common in both the Western and Northern counties during this period, and it seems likely that these forms belonged to the repertoires of both scribes (see *LALME* I maps 288, 212). Therefore we may conclude that the language of Ld^2 presents a mixture of Type III and Type IV London forms, in addition to two distinct dialectal layers. The Western layer is inherited from its exemplar, Ry^2, while the Northern layer may be attributed to the Ld^2 scribe.

Lincoln Cathedral Library MS 110 [Ln]
Localised by *LALME* to Buckinghamshire (LP 6650).

John Rylands Library MS English 113 [Ma]
Manly and Rickert described the language of Ma as East Midland, suggesting Norfolk as a likely provenance. However Dan Mosser (1990) has shown that the Ma scribe also copied Bodleian Library MS Digby 181 and has used the evidence of both manuscripts to construct a linguistic profile of this scribe. Mosser has shown that the Norfolk features identified by Manly and Rickert are found only in Ma and therefore are relicts carried over from the Ma exemplar. Mosser's analysis of forms common to both manuscripts has placed the language of the Ma scribe in Warwickshire. Spellings in the *Wife of Bath's Prologue* which support this localisation are: 'wordil' WORLD, 'yhit' YET, 'evil,' (*LALME* I map 292, 247, 977). For a full discussion with accompanying linguistic profile see Mosser 1990.

'McCormick': University of Chicago Library MS 564 [Mc]
The language of Mc contains a handful of Type IV spellings, 'but', 'such', 'not', and a large number of dialectal forms. A broadly Western area is indicated by the spellings 'bury', 'fust' FIST, 'gulteles' GUILTLESS, showing the reflection of OE *y* in ⟨u⟩, and the spellings 'lond', 'honde', showing the rounding of vowels before nasal consonants. Other spellings

within the Mc text allow us to be more precise in our localisation. The use of the form 'hure' to represent both THEIR and HER points to an area within the South-West Midlands (see *LALME* I maps 62, 23). There are however some occurrences of the spellings 'thayre' THEIR and 'thayme' THEM which are common to Northern dialects and extremely rare in the South-West Midlands (see *LALME* I maps 54, 42). In the Midlands these forms are both recorded in Oxfordshire and may therefore be accommodated within a more central Midland localisation. However it may be that these forms are relicts from a previous layer of copying and do not belong within the Mc scribe's language at all. The spelling 'þeyh' further confirms the South-West Midlands as the likely provenance of Mc, as this form is most common in Gloucestershire and Herefordshire (see *LALME* I map 201). Another spelling of THOUGH, 'þauh', found in Mc also indicates the South-West Midlands, but may be accommodated a little further east in West Oxfordshire (see *LALME* I map 195). It would therefore seem most likely that the Mc manuscript represents the language of West Oxfordshire.

Pierpont Morgan Library MS 249 [Mg]
It is generally accepted by scholars that Mg was copied from Lc. Therefore in analysing the language of Mg we may compare this with that of Lc. In fact it is striking how similar the language of these two manuscripts is. Mg contains many of the same Type III and Type IV forms observed in Lc, such as 'though', 'but', 'whiche', 'not', 'nat'. Other forms in Mg not belonging to Types III and IV, e.g. 'ȝit' YET. 'nouȝt', 'cusse' KISS, are also found in Lc. The only significant difference between the language of these two manuscripts is that Mg shows a greater degree of influence from Type IV. For example Lc contains a number of different spellings of THOUGH, 'þogh', 'þough', 'þouȝ', while Mg has the single spelling 'though' for this item. This evidence suggests that either the Mg scribe copied exactly the spellings of his exemplar or that his own spelling system was very similar to that of Lc. Given that the Lc scribe's system is largely an uncomplicated mixture of Type III and Type IV forms it seems likely that the two scribes were both working in London with similar linguistic habits.

Cambridge University Library MS Mm. 2.5 [Mm]
Localised by *LALME* to Leicestershire.

New College, Oxford, MS D.314 [Ne]
Localised by *LALME* to Norfolk.

Alnwick Castle Northumberland MS 455 [Nl]
Localised by *LALME* to Essex (LP 6040). Similar hand and language as Helmingham. See above.

Phillipps 8136: Bodmer Library MS 48 [Ph²]
See Bo[1].

Phillipps 8137: Philadelphia Rosenbach Foundation MS 1084/1 [Ph³]
Ph³ was copied by two scribes: the *Wife of Bath's Prologue* is in the hand of the second scribe. A number of forms within the Ph³ language indicate a broadly Western provenance. For instance the spellings 'churche', 'fuyre' show the reflection of OE *y* in ⟨u, uy⟩, and the spellings 'honde', 'honged', 'londe' show the rounding of vowels before nasal consonants. The West Midlands is further suggested by the consistent use of 'hur' HER (see *LALME* I map 23). The spelling 'scho' SHE is a characteristic of Northern dialects and is very rare in the West Midlands, restricting the provenance of Ph³ to Shropshire or Herefordshire (see *LALME* I map 13). The addition of initial unetymological ⟨h-⟩ to a number of forms, e.g. 'holde' OLD, 'habraham' ABRAHAM is also rare in the West Midlands and further restricts the likely area to Herefordshire (see *LALME* I map 1172).

Bibliothèque Nationale MS Fonds Anglais 39 [Ps]
Localised by *LALME* to Lincolnshire.

Petworth House MS 7 [Pw]
The language of Pw consists of a layer of Type III and Type IV spellings, 'such', 'if', 'not', 'hem', alongside a layer of West Midlands forms, 'ham' THEM, 'ʒif'. The presence of a number of West Midlands forms in Pw allows us to localise the language of the scribe to the borders of South-West Worcestershire and Gloucestershire. Diagnostic forms in Pw are 'hur(e)' HER, 'ham' THEM, 'mony', 'furst', 'sclayn', 'sclyke' etc. (see *LALME* I maps 23, 45, 91). Palaeographers have identified the hand of the Pw scribe in several other manuscripts, including Pembroke College, Cambridge, MS 307, a copy of Gower's *Confessio Amantis*, localised by Smith to the Gloucestershire/Worcestershire border (Smith 1985: 134). The hand of the Pw scribe has also been recognised in two manuscripts of Nicholas Love's *Mirror of the Blessed Life of Jesus Christ*, National Library of Scotland MS Advocates 18.1.7 and Tokyo, University of Waseda MS, manuscripts which show similar mixtures of dialectal features.[2] It has been suggested by Seymour (1997: 221) that the same scribe also copied BL Arundel 119, a copy of Lydgate's *Siege of Thebes*. However Arundel 119 has been localised by *LALME* to Essex and the linguistic evidence does not therefore support this identification.[3]

Royal College of Physicians MS 388 [Py]
This manuscript was copied by a prolific fifteenth-century copyist known as the 'Hammond scribe'.[4] The language of Py contains a number of arche-

---

[2] For an examination of the language of the Advocates and Waseda manuscripts, and a comparison of these with the Petworth manuscript see Smith 1997b.
[3] Arundel 119 is *LALME* LP 9450. For a list of manuscripts ascribed to the Pw scribe see Mosser 1996 and for further discussion of this scribe see chapter 7.
[4] For the most recent list of manuscripts ascribed to the Hammond scribe see Mooney 1996.

typal Chaucerian spelling features, such as 'nat', thurgh'. However study of the language of other manuscripts in this same scribe's hand reveals the presence of these same forms, suggesting that their appearance in Py is due to the input of the scribe and not pressure from the exemplar. Py also contains a number of Type IV forms such as 'suche' and 'but', alongside a number of spellings characteristic of the Kentish dialect. Diagnostic Kentish features are 'bien' BE, and related spellings showing ⟨ie⟩ for OE *e, eo* and OF *e*, such as 'hield', triew, 'chiere', 'thiese'. Py also contains a number of broadly Western dialect features, such as OE *y* reflected in ⟨u⟩, ⟨uy⟩, e.g. 'fuyre', 'busie' and the single occurrence of the form 'bott' BUT. However these forms are not found in any other manuscript in this scribe's hand, and are therefore likely to derive from the exemplar. Alongside the forms showing OE *y* in ⟨u⟩ are a number of spellings, common to Py and other manuscripts in the scribe's hand, with OE *y* reflected in ⟨y, i⟩, as shown in 'myrry', 'synne', 'chirche', and it seems likely that these forms represent the scribe's preferred usage. This mixture of forms suggests that the scribe's native dialect was that of Kent and that he was an immigrant to London where his prolific copying career resulted in the gradual adoption of a number of Type IV spelling features.

Bodleian Library MS Rawlinson Poetry 141 [Ra¹]
Localised by *LALME* to Shropshire (LP 237).

Bodleian Library MS Rawlinson Poetry 149 [Ra²]
Ra² was copied by a number of scribes, although the exact number is a matter of scholarly dispute. The *Wife of Bath's Prologue* is in the hand of the scribe who copied the majority of the manuscript, folios 53–136. The Ra² language comprises a number of spellings which are found in Type III London English, such as 'thogh', 'though'. In addition to these forms are a number of dialectal forms. The spellings 'besy', 'mery' point to a South-Eastern or East Anglian provenance (see *LALME* I map 371). The sporadic use of the ⟨-es⟩ inflexion in the third person singular present indicative, e.g. 'haes', indicates a provenance to the North of this area (see *LALME* I map 645). The consistent use of the spelling 'soch' SUCH confirms North Norfolk as the home of Ra² (see *LALME* I map 69).

Bodleian Library MS Rawlinson Poetry 223 [Ra³]
This manuscript was copied by the 'hooked g' scribe. See below for an analysis.

British Library MS Royal 17 D.XV [Ry¹]
Ry¹ was copied by two scribes. The first scribe was responsible for the *Wife of Bath's Prologue*, and it is the language of this scribe which will be discussed here. The second scribe is known as the 'Hammond scribe' and his hand has been recognised in a number of other manuscripts, including Py

(see above). The majority of the forms found in the language of the second scribe of Ry[1] are common to texts copied in London during this period. For instance the scribe uses the typical Type IV features 'suche', 'though', 'many', 'through'. His collaboration with the Hammond scribe, a professional London scribe, suggests that the first scribe was also a Londoner and that Ry[1] is a London production. There are however a number of other minor forms which may indicate a separate dialectal layer. For instance there is a single occurrence of the feminine pronoun 'hur' alongside 'her'. This form is more common in the West Midlands, although it is recorded in some London texts of this period (see *LALME* I map 23). The spellings 'mochell', 'yefe' IF, 'yette' YET, 'are' ERE also contribute to a West Midlands layer in the Ry[1] language (see *LALME* I maps 109, 209, 249, 232). These forms may be part of the scribe's own repertoire, perhaps indicating that the Ry[1] scribe was a Western immigrant into the capital. It is of course also possible that these Western forms are relicts from a previous layer of copying. However comparison of these forms with the equivalent forms in the section of the manuscript copied by the Hammond scribe suggests that these are not exemplar relicts. None of these Western features are recorded in the Hammond scribe's stint; his forms for these items are as follows: 'moche', 'if', 'yit', 'ere'. This of course does not rule out the possibility that the first scribe was less consistent in imposing his own spelling system upon a West Midland exemplar. However it seems more likely that the Western features in the first scribe's stint are part of his own repertoire, revealing his West Midland origins.

British Library MS Royal 18 C.II [Ry[2]]
The language of Ry[2] contains a handful of Type III and Type IV forms, mixed with a strong West Midlands layer. Forms characteristic of Type III and Type IV are 'though', 'suche', 'whiche', 'not'. Forms characteristic of the West Midlands layer are 'furst', 'buryen', 'fuyry' showing the reflection of OE *y* in ⟨u, uy⟩, and 'mony', 'londe', showing the rounding of vowels before nasal consonants. Another form in Ry[2] which is typical of the West Midlands and South-Western dialects is 'hur' for the pronoun HER (see *LALME* I map 23). Spellings of the pronoun IT with initial ⟨h-⟩ are also characteristic of the West Midlands and the form 'hit' is found regularly throughout Ry[2] (see *LALME* I map 24). The language of the Ry[2] scribe is characterised by a large variety of spellings for common items, such as the following forms of the item THOUGH: 'þauȝ', 'þauȝt', 'þouȝ', 'þeȝ'. The spellings with medial ⟨au⟩ point to a well-defined cluster of manuscripts with similar forms in the West Midlands, with a handful of other examples in East Anglia (see *LALME* I map 195). The spelling 'þeȝ' with medial ⟨e⟩ is extremely rare in all dialects of ME and is recorded in the West Midlands only in Gloucestershire (see *LALME* I map 200). The Ry[2] scribe also has a variety of different forms for the item NOT, 'naȝt', 'noȝt', not, 'nouȝt', 'noȝ'. The last of these is a particularly rare spelling, attested in the West

Midlands only in Gloucestershire and South Herefordshire (see *LALME* I map 279). The presence of these two rare forms, 'þeȝ', 'noȝ' therefore enable us to posit a Gloucestershire provenance for Ry^2.

Bodleian Library MS Arch. Selden B.14 [Se]
The language of Se consists of a mixture of Type III and Type IV London English forms, although the Type IV forms are in the majority. Type IV forms recorded in Se are 'but', 'such', 'which', 'not'. Alongside these are found some Type III forms although these are minor variants, e.g. 'swich' (1 occurrence), 'nat' (5). In addition to these forms are a number of other spellings which do not form part of either Type III or IV. For instance the spelling 'meche(l)' which is most common in the West and East Midlands, although it is also found in a number of London texts (see *LALME* I map 101). Other idiosyncratic scribal forms are 'wich' WHICH, 'yiff' IF. Neither of these forms is sufficiently dialectal to suggest a provincial origin for Se, and both may be attributed to London. Another characteristic of the Se language is the reflection of OE *y* in ⟨e, i, u⟩, e.g. 'berye', 'chirche', 'churche', which further suggests a London localisation for Se.

'Sion': Takamiya MS 22 [Si]
The language of Si consists of a blend of some Type III and Type IV features with a strong dialectal layer. Type IV spellings recorded in Si are 'not', 'suche', 'but', 'which'. There are some occurrences of Type III spellings, e.g. 'thogh', 'though', although these are frequently found with dialectal equivalents, e.g. 'þowe'. The spelling 'þowe' is common in the Midlands dialects generally, an area further suggested by spellings of GIVE, GAVE with initial ⟨g-⟩, e.g. 'gaf', 'gyff' (see *LALME* I map 197, 424). The presence of the spelling 'sich' alongside Type IV 'such' enables us to posit the Central Midlands as the likely origin of the Si language (see *LALME* I map 68). The regular use of the spelling 'schold' SHOULD is more common in the West Midlands dialects and allows us to settle on the Western limit of the Central Midlands area, suggesting that Warwickshire is the most likely home for the Si language (see *LALME* I map 159).

British Library MS Sloane 1685 [Sl^1]
The *Wife of Bath's Prologue* in Sl^1 is copied by the third scribe, who copied folios 63–222. A number of forms in the Sl^1 language closely resemble the equivalent forms in Type IV London English, e.g. 'not', 'whiche', 'if'. Other forms constitute a separate dialect layer. A broadly Western area is indicated by spellings such as 'fuyre', 'murthe' showing the reflection of OE *y* in ⟨u, uy⟩, and spellings showing the rounding of vowels before nasal consonants, e.g. 'honde', 'honged', 'þonkes'. The frequent use of ⟨th-⟩ forms of the third person plural pronouns, 'þeire', 'þere', and the feminine pronoun 'sho', 'scho' points to a Northern localisation, although there are rare occurrences of this form in some Western texts, especially those

copied in Shropshire (see *LALME* I maps 51, 13). A single appearance of the form 'sall' SHALL, alongside frequent 'schall', 'shalle', also suggests a Northern provenance, although there are occurrences of this form in Staffordshire and Worcestershire (see *LALME* I map 148). The spelling 'shude' is also rare throughout the ME dialects although this too is found in Staffordshire (see *LALME* I map 156). It seems therefore that the language of Sl[1] indicates a Staffordshire provenance.

British Library MS Sloane 1686 [Sl[2]]
This manuscript is dated to the period 1480–90 by Manly and Rickert. As a result of this late date of copying the language of the text is relatively standardised, although the presence of certain diagnostic forms allow for a definite localisation within Norfolk. The most characteristic Norfolk feature found in Sl[2] is the use of ⟨x⟩ in initial position to represent /ʃ/ in SHALL, SHOULD etc., e.g. 'xall', 'xallt', 'xolde', 'xulde' (*LALME* I map 149). These forms are found alongside the standardised equivalents 'shall', 'sholde' etc. In addition to these are a number of other spellings which support this localisation. For instance the scribe of Sl[2] uses the spelling 'soch' for SUCH alongside the Type IV form 'such' (*LALME* I map 69). Several spellings show the reflection of OE *y* in ⟨e⟩ which is a characteristic of East Anglia and the South-East, e.g. 'besy' BUSY, 'melle' MILL. Other features which strengthen the Eastern localisation are 'brenne' BURN (*LALME* I map 970) and 'wordly' (*LALME* I map 292).

Trinity College, Cambridge, MS R.3.3 [Tc[1]]
This manuscript was copied by the 'hooked g' scribe. See below for an analysis.

Trinity College, Cambridge, MS R.3.15 [Tc[2]]
Tc[2] was copied at the end of the fifteenth century and its language shows considerable influence from Type IV language. For instance the following Type IV forms are consistently employed throughout the text: 'but', 'suche', 'whiche', not', 'if', 'yet'. Despite this large number of Type IV forms a handful of Type III forms do continue to appear in Tc[2], e.g. 'hem', 'her' rather than Type IV 'them', 'their'. There are very few forms which do not belong to Types III and IV, e.g. occasional 'thow' alongside 'though', although by the end of the fifteenth century these are "colourless" forms rather than distinctive regional features.

Trinity College, Oxford, MS Arch.49 [To[1]]
The language of To[1] consists of a mixture of Type IV features with a small number of dialectal features. Type IV features found in To[1] are 'though', 'but', 'suche', 'yet'. There are a number of other spellings showing the reflection of OE *y* in ⟨e⟩, which is broadly indicative of the East Anglian and South-Eastern counties. Alongside the Type IV form 'such' are a number of

variant spellings, 'swoche', 'swiche', 'sweche', 'sueche'. Spellings of SUCH with initial ⟨sw-⟩ and ⟨su-⟩ are found in East Anglia and in the South-East, particularly in the counties of Norfolk, Sussex and Surrey (see *LALME* I maps 74, 75). The spelling 'nott' however allows us to restrict the likely area to Surrey, an area further supported by the spelling 'yitte' YET (see *LALME* I maps 286, 249).

Scribe D

Jeremy Smith's (1985) study of the spelling of all of Scribe D's manuscripts has revealed a layer of South-West Midland dialect features common to each of these texts, which suggests that this is Scribe D's native dialect usage. In addition these manuscripts reveal a number of standardised spellings which show the scribe's interaction with the language of London as a result of his central role in the metropolitan book trade. Furthermore the scribe's long association with Gower's *Confessio Amantis* left him with a number of foregrounded Gowerian spellings, such as the Kentish form 'oughne', which he introduced into his copies of Chaucer, Langland and Trevisa.

'Hooked g' scribe

A number of the features found in the three manuscripts copied by the 'Hooked g' scribe are those of Type IV, e.g. 'such', 'but', 'shal' and 'agein'. However the scribe's adoption of Type IV forms was not exhaustive, and his language also contains a number of distinctive regional features, such as 'thouȝ', 'ougne', 'wich' and 'yit'. Several of these regional forms are independently distinctive, and the presence of this combination of spellings allows a confident localisation of such features within the county boundaries of Kent. Particularly diagnostic forms are 'ougne' and 'wich', although a number of other features are also regularly found in Kentish texts of the period (see *LALME* I map 499). In addition to these are the consistent use of contracted and syncopated forms of the third person singular, e.g. 'comth', the reflex of OE *e*, *eo* in ⟨ie⟩, e.g. 'hiere' HERE and HEAR, and OE *y* reflected in ⟨e⟩, 'besy' BUSY and 'mery' MERRY. Combinations of these features may be paralleled in a number of Linguistic Profiles of localised Kentish texts, and many correspond with elements of the Kentish stratum identified within Gower's repertoire.[5] Despite the agreement in many of these core features there are a few differences between the three manuscripts, particularly apparent where Ra[3] differs against Ds[1] and Tc[1]. These differences are shown in the use of 'shall', 'owne', 'which', 'yet' in place of the forms 'shal', 'ougne', 'wich', 'yit' common to both Ds[1] and Tc[1]. However these differences may be explained as the result of the influence of the process of standardisation during the fifteenth century which saw the

---

[5] Gower's repertoire includes 'oghne' OWN, contracted 3rd person singular present indicative verbs and spellings showing the reflex of OE *e, eo* and OF *e* in ⟨ie⟩, e.g. 'lief', 'diere', 'hiere' HERE and HEAR etc. See Samuels and Smith 1988.

replacement of pronounced provincialisms with Type IV forms. The forms 'ougne', 'wich', 'yit' eradicated in Ra[3] are particularly regional forms and in Ra[3] they are replaced with their Type IV equivalents. This process can be observed in progress in the appearance of minor spellings for several items in Ra[3], such as 'though', 'right', 'how', 'thow', which represent the gradual replacement of ⟨ȝ⟩ with ⟨gh⟩ and ⟨ou⟩ with ⟨ow⟩. A further change found only in Ra[3] is the loss of syncopated and contracted forms of the third person singular, exemplified by the spelling 'comith' in place of the Ds[1] and Tc[1] form 'comth'. However some of these changes are also apparent in Tc[1] and here we witness the introduction of the Type IV forms 'right' and 'not', which are both found in increased numbers in Ra[3]. This evidence suggests that the scribe was an immigrant to London, and that his dialectal origins were in Kent. His linguistic behaviour reveals a gradual replacement of the provincial forms common to his native Kent with the accepted usage of the incipient Type IV. See further Horobin 1998a.

Appendix 2
Chronological List of *Canterbury Tales* Manuscripts

I. 1400–1425

Cp   Corpus Christi College, Oxford, MS 198
Dd   Cambridge University Library MS Dd.4.24
El   'Ellesmere': Huntington Library MS El. 26 C 9
Gg   Cambridge University Library MS Gg.4.27
Ha^4 British Library MS Harley 7334
Hg   'Hengwrt': National Library of Wales MS Peniarth 392 D
La   British Library MS Lansdowne 851
(7 manuscripts)

II. 1425–1450

Ad^3 British Library MS Additional 35286
Bo^2 Bodleian Library MS Bodley 686
En^1 British Library MS Egerton 2726
En^2 British Library MS Egerton 2863
He   'Helmingham': Princeton University Library MS 100
Ii   Cambridge University Library MS Ii.3.26
Lc   Lichfield Cathedral Library MS 29
Ld^1 Bodleian Library MS Laud Misc. 600
Ph^3 Phillipps 8137: Philadelphia Rosenbach Foundation MS 1084/1
Ps   Bibliothèque Nationale MS Fonds Anglais 39
Pw   Petworth House MS 7
Ry^2 British Library MS Royal 18 C.II
Sl^1 British Library MS Sloane 1685
(13 manuscripts)

III. 1450–1475

Bo^1 Bodleian Library MS Bodley 414
Bw   Bodleian Library MS Barlow 20
Ch   Christ Church College, Oxford, MS 152
Cn   'Cardigan': University of Texas HRC MS 143
Dl   'Delamere': Takamiya MS 32

Ds^1 'Devonshire': Takamiya MS 24
Fi   Fitzwilliam Museum MS McLean 181
Ha^2 British Library MS Harley 1758
Ha^5 British Library MS Harley 7335
Hk   Holkham Hall MS 667
Ht   Bodleian Library MS Hatton Donat. 1
Ln   Lincoln Cathedral Library MS 110
Mc   'McCormick': University of Chicago Library MS 564
Mg   Pierpont Morgan Library MS 249
Mm   Cambridge University Library MS Mm.2.5
Ne   New College, Oxford, MS D.314
Nl   Alnwick Castle Northumberland MS 455
Ph^2 Phillipps 8136: Bodmer Library MS 48
Py   Royal College of Physicians MS 388
Ra^1 Bodleian Library MS Rawlinson Poetry 141
Ra^2 Bodleian Library MS Rawlinson Poetry 149
Ra^3 Bodleian Library MS Rawlinson Poetry 223
Ry^1 British Library MS Royal 17 D.XV
Se   Bodleian Library MS Arch. Selden B.14
Tc^1 Trinity College, Cambridge, MS R.3.3
To^1 Trinity College, Oxford, MS Arch. 49
(26 manuscripts)

IV.   1475–1500

Ad^1 British Library MS Additional 5140
Cx^1 Caxton's First Edition (1476)
Cx^2 Caxton's Second Edition (1482)
En^3 British Library MS Egerton 2864
Gl   Glasgow University Library MS Hunter 197
Ld^2 Bodleian Library MS Laud Misc. 739
Ma   John Rylands Library MS English 113
Pn   Pynson (1492)
Si   'Sion': Takamiya MS 22
Sl^2 British Library MS Sloane 1686
Tc^2 Trinity College, Cambridge, MS R.3.15
Wy   Wynkyn de Worde (1498)
(12 manuscripts)

Bibliography

Alford, J.A., *A Companion to Piers Plowman* (London, 1988)

Barron, C.M., 'William Langland: a London Poet', in B. Hanawalt (ed.), *Chaucer's England: Literature in Historical Context* (Minneapolis, 1992), pp. 91–109

Baugh, A.C. and T. Cable, *A History of the English Language*, 4th edition (London, 1993)

Beadle, R., (a) 'Geoffrey Spirleng (c. 1426–c. 1494): a Scribe of the *Canterbury Tales* in his Time', in P.R. Robinson and R. Zim (eds), *Of the Making of Books: Medieval Manuscripts, their Scribes, and Readers: Essays presented to M.B. Parkes* (Aldershot, 1997), pp. 116–46

—— (b) 'The Language of a Father and a Son in the Late Fifteenth Century', paper presented at the Second International Conference on Middle English, University of Helsinki, 29 May–1 June 1997

Benskin, M., 'Some New Perspectives on the Origins of Standard Written English', in J.A. van Leuvensteijn and J.B. Berns (eds), *Dialect and Standard Language in the English, Dutch, German and Norwegian Language Areas* (Amsterdam, 1992), pp. 71–105

—— 'The Fit-Technique Explained', in F. Riddy (ed.), *Regionalism in Late Medieval Manuscripts and Texts: Essays celebrating the publication of A Linguistic Atlas of Late Mediaeval English* (Cambridge, 1991), pp. 9–26

Benskin, M. and M. Laing, 'Translations and *Mischsprachen* in Middle English Manuscripts', in M. Benskin and M.L. Samuels (eds), *So Meny People Longages and Tonges: Philological Essays in Scots and Mediaeval English presented to Angus McIntosh* (Edinburgh, 1981), pp. 55–106

Benson, L.D., 'Chaucer's Spelling Reconsidered', *English Manuscript Studies 1100–1700* 3 (1992), 1–28, reprinted in T.M. Andersson and S.A. Barney (eds), *Contradictions: From Beowulf to Chaucer* (Aldershot, 1995), pp. 70–99

—— (ed.), *Riverside Chaucer* (Oxford, 1987)

—— 'The Order of *The Canterbury Tales*', *Studies in the Age of Chaucer* 3 (1981), 77–120, reprinted in T.M. Andersson and S.A. Barney (eds), *Contradictions: From Beowulf to Chaucer* (Aldershot, 1995), pp. 100–40

—— 'Chaucer's Historical Present: its Meaning and Uses', *English Studies* 42 (1961), 65–77

Benzie, W., *Dr. F.J. Furnivall, Victorian Scholar Adventurer* (Norman, 1983)

Blake, N.F., (a) 'Geoffrey Chaucer and the Manuscripts of *The Canterbury Tales*', *Journal of the Early Book Society* 1 (1997), 96–122

—— (b) 'Chancery English and the Wife of Bath's Prologue', in T. Nevalainen and L. Kahlas-Tarkka (eds), *To Explain the Present: Studies in the Changing English Language in honour of Matti Rissanen* (Helsinki, 1997), pp. 3–24

—— *A History of the English Language* (London, 1996)

—— (a) *William Caxton and English Literary Culture* (London, 1991)

—— (b) 'Manuscript to Print', in Blake 1991a, pp. 275–303

——(c) 'English Versions of *Reynard the Fox* in the Fifteenth and Sixteenth Centuries', in Blake 1991a, pp. 259–273

——(d) 'Caxton and Chaucer', in Blake 1991a, pp. 149–165

—— *The Textual Tradition of the Canterbury Tales* (London, 1985)

—— 'The Editorial Assumptions in the Manly-Rickert Edition of *The Canterbury Tales*', *English Studies* 64 (1983), 385–400

——(ed.), *The Canterbury Tales edited from the Hengwrt Manuscript* (London, 1980)

—— 'The Relationship between the Hengwrt and Ellesmere Manuscripts of the *Canterbury Tales*', *Essays & Studies* n.s. 32 (1979), 1–18

—— *Caxton's Own Prose* (London, 1973)

—— *Caxton and his World* (London, 1969)

Blake, N.F. and P.M.W. Robinson (eds), *The Canterbury Tales Project Occasional Papers Vol. II* (London, 1997)

—— *The Canterbury Tales Project Occasional Papers Vol. I* (Oxford, 1993)

Blake, N.F., J.D. Burnley, M. Matsuo and Y. Nakao (eds), *A New Concordance to the Canterbury Tales* (Tanaka, 1994)

Blodgett, J., 'William Thynne', in Ruggiers 1984, pp. 35–52

Boffey J. and A.S.G. Edwards, 'Bodleian MS Arch. Selden. B.24 and the "Scotticization" of Middle English Verse', in Thomas A. Prendergast and Barbara Kline (eds), *Rewriting Chaucer: Culture, Authority, and the Idea of the Authentic Text 1400–1602* (Ohio, 1999), pp. 166–85

——(eds), *The Works of Geoffrey Chaucer and The kingis quair: a Facsimile of Bodleian Library, Oxford, MS Arch. Selden. B.24* (Cambridge, 1997)

Brewer, Charlotte, *Editing Piers Plowman: the Evolution of the Text* (Cambridge, 1996)

Brewer, Derek (ed.), *Chaucer: the Critical Heritage Volume I, 1385–1837* (London, 1978)

Brown, Roger and Albert Gilman, 'The Pronouns of Power and Solidarity', in T.A. Sebeok (ed.), *Style in Language* (Boston, 1960), pp. 253–76, reprinted in Pier Paolo Giglioli (ed.), *Language and Social Context: Selected Readings* (Harmondsworth, 1972), pp. 252–82

Brunner, K. (ed.), *The Seven Sages of Rome*, EETS OS 191 (London, 1933)

Brusendorff, A., *The Chaucer Tradition* (Oxford, 1925)

Burnley, J.D., 'Sources of Standardisation in Later Middle English', in J.B. Trahern (ed.), *Standardizing English: Essays in the History of Language Change in honor of John Hurt Fisher* (Knoxville, 1989), pp. 23–41

—— *The Language of Chaucer* (London, 1983)

—— 'Inflexion in Chaucer's Adjectives', *Neuphilologische Mitteilungen* 83 (1982), 169–77

Burrow, J.A. (ed.), *Thomas Hoccleve's Complaint and Dialogue*, EETS OS 313 (Oxford, 1999)

—— *Thomas Hoccleve*, Authors of the Middle Ages 4 (Aldershot, 1994)

—— *Essays on Medieval Literature* (Oxford, 1984)

Cannon, C., *The Making of Chaucer's English: a Study of Words* (Cambridge, 1998)

—— 'The Myth of Origin and the Making of Chaucer's English', *Speculum* 71 (1996), 646–75

Carver, P.L. (ed.), *The Comedy of Acolastus Translated from the Latin of Fullonius by John Palsgrave*, EETS OS 202 (London, 1937)

Chambers, R.W. and M. Daunt (eds), *A Book of London English 1384–1425* (Oxford, 1931)

Cooper, H., 'The Order of the Tales in the Ellesmere Manuscript', in M. Stevens and D. Woodward (eds), *The Ellesmere Chaucer: Essays in Interpretation* (San Marino, 1997), pp. 245–61

Corbett, J., *Written in the Language of the Scottish Nation: a History of Literary Translation into Scots* (London, 1999)

Dance, R., 'Words Derived from East and West Norse in Middle English Texts, especially *Sir Gawain and the Green Knight*', paper presented at the 11th International Conference on English Historical Linguistics, University of Santiago de Compostela, 7–11 September 2000

Davis, N., 'The Language of Two Brothers in the Fifteenth Century', in E.G. Stanley and D. Gray (eds), *Five Hundred Years of Words and Sounds: a Festschrift for Eric Dobson* (Cambridge, 1983), pp. 23–8

—— 'Chaucer and Fourteenth-Century English', in D. Brewer (ed.), *Geoffrey Chaucer: the Writer and his Background* (Cambridge, 1974), pp. 58–84

—— 'A Paston Hand', *Review of English Studies* 3 (1952), 209–21

—— 'A Scribal Problem in the Paston Letters', *English and Germanic Studies* 4 (1951–2), 31–64

De Vries, F. (ed.), *Floris and Blauncheflur* (Groningen, 1966)

Dempster, G., 'The Fifteenth-Century Editors of the *Canterbury Tales* and the Problem of Tale Order', *PMLA* 64 (1949), 1123–42

—— 'On the Significance of Hengwrt's Change of Ink in the Merchant's Tale', *Modern Language Notes* 63 (1948), 325–30

Dickins, B. and R.M. Wilson (eds), *Early Middle English Texts* (Cambridge, 1951)

Dobson, E.J., *English Pronunciation 1500–1700*, 2 vols (Oxford, 1968)

Doyle A.I., 'The Copyist of the Ellesmere *Canterbury Tales*', in M. Stevens and D. Woodward (eds), *The Ellesmere Chaucer: Essays in Interpretation* (San Marino, 1997), pp. 49–67

—— 'English Books In and Out of Court from Edward III to Henry VII', in.V.J. Scattergood and J.W. Sherborne (eds), *English Court Culture in the Later Middle Ages* (London, 1983), pp. 163–81

Doyle, A.I. and M.B. Parkes, 'Paleographical Introduction', in Ruggiers 1979, pp. xix–xlix

—— 'The Production of Copies of the *Canterbury Tales* and the *Confessio Amantis* in the Early Fifteenth Century', in M.B. Parkes and A.G. Watson (eds), *Mediaeval Scribes, Manuscripts and Libraries: Essays presented to N.R. Ker* (London, 1978), pp. 163–210

Edwards, A.S.G., 'Walter W. Skeat', in Ruggiers 1984, pp. 171–189

Ekwall, E., *Studies on the Population of Medieval London* (Stockholm, 1956)

Fisher, J.H., 'Caxton and Chancery English', in J.H. Fisher, *The Emergence of Standard English* (Lexington, 1996), pp. 121–144

—— *John Gower: Moral Philosopher and Friend of Chaucer* (London, 1965)

Fisher, J.H., M. Richardson and J.L. Fisher (eds), *An Anthology of Chancery English* (Knoxville, 1984)

Fradenburg, L., 'The Scottish Chaucer', in D.J. Pinti (ed.), *Writing after Chaucer: Essential Readings in Chaucer and the Fifteenth Century* (London, 1998), pp. 167–76

Furnivall, F.J. (ed.), *Hoccleve's Works: the Minor Poems*, revised edition J. Mitchell and A.I. Doyle, EETS ES 61, 73 (Oxford, 1970)

——(ed.), *Fifty Earliest English Wills*, EETS OS 78 (London, 1882, 1964)

——(ed.), *The Six-Text Edition of Chaucer's Canterbury Tales*, Chaucer Society 1st series 2 etc. (London, 1868–84)

——*A Temporary Preface to the Chaucer Society's Six-Text Edition of Chaucer's Canterbury Tales*, Chaucer Society 2nd series 3 (London, 1868)

Gómez-Soliño, J.S., 'Variación y Estandarización en el Inglés Moderno Temprano 1470–1540' (unpublished PhD dissertation, Oviedo University, 1984)

Gordon, E.V. and A.R. Taylor (eds), *An Introduction to Old Norse* (Oxford, 1992)

Görlach, M., *Introduction to Early Modern English* (Cambridge, 1991)

——*Studies in the History of the English Language* (Heidelberg, 1990)

Gradon, P. (ed.), *Ayenbite of Inwyt*, EETS OS 278 (London, 1979)

Hammond, Eleanor, *Chaucer: a Bibliographical Manual* (New York, 1908)

Hanna, R, III, (a) 'The Hengwrt Manuscript and the Canon of *The Canterbury Tales*', *English Manuscript Studies* 1 (1989), 64–84, reprinted in R. Hanna III, *Pursuing History: Middle English Manuscripts and their Texts* (Stanford, 1996), pp. 140–55

——(b) (ed.), *The Ellesmere Manuscript of Chaucer's Canterbury Tales: a Working Facsimile* (Cambridge, 1989)

——(c) 'Sir Thomas Berkeley and his Patronage', *Speculum* 64 (1989), 878–916

Hanna, R, III and A.S.G. Edwards, 'Rothely, the De Vere Circle, and the Ellesmere Chaucer', *Huntington Library Quarterly* 58 (1996), 11–35

Hellinga, L., 'Nicholas Love in Print', in S. Oguro, R. Beadle and M. Sargent (eds), *Nicholas Love at Waseda* (Cambridge, 1997), pp. 143–62

Horobin, S.C.P., (a) 'J.R.R. Tolkien as a Philologist: a Reconsideration of the Northernisms in Chaucer's *Reeve's Tale*', *English Studies* 82 (2001), 97–105

——(b) 'The Language of the Fifteenth-Century Printed Editions of the *Canterbury Tales*', *Anglia* 119 (2001), 249–58

——(a) 'Some Spellings in Chaucer's *Reeve's Tale*', *Notes and Queries* n.s. 47 (2000), 16–18

——(b) 'Chaucer's Spelling and the Manuscripts of the *Canterbury Tales*', in Irma Taavitsainen et al. (eds), *Placing Middle English in Context* (Berlin, 2000), pp. 199–208

——(a) 'The "Hooked g" Scribe and his Work on Three Manuscripts of the *Canterbury Tales*', *Neuphilologische Mitteilungen* 99 (1998), 411–17

——(b) 'A New Approach to Chaucer's Spelling', *English Studies* 79 (1998), 415–24

——(a) 'Editorial Assumptions and the Manuscripts of the *Canterbury Tales*' in Blake and Robinson 1997, pp. 15–21

——(b) 'A Transcription and Study of British Library Additional 35286' (unpublished PhD dissertation, Sheffield University, 1997)

Horobin, S and J.J. Smith, 'A Database of Middle English Spelling', *Literary and Linguistic Computing* 14 (1999), 359–73

Hudson, R.A., *Sociolinguistics* (Cambridge, 1996)

James, M.R. (ed.), *Vulgaria by William Hormon* (Oxford, 1926)

Jefferson, Judith A., 'The Hoccleve Holographs and Hoccleve's Metrical Practice', in D.A. Pearsall (ed.), *Manuscripts and Texts: Editorial Problems in Later Middle English Literature* (Cambridge, 1987), pp. 95–109

Jordan, R., *Handbook of Middle English Grammar: Phonology*, trans. E.J. Crook (The Hague, 1974)

Kane, G., 'John M. Manly and Edith Rickert', in Ruggiers 1984, pp. 207–29

Kane, G. and E.T. Donaldson (eds), *Piers Plowman: the B Version*, revised edition (London, 1988)

Kerling, J., *Chaucer in Early English Dictionaries: the Old-Word Tradition in English Lexicography down to 1721 and Speght's Chaucer Glossaries* (Leiden, 1979)

Kingsley, G.H. (ed.), *Francis Thynne, Animadversions* EETS OS 9 (London, 1865)

Kratzmann, G., *Anglo-Scottish Literary Relations, 1430–1550* (Cambridge, 1980)

Labov, W., 'Hypercorrection by the Lower Middle Class as a Factor in Linguistic Change', in W. Labov, *Sociolinguistic Patterns* (Oxford, 1972), pp. 122–42

Laing, M. (ed.), *Middle English Dialectology: Essays on Some Principles and Problems* (Aberdeen, 1989)

Lewis, R.E. and A. McIntosh, *A Descriptive Guide to the Manuscripts of the Prick of Conscience* (Oxford, 1982)

Macrae-Gibson, O.D. (ed.), *Of Arthour and of Merlin, Volume I: Text*, EETS OS 268 (Oxford, 1973)

—— 'The Auchinleck MS.: Participles in *-and(e)*', *English Studies* 52 (1971), 13–20

Manly, J.M. and E. Rickert (eds), *The Text of the Canterbury Tales: Studied on the Basis of All Known Manuscripts*, 8 vols (Chicago, 1940)

Mann, J., 'Chaucer's Meter and the Myth of the Ellesmere Editor of the *Canterbury Tales*', *Studies in the Age of Chaucer* 23 (2001), 71–107

McClure, D., 'English in Scotland', in R. Burchfield (ed.), *The Cambridge History of the English Language V: English in Britain and Overseas: Origins and Development* (Cambridge, 1994), pp. 23–93

McIntosh, A., 'Word Geography in the Lexicography of Mediaeval English', in Laing 1989, pp. 86–97

—— 'A New Approach to Middle English Dialectology', *English Studies* 44 (1963), 1–11, reprinted in Laing 1989, pp. 22–31

McIntosh, A., M.L. Samuels and M. Benskin (eds), *A Linguistic Atlas of Late Mediaeval English* [*LALME*], 4 vols (Aberdeen, 1986)

Mersand, J., *Chaucer's Romance Vocabulary* (Brooklyn, 1937)

Milroy, J., *Linguistic Variation and Change* (Oxford, 1992)

Milroy, J. and L. Milroy, *Authority in Language: Investigating Language Prescription and Standardisation* (London, 1985)

Mooney, L., 'More Manuscripts Written by a Chaucer Scribe', *Chaucer Review* 30:4 (1996), 401–7

Moore, S., 'Patrons of Letters in Norfolk and Suffolk, c. 1450: Part II', *PMLA* 28 (1913), 79–105

—— 'Patrons of Letters in Norfolk and Suffolk, c. 1450: Part I', *PMLA* 27 (1912), 188–207

Mosser, D.W., 'Witness Descriptions', in P.M.W. Robinson 1996

—— 'The Scribe of Chaucer Manuscripts Rylands English 113 and Bodleian Digby 181', *Manuscripta* 34 (1990), 129–47

Nelson, W., 'The Teaching of English in Tudor Grammar Schools', *Studies in Philology* 49 (1952), 119–43

Owen, C.A. Jr., *The Manuscripts of the Canterbury Tales* (Cambridge, 1991)

—— Review of Blake 1985, *Studies in the Age of Chaucer* 9 (1987), 183–7

Parkes, M.B. and R. Beadle (eds), *The Poetical Works of Geoffrey Chaucer: a Facsimile of Cambridge University Library Gg.4.27*, 3 vols (Cambridge, 1979)

Partridge, S., 'The Vocabulary of The Equatorie of the Planetis and the Question of Authorship', *English Manuscript Studies 1100–1700* 3 (1992), 29–37

Pearsall, D.A., 'The Weak Declension of the Adjective and its Importance in Chaucerian Metre', in G.A. Lester (ed.), *Chaucer in Perspective: Middle English Essays in honour of Norman Blake* (Sheffield, 1999), pp. 178–93

——'Langland's London', in S. Justice and K. Kerby-Fulton (eds), *Written Work: Langland, Labor, and Authorship* (Philadelphia, 1997), pp. 185–207

——'*The Franklin's Tale*, Line 1469: Forms of Address in Chaucer', *Studies in the Age of Chaucer* 17 (1995), 69–78

——*The Life of Geoffrey Chaucer* (Oxford, 1992)

——(ed.), *Manuscripts and Texts: Editorial Problems in Later Middle English Literature* (Cambridge, 1987)

——'Thomas Speght', in Ruggiers 1984, pp. 71–92

——(ed.), *Manuscripts and Readers in Fifteenth-Century England* (Cambridge, 1983)

——*John Lydgate* (London, 1970)

Rand Schmidt, K.A., *The Authorship of the Equatorie of the Planetis* (Cambridge, 1993)

Reinecke, G.F., 'F.N. Robinson', in Ruggiers 1984, pp. 231–51

Riddy, F. (ed.), *Regionalism in Late Medieval Manuscripts and Texts: Essays celebrating the publication of A Linguistic Atlas of Late Mediaeval English* (Cambridge, 1991)

Robinson, F.N. (ed.), *The Works of Geoffrey Chaucer* (Oxford, 1957)

——(ed.), *The Complete Works of Geoffrey Chaucer* (Oxford, 1933)

Robinson, P., 'Geoffrey Chaucer and the *Equatorie of the Planetis*: The State of the Problem', *Chaucer Review* 26 (1991), 17–30

Robinson, P.M.W., 'Can We Trust the Hengwrt Manuscript?', in G.A. Lester (ed.), *Chaucer in Perspective: Middle English Essays in honour of Norman Blake* (Sheffield, 1999), pp. 194–217

——'A Stemmatic Analysis of the Fifteenth-Century Witnesses to The Wife of Bath's Prologue', in Blake and Robinson 1997, pp. 69–132

——(ed.), *The Wife of Bath's Prologue on CD-ROM* (Cambridge, 1996)

Root, R.K., Review of Manly and Rickert 1940, *Studies in Philology* 38 (1941), 1–13

Ruggiers, P.G. (ed.), *Editing Chaucer: the Great Tradition* (Norman, 1984)

——(ed.), *The Canterbury Tales: a Facsimile and Transcription of the Hengwrt Manuscript with Variants from the Ellesmere Manuscript* (Norman, 1979)

Samuels, M.L., 'Scribes and Manuscript Traditions', in Riddy 1991, pp. 1–7

——(a) 'Chaucerian Final -*e*', in Smith 1988a, pp. 7–12

——(b) 'Chaucer's Spelling', in Smith 1988a, pp. 23–37

——(c) 'The Scribe of the Hengwrt and Ellesmere Manuscripts of *The Canterbury Tales*', in Smith 1988a, pp. 38–50

——(d) 'Langland's Dialect', in Smith 1988a, pp. 70–85

——(e) 'Spelling and Dialect in the Late and Post-Middle English Periods', in Smith 1988a, pp. 86–95

——(f) 'Dialect and Grammar', in J.A. Alford (ed.), *A Companion to Piers Plowman* (London, 1988), pp. 201–22

——*Linguistic Evolution with Special Reference to English* (Cambridge, 1972)

——'Some Applications of Middle English Dialectology', *English Studies* 44 (1963), 81–94, reprinted in Laing 1989, pp. 64–80

Samuels, M.L. and J.J. Smith, 'The Language of Gower', in Smith 1988, pp. 13–22

Sandved, A.O., 'Prolegomena to a Renewed Study of the Rise of Standard English', in M. Benskin and M.L. Samuels (eds), *So Meny People Longages and Tonges: Philological Essays in Scots and Mediaeval English presented to Angus McIntosh* (Edinburgh, 1981), pp. 31–42

Scott, K.L., 'An Hours and Psalter by Two Ellesmere Illuminators', in M. Stevens and D. Woodward (eds), *The Ellesmere Chaucer: Essays in Interpretation* (San Marino, 1997), pp. 87–119

Seymour, M.C., *A Catalogue of Chaucer Manuscripts, Volume II: the Canterbury Tales* (Aldershot, 1997)

—— *A Catalogue of Chaucer Manuscripts, Volume I:. Works before the Canterbury Tales* (Aldershot, 1995)

Skeat, W.W. (ed.), *The Complete Works of Geoffrey Chaucer*, 6 vols (Oxford, 1894–5)

Smith, J.J., (a) 'The Language of the Ellesmere Manuscript', in M. Stevens and D. Woodward (eds), *The Ellesmere Chaucer: Essays in Interpretation* (San Marino, 1997), pp. 69–86

—— (b) 'Dialect and Standardisation in the Waseda Manuscript of Nicholas Love's *Mirror of the Blessed Life of Jesus Christ*', in S.Oguro, R.Beadle and M. Sargent (eds), *Nicholas Love at Waseda* (Cambridge, 1997), pp. 129–41

—— *An Historical Study of English: Function, Form and Change* (London, 1996)

—— 'The Great Vowel Shift in the North of England, and Some Forms in Chaucer's *Reeve's Tale*', *Neuphilologische Mitteilungen* 95 (1994), 433–7

—— 'Dialectal Variation in Middle English and the Actuation of the Great Vowel Shift', *Neuphilologische Mitteilungen* 94 (1993), 259–77

—— (a) (ed.), *The English of Chaucer and his Contemporaries* (Aberdeen, 1988)

—— (b) 'The Trinity Gower D-Scribe and his Work on Two Early *Canterbury Tales* Manuscripts', in Smith 1988a, pp. 51–69

—— (c) 'Spelling and Tradition in Fifteenth-Century Copies of Gower's *Confessio Amantis*', in Smith 1988a, pp. 96–113

—— 'Some Spellings in Caxton's Malory', *Poetica* 24 (1986), 58–63

—— 'Studies in the Language of Some Manuscripts of Gower's *Confessio Amantis*' (unpublished PhD dissertation, Glasgow University, 1985)

Solopova, E., 'Chaucer's Metre and Scribal Editing in the Early Manuscripts of *The Canterbury Tales*', in Blake and Robinson 1997, pp. 143–64

Speght, T. (ed.), *The workes of our antient and learned English poet, Geffrey Chaucer* (London, 1598, 1602)

Strohm, P., 'The Textual Vicissitudes of Usk's "Appeal"', in P. Strohm, *Hochon's Arrow: The Social Imagination of Fourteenth-Century Texts* (Princeton, 1992), pp. 145–60

—— 'Politics and Poetics: Usk and Chaucer in the 1380s', in L. Patterson (ed.), *Literary Practice and Social Change in Britain 1380–1530* (Berkeley, 1990), pp. 83–112

Stubbs, E.V., 'Clare Priory, the London Austin Friars and Manuscripts of Chaucer's *Canterbury Tales*', in A.J. Minnis (ed.), *Middle English Poetry: Texts and Traditions. Essays in honour of Derek Pearsall* (York, 2001), pp. 17–26

—— (ed.), *The Hengwrt Chaucer Digital Facsimile* (Leicester, 2000)

Tatlock, J.S.P., 'The Canterbury Tales in 1400', *PMLA* 50 (1935), 100–39

Thompson, John J., 'A Poet's Contacts with the Great and Good: Further Consideration of Thomas Hoccleve's Texts and Manuscripts', in F. Riddy (ed.), *Prestige, Authority and Power in Late-Medieval Manuscripts and Texts* (York, 2000), pp. 77–101

Thrupp, S., *The Merchant Class of Medieval London* (Chicago, 1948)

Thynne, William (ed.), *The workes of Geffray Chaucer* (London, 1532, 1542)

Tolkien, J.R.R., 'Chaucer as a Philologist: *The Reeve's Tale*', *Transactions of the Philological Society* (1934), 1–70

Turville-Petre, T. and H. Duggan (eds), *The Piers Plowman Electronic Archive, Vol. 2: Cambridge, Trinity College, MS B.15.17 (W)* (Ann Arbor, 2000)

Tyrwhitt, T. (ed.), *The Canterbury Tales of Chaucer* (London, 1775–8)

Vollmer, Erich, 'Sprache und Reime des Londoners Hoccleve', *Anglia* 21 (1899), 201–21

Windeatt, B.A. (ed.), *Geoffrey Chaucer: Troilus & Criseyde. A new edition of 'The Book of Troilus'* (London, 1984)

—— 'The Scribes as Chaucer's Early Critics', *Studies in the Age of Chaucer* 1 (1979), 119–41

Wright, L., (ed.), *The Development of Standard English 1300–1800: Theories, Descriptions, Conflicts* (Cambridge, 2000)

—— 'About the Evolution of Standard English', in M.J. Toswell and E.M. Tyler (eds), *Studies in English Language and Literature: 'Doubt Wisely'. Papers in honour of E.G. Stanley* (London, 1996), pp. 99–115

Wright, T. (ed.), *The Canterbury Tales* (London, 1847–51)

Wyld, H.C., *A History of Modern Colloquial English* (London, 1920)

Index of Words

Index of Subjects

Undergraduate Lending Library

CHAUCER STUDIES